Basia Sliwinska is an art historian
twentieth- and twenty-first-century art with a focus on the feminist practices of contemporary women artists. She is a senior lecturer at the University of the Arts London. Previously, she worked at the School of Art and Design at Middlesex University and was a research fellow at Winchester School of Art, the University of Southampton and an associate editor at the academic journal *Third Text*.

'"Curiouser and curiouser" – taking its cue and organisational frame from *Alice in Wonderland*, Basia Sliwinska explores the effects generated by works from Eastern European contemporary women artists. Inverting the pre-determined expectations of pornography (male arousal, female objectification) and current mass-media standards of beauty (glamour, spectacle, female desire), she opens up the mirror to show that it is precisely these artists' point of view of the 'Other' side of the real that aims to shock, disturb and unsettle realities and conventions about looking/being/acting.'

Katy Deepwell, Professor of Contemporary Art, Theory and Criticism, Middlesex University and editor of *n.paradoxa*

THE **FEMALE BODY** IN THE LOOKING-GLASS

CONTEMPORARY ART, AESTHETICS AND GENDERLAND

BASIA SLIWINSKA

I.B. TAURIS
LONDON · NEW YORK

New paperback edition published in 2018 by
I.B.Tauris & Co. Ltd
London • New York
www.ibtauris.com

First published in hardback in 2016 by I.B.Tauris & Co. Ltd

ISBN: 978 1 78831 101 4
eISBN: 978 1 78672 008 5
epdf: 978 1 78673 008 4

A full CIP record for this book is available from the British Library
A full CIP record is available from the Library of Congress

Library of Congress Catalog Card Number: available

Typeset by Newgen
Printed and bound by CPI Group (UK) Ltd, Croydon, CR0 4YY

MIX
Paper from responsible sources
FSC® C013604

'Curiouser and curiouser.'
Lewis Carroll, *Through the Looking-glass, and What Alice Found There*

For my mother Helena
Filon

... and for all those who are 'curiouser and curiouser'

Contents

List of Illustrations

Acknowledgements

This book was conceptualised after I attained my PhD. Then I travelled with it, writing some passages when sitting in my mother's garden back at home in Wrocław, Poland. This was pure pleasure, as writing was accompanied by seasonal fruit and motherly care. Some paragraphs were born in the flat I rented, some in one of the parks in Leicester, England, and some when sitting on a plane. A big part of this book was written in a small café on a beach in Portugal, where I was surrounded by sandy dunes that opened up a perspective towards an infinite dark blue ocean. This book grew up with me and travelled. All the places I visited and worked in are significant to me and deeply personal, so my first thanks go to the different sites that enabled wondering and to people who made my writing possible and who often said things that inspired my thinking.

A number of my colleagues read passages of this book and helped immensely to make it better. I owe more than I can ever acknowledge to Dr Marion Arnold, a dear friend, who offered her support throughout the whole process and read (and reread) the whole text, providing me with invaluable comments and suggestions for improvement. She was instrumental in helping me strengthen my argument. I am most indebted, and would also like to thank Marion for her friendship and for teaching me to believe in myself. I am particularly grateful to Dr Malcolm Barnard for his astute criticism and sound advice, and for introducing me to a number of theoretical texts that shaped my analysis of the chosen artworks. I also acknowledge the support of Baillie Card and Lisa Goodrum of I.B.Tauris for guiding this book into publication and Pat FitzGerald for her thorough copy-editing. I am greatly indebted to the artist Joanna Rajkowska for providing me with the cover image, and for her participation (and sharing her 'self') in a symposium that was part of my *Migratory Homes* project in 2013. I also thank all individuals and institutions that generously provided images for this book.

Finally, I express my gratitude to all those who motivated me and helped me remain calm, in particular my mother, Helena Śliwińska, whom I love dearly, who was the first strong woman (feminist, I dare say, even if not conscious of it) I encountered and who introduced to me *Alice's Adventures in Wonderland* (1865); Dr Michał Fornalczyk, because he supported me throughout my journey, went for countless walks with me and patiently listened to me over coffee; my family and especially my aunt Basia Karwat for their encouragement; and Dr Ania Wójt, who has been my friend since teenage years and who never doubted me. I also thank Dr Maria Photiou for keeping me on track and always finding time for a coffee conversation, and Dr Kasia Zimna for always being there for me.

Preface

When I was flirting with the idea of an academic career as an art historian and was maturing as a woman, I migrated from Central to Western Europe, moving from Poland to England. I found crossing borders, physically and metaphorically, meaningful for enabling wholeness, rather than entrenching thinking in terms of 'either/or'. While considering my research options, I decided to focus on Central and Eastern European artistic practice *through* and from the theoretical perspective of the West, and to relate this to my belief that the body establishes one's identity and plays a significant role in contemporary female artistic practice.

This book has become very personal as it travels into the routes and roots of my homeland. Writing it was a process of self-discovery and a journey into my beliefs and thoughts about the female body, its mystery and its capacity to influence the world. This might be seen as idealistic but I cannot escape the conviction that women's artistic practice, encompassing collaboration, solidarity and friendship, enriches contemporary visual culture and opens up opportunities for social change and dialogue.

Readers might wonder about my references to Lewis Carroll's *Alice's Adventures in Wonderland* (1865) and *Through the Looking-Glass, and What Alice Found There* (1871) but in Poland I grew up with Alice, a book that is published all over the world. When I was a child, my mother introduced me to the Alice books and she has always encouraged me to believe in Wonderland and be idealistic. Without her, this book would never have happened. I was attracted to the fantasy world and the little girl who was curious about everything. She could do anything she wanted and she made her own decisions. She escaped from what she did know and into what she didn't know, but she explored and learnt about the world around her and herself. Alice participated in different scenarios – being a nursing mother or a ruthless queen, or being subjected to the dictatorial, phallic

Caterpillar, sitting above her on a female-shaped mushroom. She refused to commit herself to the passivity demanded of Victorian girls and women.

I returned to Alice decades later to play with some of the issues I had found fascinating years before. The books became a platform from which to think symbolically and metaphorically. In Wonderland Alice had plenty of time to look around her and wonder, and so did I, and this book is my first tumble down the rabbit hole to discover what will happen next.

Introduction

The female body is the defining idea and reality of this book, which focuses on feminist themes through metaphors from Lewis Carroll's books, *Alice's Adventures in Wonderland* (1865) and *Through the Looking-Glass, and What Alice Found There* (1871).[1] These classic English texts, which have stimulated a huge body of scholarly research on Carroll, British academic culture, nineteenth-century adult/child relations, the class system, Victorian children's literature and so on, are not my primary concern here.

Growing up in Poland, as a child I read Alice through translation. I was captivated by Carroll's imagination and entranced by Alice's adventures. Later, as an adult reader, English cultural history and values remained in the background of my relationship with the text. Instead, I responded to the Alice texts as metaphors of experience: the looking-glass (the other side enabling ways of seeing the female body beyond lack, and acknowledging otherness); Alice's journey down the rabbit hole (challenging different beauty myths); the White and the Red queens (resonating with narratives around beauty and ugliness); the Cheshire Cat (concerning strategies of embodiment and fluidity of representation); the rose garden (articulating identification with difference and dispersal of either/or structures). In recent decades, these same issues that these metaphors represent have been explored in art made by women. Opportunities to experiment with alternative media and the use of art as a space apart from usual social norms have allowed identity art and activist art to emerge, within which issues around the female body can be addressed *through* the female body itself.

Carroll's Alice novels provide a rich reader experience, being popular with adults and children. Many adults approach them as classics of Victorian literature that are entertaining to read. Some see them as metaphorical. Metaphors have been recognised as crucial in the development of natural and constructed languages. They activate understanding through theoretical engagement. This book is indeed primarily theoretical and tests Central and Eastern European women's art *through* metaphor. The figure of Alice is well recognised in popular culture and even though she was re-imagined in movies, different versions of the book, comics, cartoons and so on, I refer to the original books. They describe a world in which a young woman explores her identity and, in presenting many options for her to choose from, they also offer many levels of interpretation.

The Alice books can be used to investigate and discuss women's art because they offer metaphors relating to a woman's entrance into the world of representation. This world is guided by and subjected to patriarchal ideologies and the coercive mechanisms of seeing and defining the female body. Perhaps despite the books being written by a white middle-class male, the metaphors can be used to deconstruct stereotypical representations of the female body. Alice refuses to be caught up in her own reflection in the mirror. She goes *through* the looking-glass but this going *through* is not a symmetrical reversal. She goes *towards* asymmetry, displacement and the destabilisation of the subject. Alice enters a world where there is no possibility of naturalistic identification. Alice's journey is about awakening, learning to communicate, travelling and wandering, and even though Carroll controls Alice (or her journey towards womanhood) through the presence (or lack) of food (she is allowed to eat or drink items of food which are clearly labelled and only then is she able to transform), Alice gains her own life and her own identity in the process. She learns to make decisions. Presented with different opportunities (to eat or not to eat and so on), she learns how to make judgements, become decisive and confident and gain a voice.

The metaphor of the looking-glass and its role in Carroll's classic Victorian Alice novels led me towards the concept of 'genderland'. This concept emphasises gender and place to enable discussion about the aesthetics and practice of contemporary art made by women. More specifically, it presents projects by women artists from Central and Eastern Europe who use their bodies to engage with questions around the construction of body and gender and the performativity of feminine identity, and to situate their practices within activist trajectories. They tell personal stories through their bodies, acknowledging the legacy of earlier generations of feminist artists.

In my journey I bring together different theoretical perspectives arising from different disciplinary fields in order to question the visualising strategies of images and demystify the ways in which certain images are constructed to encourage particular ways of seeing the female body. This book offers a theoretical discourse on genderland and corporeality explained through its application to analysis of specific artworks from Eastern and Central Europe. Geography is important because contemporary art practice is diverse in terms of both ethnicity and location. Globalisation of the 1980s, migrations within and beyond Europe and increased transnationalism shifted sites of contemporary art production beyond the West. Earlier feminist art was mostly Western (in a broad sense), academic and middle class. Art production in Eastern and Central Europe remained overlooked by Western scholars and was discouraged in post-communist societies. In their efforts to orientate their art-making, women artists from those locations often use and reinterpret tactics and theories from the West to underpin their personal and cultural agendas.

My choice of examples from geographical locations beyond Western Europe is determined by the fact that little is known about them or that art world in general. My methodology prioritises theory and cites art to demonstrate the mechanisms that guide practice towards social and cultural engagement and beyond merely aesthetic production. This research is not about feminism and the sociology of art or theories of the body, but it has been greatly affected by these fields of enquiry.

During my journey of discovering women artists from Eastern and Central Europe, as I become 'curiouser and curiouser' I apply different theories referring to issues emerging from the Alice books – the different reversals in the looking-glass, mirror images, appearances and disappearances, and the multiple options for identity existing in Wonderland. These are used to articulate and analyse tactics employed by women artists to comment on the mechanisms to which the female body has been subjected in the postmodern and post-postmodern world. Visual tropes and narratives from the Alice books are also useful in introducing ideas about embodiment.

The body is a material organism but it is also a site of identification where a strong 'I' emerges and is shaped. In fact, it is a 'land' full of wonders which for far too long were forbidden, mysterious, secretive and undiscovered by Western women. Woman was a 'no body'. She had neither responsibility for her body nor support until early feminists claimed their bodies and identities as women. They desired to be 'some body' and started writing in their own voices *as* women and expressing themselves *with* and *through* the body. This freedom provided women with opportunities and responsibilities with regard to their bodies.

I approached research for this book as a curious enquirer. My thinking has been shaped by women who fight against patriarchal repression and the sustained male gaze, which violates women's bodies and their 'selves', but there are also women who condone sexism. Their tactics and language harms women, instead of challenging the gender inequality inherent in patriarchal culture(s), rascism, neo-colonialism and global capitalism.

'Genderland' is not an easy territory to negotiate, and the actions of groups of women from Central and Eastern Europe exemplify the contradictory relationships that exist among place, cultural values and the role of the female body in socio-political activism (and art practice). Women belonging to Femen, a group started in 2008 in Ukraine, claim that they use their topless bodies to raise awareness of women's rights in a nation trying to come to terms with democracy in a post-communist era. When entering Femen's website, one is welcomed with an image of a topless woman personified as death with 'Sextremism' written across the scythe. Next to the figure, there is a slogan – 'Femen is a death for patriarchy'.[2] When clicking on the 'Femen' tab, one is introduced to a 'Witch Bitch' wearing a floral hair wreath and gothic make-up. The statement below notes 'FEMEN is an international women's movement of brave topless female activists painted with the slogans and crowned with flowers'. We are also informed its ideology is founded upon 'Sextremism; Atheism; Feminism'.

In the 'Tactics' section of the text is the statement: 'Sextremism is a fundamentally new form of women's feminist actionism developed by FEMEN.'[3] Femen therefore claims to have invented an entirely new form of feminist activism based on naked protest, and argues that empowered and enlightened women signal their emancipation by embracing nudity. According to the documentary *Ukraine is not a Brothel* (2013; dir. Kitty Green), the founder of the group was a man, Victor Svyatski, who was initially acknowledged as a consultant of the group. Perhaps this explains the looks of members of Femen, who are all thin, blonde and pretty and so easily attract media attention. In the film Svyatski says: 'These girls are weak.' Femen not only misunderstands but, more worryingly, is disrespectful towards objectification and sexualisation of the female body, either neglecting or being unaware of the histories and traditions of feminist discourse long established in the United States and Western Europe. Their tactics seem to be founded solely on the shock factor and the fact that sex still (unfortunately) sells, and reinforces the female body as a sexualised object.

On the other side of the performative spectrum are groups that engage thoughtfully and knowledgeably with feminist activism. Pussy Riot, a feminist punk rock protest group founded in 2011 in Russia, follows the route of female activism established by the Guerilla Girls; Riot Grrrl, a 1990s feminist punk movement; Bikini Kill, a punk rock band; and Ladyfest, a global music and arts festival for women artists. Pussy Riot fights for the freedom of speech, human rights and democracy, or freedom of individuals in general. This was a message of their famous guerilla performance in Moscow's Cathedral of Christ the Saviour in 2012, for which three members of the group were imprisoned. Pussy Riot stands for ideas. They wear balaclavas, which de-individualises them and, as Slavoj Žižek suggests, demonstrates that ideas matter and will be seen as dangerous by some, especially in authoritarian Russia under Vladimir Putin's regime. Žižek says,

> The message of their balaclavas is that it doesn't matter which of them got arrested - they're not individuals, they're an Idea. And this is why they are such a threat: it is easy to imprison individuals, but try to imprison an Idea![4]

The group attacks the patriarchal state and reinforces the political dimensions, which are part of subculture and actionist art. Post-Soviet conditions of relative stability under Vladimir Putin's rule resulted in a lack of trust in public politics opposing official state politics, but Pussy Riot disputes this.

Since the late nineteenth century in the Western world, women have fought for the freedoms we enjoy today. The priorities of the feminist movement might vary depending on the location of activism but always concern women's selves and their right to their bodies, whether literal and physical or as signifiers of their social, political and cultural dimensions. These struggles are forcefully expressed in feminist art, confronting questions around women's freedoms and experiences, challenging stereotypes and intervening in representational strategies concerning the female body based on rigid art historical canons and cultural attitudes. Contemporary art practice continues interrogating these issues, making them relevant to late twentieth- and twenty-first-century cultures.

Women artists' practices acknowledge bodies that are often socially despised, inviting the self to play with the privileging looks attached to tropes of femininity present in contemporary culture. As such, they not only actively use ideality embedded in the image of Venus but also identify with monstrosity, associated with the figure of Medusa. Interpretations of their works can be ambivalent and often dependent on how one approaches Eastern and Central Europe, which for most of the twentieth century was dominated by repression that permeated politics, culture, economic and social structures. The freedom that came in 1989 with the fall of the Berlin Wall gave women in Eastern and Central Europe an opportunity to act and test different scenarios, enabling them to interpret their bodies and use them to claim their identities.

Even though contemporary feminist and gender discourse on visual culture is a burgeoning field,[5] the post-colonial dimension of contemporary feminist and gender discourse on visual culture only marginally expands towards Central and Eastern Europe, which remains a 'grey zone', as suggested by Susan Gal and Gail Klingman and Janet Elise Johnson and Jean C. Robinson.[6] The feminist and gender agenda, which was an integral part of Western discourse, was difficult to communicate across the Iron Curtain.[7] After the fall of the Berlin Wall and the subsequent dissolution of communist regimes in Eastern and Central Europe, liberal democracy was introduced to the newly established states. It caused a further division in the social fabric of Europe in relation to the economy and gender.

Since then, women artists working in Europe have been addressing these processes, providing radical critiques and deconstructing values accepted by the new post-socialist societies, such as patriarchy, class, sexism and nationalism, as proposed by Edit András and Ekaterina Dyogot.[8] These visual artists demonstrate that post-1989 tropes of femininity that are discussed in this book – for example Venus and Medusa – still embody the male ideas instituted in the mid-nineteenth century. The practices of women artists I analyse dissolve the ideal form, the pretty and youthful look described by Naomi Wolf in 1991 as the 'beauty myth'.[9] Their work is embedded in the post-1989 free capitalist doctrine, governed by mass culture and consumerist Europe, and they respond to the new socio-cultural phenomena and their access to theories from the West. This plural world necessitates a search for female and feminine identity, which becomes one of the key themes in their work. The newfound freedom has offered an opportunity to act and a right to act provocatively. Their work resonates with the contemporary world and its technologies that make everything accessible instantly.

My choice of artworks was dictated by women using their bodies to negotiate gender inequalities imposed by stereotypical constructions of femininity. They tamper with representations of femininity to demonstrate that difference can be sustained, not annulled. Anetta Mona Chişa & Lucia Tkáčová, Grupa Sędzia Główny (Chief Judge Group), Katarzyna Kozyra, Joanna Rajkowska, Boryana Rossa and Alicja Żebrowska, among others, denaturalise processes of representation to contest images of the female body imposed on them, usually by men. As a result, a more complicated conception of gender and identity emerges, which is articulated through Western concepts and theories, and addresses general issues concerning the female body, however embedded within the context of Eastern and Central Europe.

This volume is an invitation to a longer discussion on the issues that are mobilised. Ulf Brunnbauer described the post-1989 transformation of women's position as 'from equality without democracy to democracy without equality',[10] which points to the economic, social and cultural change that largely shaped women's practice and their thinking about their bodies. My main concern is to investigate practices of women artists from Central and Eastern Europe and explore how they seek structures for their identity, challenging the dominant ideas and undermining stereotypes of the patriarchal iconosphere. I am also implicitly drawing attention to difference in feminist thinking and practice in the emerging Eastern and Central European democracies and the established democracies of Western Europe.

This is a story of passion and sometimes violence towards bodies injected into practices that are deliberately confrontational, subversive and challenging. The artists dream of the 'other side' and decode cultural constructions producing guilt, shame and inferiority. They are like Alice – curious and rebelling – questioning their identity and refusing to accept what has been imposed on them. They are discovering their female selves, flexible and multiple, as once noted by Luce Irigaray,[11] and rejecting associations with categories of 'proper' and 'property'. They transition and go underground/to the other side of the mirror, where the law of the father is subverted.

Some of the artworks I describe are so overtly sexual that they might be seen as pornographic. I position them in relation to a specific theoretical framework and argue that, contrary to Femen's eagerly showing off their breasts, allusions to widely circulated and easily accessible porn images allow women artists to develop serious discussion on sexualisation and the objectification of the female body. The artists reach out to representations, which can be encountered on an everyday basis when looking at any newspaper stand, flicking through pages of any women's magazine or watching music videos. This familiarity with images of naked female bodies anaesthetises individuals to pertinent values that are hidden behind pouting lips, a seducing gaze and widespread legs.

In the West in particular, the right to freedom of expression, upheld by the Universal Declaration of Human Rights[12] as crucial in any democracy, and the culture of permissiveness blurs the line between pornography and eroticism. Pornography is defined in dictionaries as a depiction of sexual behaviour that causes sexual arousal. The artworks I discuss are created by artists from a non-Western world with more conservative values. Their use of 'pornographic' imagery is not arousing, self-indulgent or desiring of salacious attention (although it certainly helps to attract a male audience). It is deliberately chosen and validates their arguments around the objectification of the female body as demeaning, reinforcing sex myths and often causing violence. Women artists push gender boundaries by directly quoting poses and camera moves from porn movies and nudity, and they articulate feminist concerns around the consumption of the female body, eroticisation and male domination.

Similarly, I discuss artworks in which women control the ways in which they intentionally violate their bodies and tamper with their most private parts. They may inflict pain on themselves at times as a form of referencing the violence against women, now more prevalent than ever globally. It is difficult and deeply unsettling to watch some of these performances. Nonetheless, violating the body is employed deliberately to respond to issues of today rather than to bask in the newfound freedom of expression or promote oneself. Fifty years ago the latter was a part of the artistic strategy of Rudolf Schwarzkogler, one of Viennese Actionists, in a staged performance in 1965 in which it was believed that he mutilated his penis, which helped him gain publicity to promote his gallery.

The artworks I analyse can be understood by knowledgeable audiences but they can also be misunderstood or spark different, often visceral, responses. I chose the artworks carefully because they demonstrate my methodology of illustrating theory in action through analysis of selected examples. I argue that they mobilise the theoretical issues I prioritise, which cannot be ignored, for example in Boryana Rossa and Oleg Mavromatti's performance *SZ-ZS* (2005; discussed in Chapter 1). No interpretation is fixed and some performances might be seen differently by audiences who do not know or share the theoretical and philosophical perspectives intended by the practitioners. Some might see female bodies doing shocking things in a troubled world with contradictory cultural values and attitudes towards women, sex and gender. The artists I discuss use their performing bodies as metaphors for the physical and psychological violence to which the female body is repeatedly subjected. Their acts, some of which are harmful, are anarchic and point to issues of mastery and domination. They also address the female self-depreciation that may result from patriarchal structures.

I am conscious of the fact some of the actions are reminiscent of the artistic practices and sensationalism of 1970s feminist art. Some might even claim that violating the body and subjecting it to pain and danger in order to claim subjectivity has already been done, for example by Valie Export or Carolee Schneemann, among others, but I suggest that it was done differently, under different cultural, social and political conditions and by different people. Even though representation of the female body was tested in numerous performances in Western countries, women from the end of twentieth- and twenty-first-century Central and Eastern Europe approach it from a different perspective and in a different context, guided by recent experiences of repression and lack of democracy. Some artists are idealistic, aspiring for a better society and a more equal global world and, like the Suffragettes, they become militant and choose ways which are often painful in order to acknowledge and contest issues that concern them. They tease out and reinforce Western theory and apply it to work in the contemporary realm of sexual identities to question the female body and female identity.

This book was conceptualised to develop Western readers' awareness of women's art in Eastern and Central Europe through discussion of theory in action. The chapters are structured to interweave theoretical issues with visual analysis of selected examples, thus demonstrating an application of theory in artistic practice in different geographical and cultural locations. Each artwork is analysed in a theoretical setting to test some theoretical claims overarched by the concept of the mirror, whose reflective side belongs to men. In consequence, women are defined as lacking and are excluded from active looking by being subjected to the patriarchal gaze. The mirror is an object that simply reflects, but the mirror also combines the senses of sight and touch. It is a complex tool that enables one to get to know the self through looking and touching. Some of the artworks discussed involve actual mirrors and some of them refer symbolically to structural aspects of the mirror, alluding to Jacques Lacan's mirror stage of development.[13] Sometimes skin and cutaneous sensations become important in taking possession of the body as an object and subject. The mirror offers opportunities to see and feel multiple aspects of identity, blurring the border between self and other, same and different, active and passive. Seeing through the mirror articulates gendered scenarios arising from the conflict between nature and culture, which imposes restricting social norms governed by heteronormativity and bipolar logic.

The first chapter, 'Looking-glass Reality', addresses 'the other side', which might offer a new beginning for conceptualising the female body beyond narratives imprisoning it in lack and deficiency. I suggest that the space in between – the fragile border between the 'into' and 'out of' – enables identification with otherness and difference through acknowledging culturally structured distinctions such as gender. My analysis of looking and the 'motility of the look' relies on Kaja Silverman's account of the look, the gaze and the cultural screen, which she traces with regard to the body and the unequal gender relations which influence formation of one's identity.[14] My concern is with Lacan's 'mirror stage' and the metaphor of the mirror, which determine idealising and de-idealising representations of the female body. The mirror, as a tool modelling representational strategies of the body, enables thinking *across* and *through*, which makes multiplicity possible. Sometimes it creates conditions of violence, which are adopted by women artists who violate their bodies in order to reach the transformative state enabling them to reclaim their subjectivity. The mirror is also employed to map issues of exclusivity and removal from fraternalist narratives. This scenario can be exemplified by the practice of Anetta Mona Chişa & Lucia Tkáčová, who revisit the politics of female friendship, which becomes a tool to emphasise a politics of difference and tease out oppositional structures inherent in bipolar narratives. The chapter revisits the field of vision through the mirror, searching for options that would allow the subject to be mobile and polymorphous, which in turn leads to a range of bodily identifications. My thinking stems from my engagement with theories put forward by Jacques Lacan, Sigmund Freud, Michel Foucault, Jean Baudrillard, Luce Irigaray and Hélène Cixous. These are tested to analyse practices of female artists who demonstrate – as does, for example, Alicja Żebrowska in *The Mystery is Looking* (1995) – that through the body woman can become a self-aware subject seizing the male gaze and emancipating her 'self'.

Chapter 2, 'Down the Skin-deep Hole', mobilises various Western 'beauty myths' perpetuated by consumer culture that shape images of femininity and reinforce unequal representations of gender. Referring to theories of Jacques Rancière[15] and John Berger[16], among others, and exploring the changing status of the concept of beauty (following the writings of Jean-François Lyotard), this chapter discusses practices of women artists who question the skin-deep portrayals of the female body and prove that the body can become an active subject intervening into its stereotypical association with physicality and objectivity. To demonstrate this, I point to a performance by Rossa and Mavromatti, *Vitruvian Body* (2009), in which corporeality becomes a site of social exchange. This work manipulates cultural imaginings of femininity and, by emphasising the role of skin, articulates the need to penetrate the boundary separating subject from object. I also discuss practices that tamper with pornographic images of the female body to contest the relations of power and possessiveness that inflict violence on one's 'self'. Finally, I analyse in detail Joanna Rajkowska's work *Satisfaction Guaranteed* (2000), which emphasises a number of issues attached to vision and gaze under the rule of consumption. Rajkowska deliberately uses the language of branding and advertising to draw attention to categories that have been used to oppress women and invert subordination into affirmation.

'White and the Red Queens or Venus and Medusa', discussed in Chapter 3, plays with metaphors of the white and the red queens from the Alice books and replaces them with figures of Venus and Medusa. This chapter addresses a cultural gaze producing associations of the female body and beauty implied by the myth of Venus and the 'lack' associated with Medusa. These are traced after the theoretical and conceptual framework has been established in Alicja Żebrowska's video installation *Grzech Pierworodny* (*Original Sin*) (1993/4). I merge narratives of wholeness and incompleteness, whose exclusivity negates difference, and embrace Silverman's 'incorporative logic' that enables heterogeneity. Drawing on Silverman's theories and Lacan's separation between the gaze, the look and the screen, I explore scenarios in which the subject acknowledges its visual identity *through* culturally structured images. 'Incorporative logic' enables the integration of difference through excorporative identification. This necessitates addressing bodily fragmentation, castration and mutilation, which I discuss in relation to the writings of Freud and Lacan, in the light of Lyotard's metaphor of travel, opening up the possibility of disrupting 'neither/nor' narratives through passage, journey and threshold. Next, I investigate more closely Mieke Bal's discourse concerned with visual framing and the different gazes (from Laura Mulvey's 'male gaze'[17] and Bracha Ettinger's 'matrixial gaze')[18] disempowering or empowering and demystifying the object of look. This leads me to narratives of dependency, deformation and physicality that are stigmatised as wrong (as suggested by Lennard Davis)[19]. The lacking body, represented by cultural figures of femininity, implies limitation, incapacity and monstrosity. I look more closely at oppressive body politics and embodiments of beauty, sublimity and ugliness and argue that, if read in line with Mark Cousins, Judith Butler, Irigaray and Cixous's writings, the lack can be acknowledged and can help demonstrate the other, which is too often pushed aside to peripheral vision.

In Chapter 4, 'The Cheshire Cat and the Disappearing Appearances', I start with Anetta Mona Chişa & Lucia Tkáčová's enactment in the video *The Descent of Man, and Selection in Relation to Sex* (2010) of the Chinese whispers or telephone game, which is used to challenge gender stereotypes. The metaphor of the Cheshire cat proves useful when demonstrating that the different strategies of embodiment can enable fluidity of representation and can manipulate corporeal passivity into activity. It symbolises the space in between, the 'into' and 'out of', what I call the 'looking-glass', in which processes of appearance and disappearance merge. The dynamics of the mirror help acknowledge this eclipsing of presentation with representation and dismantling the inaccuracies, asymmetries and gossip (as in Chinese whispers) concerning the gendered identity. I propose the logic of 'trans' and through engagement with the writings of Jean Baudrillard, Leslie Heywood's notion of 'anorexic logic'[20] and Wendy Steiner's 'anorexic aesthetics'[21], I argue for making practices of presence and absence ambivalent within a 'third space', which has many affinities with the concept of androgyny. I analyse a painful and visceral performance by Boryanna Rossa, *The Last Valve* (2004), in which the artist portrays the mechanisms that govern gender in the contemporary world. Rossa inflicted pain on her body in a politicised gesture, blurring the distinction between maleness and femaleness. She proposed a hybrid body that erases heteronormative structures and bipolar determinations. Referring to Irigaray, I go to 'the other side', which is a new land free from systems of oppression imposed on the female subject. It is a space of multiplicity and plurality, which is embraced by the performances by the collective, Grupa Sędzia Główny, who employ what Silverman calls 'a productive look' to speak about and *through* femininity. They act as a judge in control of the final verdict concerning female identity and sexuality.

The final chapter, 'A Rose Garden', alludes to the Red Queen's rose garden from *Alice's Adventures in Wonderland*, in which white roses are painted red. This points towards acceptance of 'either/or' structures and a lack of identification with difference. I see the rose garden, which I call a 'genderland', as a site of transformation and possibility, in which everything is possible and in which one can belong only to seemingly contradictory logics. This threshold land is inhabited by creatures such as Onone, visualised by Żebrowska in her project *Onone. The World after the World* (1995–9). Genderland is not governed by the primary sexual identity or grammatical conceptualizations of gender. It is a world of transformational potentiality, in which the subject becomes emancipated and identity is communicated through different socially and culturally produced borders. It is envisioned through double or multiple gazes and brings to light human anxieties and longings that imprison identity. My argument is founded on the writings of Gilles Deleuze and Félix Guattari, Butler, Baudrillard and Cixous and relies largely on the different conceptualisations of 'seduction', 'desire' and 'androgyny', which enable the despecularisation and the destruction of the phallogocentric order. Cixous's essay 'The laugh of Medusa'[22] and the concept of the 'merger type sexuality', and Irigaray's 'mimesis'[23] are instrumental in shaping my argument around the ungendered, boundaryless space and multiple identity that is defined by oneness. In genderland the female body becomes a powerful subject *and* object that, through different practices of embodiment, cuts through myths that imprisoned women. It is a space in which the look is mobilised in order to, as Silverman proposes, re-view and demystify things, which affords nonviolent acknowledgement of difference and the emergence of new singularities.

This book is an invitation to further dialogue on alternative gazes that challenge the gendered politics of looking. It opens up a discussion introducing theory in action through some lesser-known practices of Eastern and Central European women artists and demonstrates that Western theory could be read differently through the lens of site specific works from beyond the West. At the same time, some issues concerning the female body are common globally for women and only through solidarity and friendship can they be mobilised to invert patriarchal vision.

In Chapter 2 of *Alice's Adventures in Wonderland*, 'The Pool of Tears', Alice asks herself: 'Who in the world am I? Ah, that's the great puzzle.' I suggest that through slipping down the rabbit hole towards the looking-glass realm, the female subject might be discovered and reclaimed. However, whether this really can be achieved is part of a conversation between Alice and the White Queen[24] about what is possible and what we believe. When Alice states 'I can't believe that!', the White Queen replies:

> 'Can't you?' the Queen said in a pitying tone. 'Try again: draw a long breath, and shut your eyes.' Alice laughed. 'There's no use trying,' she said: 'one can't believe impossible things.' 'I daresay you haven't had much practice,' said the Queen.

1

Looking-Glass Reality

My primary concern in this chapter is with the images of the female body, which have been rendered inferior, sexualised and objectified by men. I trace gendered encounters of the female body *within* the mirror. In short, the dynamics of the mirror enable one to explore both the body and the self and this is discussed in relation to specific art projects. This chapter deals with issues of crossing borders and entering a space of possibilities and otherness, which can be playfully called a 'looking-glass' reality. It explores the formation of identity in relation to spatial and specular identifications enabled by Lacan's 'mirror stage'.

The looking-glass

When Alice from Lewis Carroll's *Through the Looking-Glass, and What Alice Found There* (1871) held her kitten in front of the looking-glass, she said,

> I'll tell you all my ideas about the Looking-glass House ... the books are something like our books, only the words go the wrong way ... how nice it would be if only we could get through into it ...[1]

The next moment Alice found herself on the other side of the 'looking-glass', where even things that seemed common from 'her' side of the mirror were utterly transformed. Here, 'everything was as different as possible'.[2] Alice first vanished into the rabbit hole in the novel *Alice's Adventures in Wonderland* (1865; commonly called *Alice in Wonderland*) and then finding herself on the other side of the mirror allows her to experience and explore a world of fantasy and otherness. It seems unsettling and frightening at times and Alice often needs to make decisions and choose which way to go or whether to play certain games (or not). Her body shrinks and grows, allowing her to reach the key or go through the door or not, and her identity is also continuously transforming. Alice's inquisitive nature expresses her desire to explore options and go beyond anything that is obvious.

This is what Carroll describes as 'the law of the mirror' or the law of divergence.[3] On the other side of the looking-glass, everything seems to be displaced and shifted. Contrary to Alice's confusion expressed in her adventures in *Alice in Wonderland*, in *Through the Looking-Glass, and What Alice Found There*, Alice, as I suggest after Deleuze, 'enters the game' and 'takes up the task of becoming queen … [which] refers to the phallus as the agency of coordination'. She

> apprehends the mirror as a pure surface, a continuity of the outside and the inside, of above and below, of reverse and right sides, where 'Jabberwocky' [the word that brings the disjunctive synthesis and makes what is divergent resonate] spreads itself out in both directions at once.[4]

It is clear that going through the looking-glass will enable Alice to enter a different realm. The question is whether this space on the other side is a new beginning, a new perspective or, perhaps, what is interesting is the leap *through* the mirror, which creates a passage from one surface and dimension to another, 'out of' and 'into'. In this 'in-between' the surface of the mirror, which is not neutral and, if understood in Lacanian terms, produces the female body as lacking and incomplete, becomes deconstructed and, in consequence, the border it implies dissolves. This undefined space marking a world of otherness grants a possibility to explore what is 'other', transformed, hybridised and what goes beyond the binary logic and dichotomies of femininity and masculinity.

The mirror is a non-territorialised realm that is experienced as presentable *and* representable. The self, emerging in the process of the mirror stage, is fragmented into the body *in front of* the mirror and its representation is seen *in* the mirror, which is often imagined, fantasised and problematised by traditional cultural and social identifications of the body. These arise from Sigmund Freud's Oedipal scenario, which is gender-inscribed and which has implications when it comes to men claiming possession of women and marking them as their territory and objects. The Oedipal scenario is extended in Lacan's mirror stage to differentiate between male and female children. Identifying the self in the mirror involves entering into a two-dimensional realm of representation. At first, the child is surprised by the surface of the mirror and can often be seen touching it, which suggests the mirror involves experience of sight and touch.

Kaja Silverman argues that '[t]o look is to embed an image within a constantly shifting matrix of unconscious memories, which can render a culturally insignificant object libidinally resonant, or a culturally significant object worthless'.[5] The female body has been subjected to the 'look' and – the key interest in this book – the male gaze for centuries. This look and gaze have often been demeaning, sexualising, subordinating, idealising, projecting phantasies and subjugating that body. Silverman reminds us that the experience of the 'self' originates in the body, so a restraining look not only inscribes the body in unequal power relations, thus privileging the male over the female, but also influences the bodily ego. She argues that culturally constructed distinctions such as gender, sexuality and race, among others, imprison the self and deny otherness and difference. Silverman is concerned with the mirror image, the cultural 'screen', or in other words, the image repertoire and the gaze.[6] The gaze and the metaphor of the mirror will be used throughout the following discussion to analyse some artworks produced by women artists to test how the look shapes the body and how it structures idealising and 'de-idealising' identifications of the body with difference.

Mystery of looking

The female body is believed to be a spectacle to be looked at. This assumption derives from the disjunction between the gaze, which is external, and the eye, which is described by Lacan. He says:

> What determines me, at the most profound level, in the visible, is the gaze that is outside. It is through the gaze that I enter light and that is from the gaze that I receive its effects. Hence it comes about that the gaze is the instrument through which light is embodied and through which … I am photographed.[7]

The mirror and its mechanisms constitute a central metaphor in this chapter and contribute to the explanation of some of the artworks discussed. My understanding of the mirror derives from Freud's notion of the Oedipus complex, describing the process of looking and the stages of a child's psychosexual development.[8] It is guided by Freud's account of subject formation, extended in Lacan's concept of the mirror stage, which explains the phases in which subjectivity is constructed. The mirror 'swallows' the subject and objectifies it, which further complicates the act of looking itself. Mechanisms associated with the mirror enable me to discuss artworks in which the constructed subject desires to go beyond objectification and narcissism and align itself with difference. I will look more closely at the concept of the mirror after I have discussed the differences between the look and the gaze and the 'lack' determining the female subject.

To understand the mechanisms 'operating' the mirror, it is necessary to investigate the act of looking itself, which is paramount in image-dominated contemporary culture. We recognise the outside world and obtain visual information about it through our eyes. Our perception of reality is filtered through our nervous system and the brain that processes images seen by the eye. There are different types of looking and not all of them are innocent. Freud referred to scopophilia, which defines pleasurable looking at other bodies as objects (mostly erotic). Looking can be voyeuristic, controlling the gaze and often being associated with sadism. It may be fetishistic, transforming a fetish object into something reassuring and satisfying, often over-evaluating it. The 'gaze' defines fixing the eyes in an intent look, embodying the relationship between the observer or the agent of gazing (beholder, viewer, spectator) and the observed. It is attributed to others, not the self.

Discourses on the gaze are prominent in myths concerning the eye, such as the myth of Medusa, which is a key concept in this book. The gaze is clearly differentiated from the eye *and* the look, which determines how one's eyes and one's gaze are directed to inspect something and exercise visual power. The term 'gaze' is associated with power. The domain of the visible is investigated by Lacan, who emphasises that perception involves other modes of apprehension beyond sight and operates within space, which means that vision extends beyond that which is literally visible.

In psychoanalysis identity is shaped through internalisation of things that seem external. This is explained by Freud, who differentiates between ego and super-ego, and according to whom absence of a particular visual attribute signifies lack. Freud's conception of constituting the subject is taken further by Lacan, who also redefines Freud's idea of castration by shifting from anatomical lack towards the void of language. The Lacanian model, providing an account for the whole field of vision – including the gaze, the look and the screen – is explained by Silverman, who explores practices of representation and spectatorship with relation to difference. She questions the narcissistic identification of the subject with its mirror image and the impact of the look and the gaze upon the body. Silverman refers to Lacan's concept of the mirror stage, which elaborates on Freud's exteriority of a bodily image. In Lacan's account, this external bodily image is first created by the subject in the guise of the mirror image and then through different cultural representations. The mirror provides the subject with a frame or screen that allows it to recognise its own image as idealised and to relate to others within the field of vision. This relation of the subject to others is guided by narcissism and the ego surpassing other libidinal transactions. The external manifestations of the bodily image are designated by Lacan as the gaze. It is an instrument that determines the subject and enables it to see itself being seen and become responsible for operating the gaze.

Silverman further complicates Lacan's account of the mirror stage in her account of the bodily ego reformulating identification with difference. She articulates the asymmetry of seeing and links gaze not only with gender but also class, race and power similarly to Foucault, demonstrating the different looking relations that form the subject. Silverman emphasises the oscillation between sameness and otherness in constructing the self through ideality and identification. She also further separates the look from the gaze and indicates that even if the look is central in articulating the field of vision, this does not mean that the looking subject possesses the gaze. Lacan's eye or Silverman's look are distinct from the gaze, which is multidirectional, and from its otherness. Silverman compares the relationship between the look and the gaze to the relationship between the penis and the phallus, in which the former can replace the latter but they are not equal because one is anatomical and the other is conceptual. The gaze is situated beyond voyeuristic looking and, according to Lacan, it resides outside of desire, whereas the look remains within the desire for self-completion through the other. In other words, all subjects form their identity upon a repertoire of culturally available (and dependent) images and a gaze. This is addressed in the pink, oval, soft and delicate objects created by Maria Pinińska-Bereś (from Poland) from 1960s onwards, in which she mobilised issues related to women's experiences. *Corsets* (created between 1966 and 1967) represent the image of woman depicted according to male desires. In the *Psycho-furniture* series (from 1968), Pinińska-Bereś addressed female social roles. The softness of materials (often quilted), delicacy and pink and white colouring, indicating that the female body might be seen as a hard candy, resonate with female sexuality and illustrate its enslavement and oppression. The artist challenges 'pinkness' defining women's identity. It is a colour of icing, sweetness, cuteness, princesses; it is the favourite colour of little girls but also a colour associated with the female body and porn industry.

Silverman agrees with Lacan in connecting the gaze and the look to a certain ahistoricism. Yet the latter, as she says, is always finite and embedded within spectacle. It resonates with both visual and psychic categories and, as such, is demarcated by lack. Nonetheless Silverman recognises cultural specificity influencing the field of vision on at least three levels. She argues:

> These variations pertain to how the gaze is apprehended; how the world is perceived; and how the subject experiences his or her visibility … I would like to propose that the screen is the site at which social and historical difference enters the field of vision.[9]

This perspective is employed in my analysis of some artworks through the narrative of subject as spectacle and subject as look, which, as Silverman reminds us, can be manipulated through changing the screen. Lacan commented on the possibility of camouflage and travesty and the 'mediation' of the screen in masking (or unmasking?) the feminine and the masculine. What I hope to achieve through my discussion of the artworks I have selected is to intervene in the representational consistency concerning the female body and allow for difference. I believe art enables this.

Silverman suggests that subjects identify not with other 'disprized' bodies (conventionally taken to be disadvantaged) but desire to replicate the cultural ideal with which they are familiar. For example, the female subject aspires to be whole and, as such, 'one' with masculinity and the idealising mirror. The struggle to reach the ideal is moderated and supported by the cultural gaze. This results in manifestations of difference both on social and personal levels.[10] Silverman refers to Freud whose concept of fetishism embeds the female body in the male subject. She also reminds us of Irigaray's *Speculum of the Other Woman*, in which the author argues masculinity is never fully realised as it desires 'the self-identical' which results in sexual difference being defined within 'the projection, the sphere of representation, of the same'.[11]

The visibility of the male over the female who is desiring and haunted by the phallus derives from the absence of the mother, which in Freud's game called 'fort-da', discussed in *Beyond the Pleasure Principle*, is represented as an object, namely a toy. The game was invented by Freud's grandson, who played with a wooden spool on a piece of string, which he threw away and then pulled back shouting 'o-o-o-o' and 'da' respectively. These sounds were interpreted by Freud as signifying something going away and reappearing ('fort' as gone away in German and 'da' as there). Further he saw the game as a compensation for emotional distress and psychic trauma associated by the child with the mother occasionally leaving the household and not taking the child with her. This simple play empowered the child and a few years later, when the boy showed little reaction to the death of his mother, Freud attributed this to the effect of the game. He also used the game to explain the mechanisms of pleasure and the concept of the return of the repressed (woman).[12] Such association further victimises women as, according to the rules of the game, the female is an object to play with that can be easily discarded. Derrida pointed out the incompletion of the game, contrary to Freud, who claimed that the toys can be used by the child only to make them go. He exposed the possibility of going elsewhere and applied it to his own theory of writing, emphasising the eternal motion of the return and difference.[13] Derrida says: 'In order to think of play in a radical way, perhaps one must think beyond the activity of a subject manipulating objects according to or against the rules.'[14]

Irigaray aims to unbury the mother and offer woman, who is seen as lacking and homeless, a 'house of language' in which her body can be brought into language and liberated from the patriarchal monological speech. She also calls on women to rethink the cultural female imaginary and make it active, acknowledging its polymorphous and plural character.[15] This will be discussed further in Chapter 2.

The male is performing a narcissistic act and projecting his ego onto the world. The reflective side of the mirror belongs to men. Consequently, women lack reflection and are unable to reflect. They are defined by the lack of voice, phallus and the gaze. This is believed to be their anatomical destiny that makes them an error and an inverted masculine subject that cannot enter Lacanian symbolism. Irigaray argues that masculine and specular representation excludes women from looking and subjects them to the cultural, and so patriarchal, gaze. Women's social surveillance is also discussed by John Berger, who describes how men are watching women, who internalise their gaze and watch themselves but do not look back.[16] The gaze belongs to men and it personifies their power over women and their speechless bodies. Irigaray deconstructs the bipolar system and proposes that women need to reclaim their bodies to become autonomous subjects who resist the patriarchal hierarchy through appropriating their roles and making them their own. This is further elaborated in the concept of mimicry, which in Irigaray's account is positive and embracing female difference. This is discussed in detail in Chapter 2.

Looking is a complex and gendered process that is addressed by Alicja Żebrowska (from Poland) in the 1.40-minute video and accompanying series of photographs entitled *The Mystery is Looking* (1995). The video portrays a lifelike glass eye shamelessly gazing back at the spectator. Only after some time does the viewer realise that he or she is, in fact, pushed into a vagina whose lips, resembling eyelids covered in blue eyeshadow, are

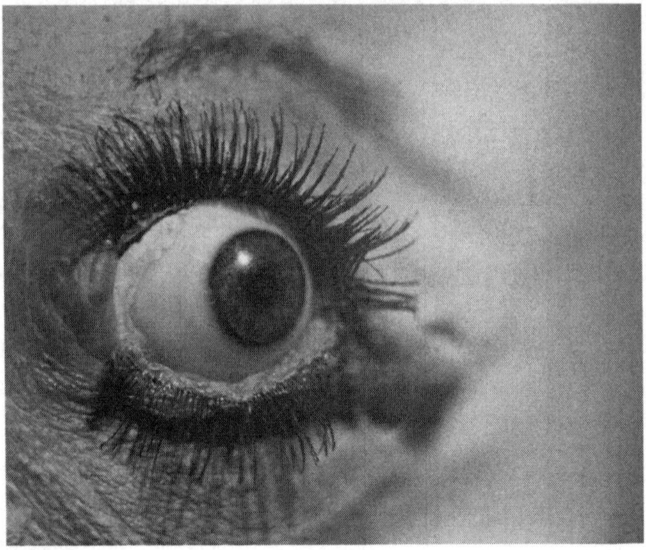

Image 1 Alicja Żebrowska, *The Mystery is Looking*, 1995, video, photography. Courtesy of the artist.

wide open, and the fluttering eyelashes attached to them reveal an eye. The inner contractions of the vagina move the eye, opening and closing it and finally spitting it out. Żebrowska says that '[e]xtremity purifies' and enables transformation.[17] In her works she refers to the experience of female sexuality and through this personal, intimate experience she comments on gender issues projected onto a wider cultural mirror. Her interest in gender indeterminacy and fluidity and the foundations of individual identity lies at the core of her practice, which undermines the dichotomous and bipolar power structures understood by Foucault as the disciplining of the body.[18]

In *The Mystery is Looking*, Żebrowska is playful yet serious, having placed the eye – presented in full make up – in her vulva. The female sexual organ transformed into a looking eye is staring at the male and female audience provocatively and fiercely. The artist intervenes in the power structures here. Usually, it is the female body being looked at by the male spectator, who dominates and controls her sexuality through his penetrating gaze. She is objectified and subjected to patterns of thinking about the female body and the perpetuated tropes of femininity compartmentalising their representations.

Woman is constrained by the phallic male gaze when it comes to her body, her role in society and in the economy (and as such the labour market) and also her participation in politics. Here the eye is placed in the vagina, which is ogling the spectator, taking the position of an object being viewed and of the viewer. It is not a silent and passive 'lack' defining the female body. It is in full view, no longer imprisoned in patriarchy, hidden and shameful, waiting to be possessed by the man. The abyss, hole or lack is demystified. It no longer functions as the site of male desire as it stares back subverting the cultural code. The vagina *is* the eye that dominates and captures objects. Through opening the eye, it becomes a self-aware subject, not an object to be looked at. It possesses and seizes the male spectator.

Żebrowska portrays the emancipation of the vagina and its becoming a subject. The secrecy of the female organ is demystified, yet it is often still seen as scary and grotesque. It is worth recalling Freud's account of 'the more' and 'the less' when it comes to genital differentiation in which the clitoris is a small organ, on the side of the 'less'. It is inefficient and insufficient, yet it poses a threat to the male corporeal ego.[19] Its ostentatious display, as in the case of Żebrowska's work, provides a threat to the male and causes anxiety regarding male corporeal integrity. His claim for the phallus, which for obvious reasons cannot be abstracted from the penis, is impaired. It is interesting to bring in Jean-Joseph Goux's perspective, which aligns the phallus with *logos*.[20] In other words, the paternal signifier is equated with rational power and intelligence that is at the core of Lacan's theory of the phallus, as recalled by Silverman.[21] Although I shall be discussing these concepts later, I want to emphasise at this point that the absurdity of the 'eye vagina' portrayed by the artist could be interpreted as referring to Cixous' laughing Medusa, who is often considered monstrous, ugly and disgusting when, in fact, she is beautiful (and she is laughing). Viewing it in full sight in a culture in which female sexual organs and sexual pleasure still cause animosity or fear, or even pain, in particular among men, demystifies myths associated with the passive and disgusting vagina. Żebrowska applies full make-up to her vagina, aestheticising it, but she does not caricature or deform it, or reject the female. The dark spell around the female body and sexuality is broken and the male fear originating in secrecy and the monstrosity of female organs is ridiculed. It does not need to suffer from being an object of male pleasure.

At the same time, the artist demonstrates that there is an alternative to the common representations of the female body. It does not need to conform to Western ideals, mostly produced by men, and it does not need to be beautiful. It does not have to be spread passively on a chaise longue, as in common representations of the reclining female nude in art, looking at him seductively, waiting to be possessed or not looking directly and submissively averting the gaze. It can be a fragment that does not need to be hidden. Yet this partiality is not arousing to men; quite the opposite for porn movies, in which the female body in pieces is prepared for the male observer. In *The Mystery is Looking*, the eye vagina fills the entire screen to the extent that it is unrecognisable at the beginning. Only later in the video does the camera move away, portraying the female crotch between open thighs and, seen beyond, breasts and face of the artist. The active staring eye protects the vagina, preventing access into it. It catches the viewer ogling it and stares back, provocatively and fiercely, as though saying, 'so what?' and 'what now?'

The mirror

In 2004 Boryana Rossa, from Bulgaria, and Oleg Mavromatti, from Russia, established ULTRAFUTURO, an international collective of artists addressing interactions between technology and science, and explaining their social implications. Their work, which will also be discussed in the following chapters, often mobilises issues of gender inequality and cross-cultural gender re-enactments, in particular within post-Cold War Russian and Bulgarian films.

In 2005 the audience of the Sofia City Art Gallery in Bulgaria encountered a naked woman wrapped in a transparent foil, sitting on a stool. She was positioned with her left side almost touching a mirror mounted on a ladder. Two round holes were cut out of the mirror, one at the top and one at the bottom, through which the woman stuck out her left leg and arm. Next to the mirror there was a table on which were some surgical tools. The audience could only observe the female body parts visible through the

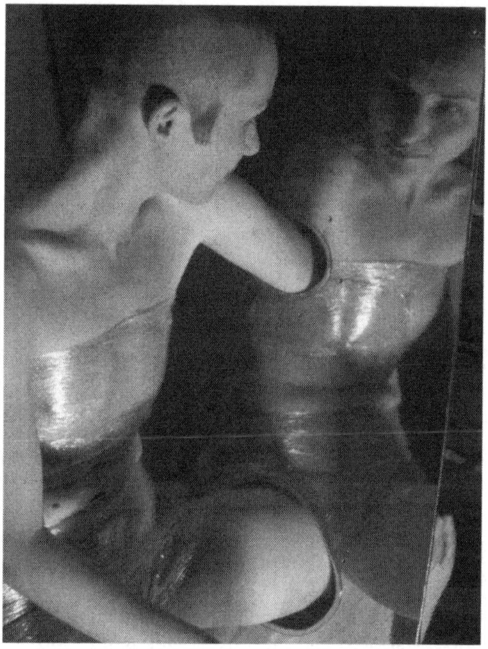

Image 2 Boryana Rossa *SZ-ZS performance*, 2005, performance, together with ULTRAFUTURO. Sofia City Art Gallery, Sofia. Photographer: ULTRAFUTURO. Courtesy of the artist.

holes. What they couldn't see was Oleg Mavromatti, who stitched Boryana Rossa to her mirror reflection with a surgical thread.

The performance, entitled *SZ-ZS* (2005), was documented by two cameras, one recording the performance and one (a surveillance camera) attached to Mavromatti's head. The images of the movement of the hand stitching the body, the pulling of the surgical thread through the skin and through small holes drilled in the mirror, the blood slowly dripping to the floor and the cleansing of the body with water were transmitted in real time from the camera to a monitor placed close to the ladder. The camera became the eye of a voyeur that facilitated delivery to the audience of a mediated image that could also be traced in real time. The act of documentation enabled by the surveillance camera was accompanied by the performance itself. After Rossa's limbs were stitched to the surface, the audience was invited to the other side of the mirror to look at the body and its reflection.

Rossa has said that the *SZ-ZS* performance offers a visual interpretation of Jacques Lacan's triad of the psychoanalytic order – the symbolic, the imaginary and the real – that forms different levels of psychic phenomena and situates subjectivity within a system of perception and representation.[22] Rossa's and Mavromatti's action demonstrates that these three Lacanian orders can function simultaneously, resonating with the internal and external world and enabling the interplay between subject formation and its external image, internalising the production and consumption of the outside reality. I will explain this point further in the section below, looking more closely at the concept of the mirror. Stitching Rossa's body to her mirror reflection addresses the fragile border between the inside and the outside, which influences the way in which the reproduction of subjectivity is aligned with the influences of external stimuli; Chapter 2 will focus on the images of perfection imposed on women's bodies. This chapter argues that the trope of the mirror can be useful in offering a new thinking *across* and *through* the mirror, which enables a future free of gender distinctions.

The mirror involves looking, creating a 'double' image (it has the capacity of creating two images of the subject) and another reality. It also suggests searching for the other and for an alternative visual order. It is a trap catching the subject and transforming it. In this sense, it is an indispensable concept through which otherness is recognised. The mirror allows us to scrutinise the journey from the self to the other through the gaze and through looking back. The mirror as a trope reflecting becoming subjects, ideologies, identities and the perpetuation of stereotypes often attracts attention from art history and theory, gender studies and psychoanalysis, evoking the myth of Narcissus (as discussed by Luce Irigaray, Julia Kristeva, Elizabeth Grosz, Christine Battersby, Hilary Robinson, Kaja Silverman and Anneke Smelik, among others)[23]. The mirror implies the 'other' and different relationships, constituting an axis of visuality that, if read in relation to Lacanian 'mirror stage's' labyrinth, becomes a metaphor for the social self. Critical cultural and visual theories assume a close connection between the mirror, the gaze, body, patriarchy and gender, best exemplified by the body of thought produced after Lacan's introduction of the 'mirror stage', indicating a becoming subject. Technically the gaze describes the ways in which we consume images. It is a psychoanalytical term linked to fantasy and desire, defining the relationship between the subject and the object, as in Lacanian discourse.[24] Similarly to the mirror, the gaze enables the building of power relations, as suggested by Foucault.[25] In feminist theory the gaze highlights gender asymmetries and inequalities, challenging the notion of the female body as castrated as suggested by, for example, Bracha Ettinger, Atara Stein, bell hooks, Silverman and Smelik.[26]

When associated with the 'male gaze', the mirror also represents a model guiding strategies for representing the female body. The metaphor of the mirror has a long tradition in visual studies and plays a major role in discussion of aesthetics/representation, and politics/power structures. It is a space of otherness as the mirror evokes an ideologically loaded image of the same. The mirror has layers of meaning that extend beyond what is directly captured by the eye. It is a trope of duality and contradiction, as it is a real object which, at the same time, shapes one's reflection.

The mirror in Lacan's mirror stage theory enables the constitution of the being as a subject in relation to others. The body, previously seen as fragments, recognises and identifies itself with its image and is seen as a totality. The mirror stage comes to an end at a point when the subject enters into relations with other 'I's' or subjects and, consequently, transforms into a social being. This is when subjectivity becomes decentred and realises its power to shape itself within the world it operates. According to Foucault, this happens through objectification within the human sciences (including psychiatry, sociology and psychology), which enables the possibility of representation. Foucault suggests that the mirror might be seen as heterotopia, which negates conventions of order and describes sites of slippage between what is familiar and what is unfamiliar.[27] Heterotopia undermines what is stable and enables the experience of otherness, collapsing the fixed to the mirror distortion between the Same and the Other.[28] Such dissolution of the boundaries underscores the concept of the mirror stage which, in Lacanian psychoanalytical theory, constructs the female body as lacking, and demonstrates the underlying complexity of this visual device and its ability to destabilise what might seem a straightforward transcription of real space. The reflection of verisimilitude, which is generated in the mirror, resonates with Foucault's ordering systems, which define the relationship between repetition and resemblance that in Western culture generates knowledge. The mirror's ideological function in the construction of space and identity also exposes what he conceptualises as interconnectivity and 'aemulatio', 'emulation of the reflection of the mirror: it is the means whereby things scattered through the universe can answer one another'.[29] The mirror unites realms. The mirror as a heterotopic space has the capacity to make accessible and isolate realms. Foucault suggests: 'Everyone can enter into these heterotopic sites, but in fact that is only an illusion: we think we enter where we are, by the very fact that we enter, excluded.'[30]

This correlation between the mirror and space further uncovers the longstanding connection between mirrors and the formation of the self. Within the mirror the real and the fictional blur and converge, creating a utopian realm in which, behind the screen, a virtual space is created. This imagined non-place is occupied by reflections that seem 'present'. Foucault argues:

> it makes this place that I occupy at the moment when I look at myself in the glass at once absolutely real, connected with all the space that surrounds it, and absolutely unreal, since in order to be perceived it has to pass through this virtual point which is over there.[31]

The mirror functions as utopia, an immaterial space uniting self-referentiality with the gaze of the reflected image. When applied to discussions around the female body, it enables the embracing of otherness associated with representations of the social and cultural 'other' embedded in visual tropes of femininity.

The mirror is a threshold between the real and the imaginary and, at the same time, a magnifying glass that allows us to finally 'see' the other. Jorge Luis Borges wrote about the invasion of the 'mirror people' who are imprisoned behind the mirror, condemned to reflect the image of the ones who defeated them.[32] They no longer reflect the conquerors but a distorted image. However, one day they will go through the mirror again and resume the war. The mirror image implies the idea of the double, and can be traced in the myth of Narcissus and Freud's 'narcissism'.[33] Lacan's 'mirror stage' and Baudrillard's 'swallowing the mirror', discussed in the following chapters, also lead through ideas of duplications and multiplications towards the return from the other side of the mirror and the collapse of binary systems into, as I would like to propose, 'genderland', the multiplicity and celebration of otherness, which stems from Hélène Cixous's 'merger type sexuality'.[34] Alicja Żebrowska addresses this dissolution of the 'either/or' logic in her 1998 installation *When the Other Becomes One's Own*. The video introduces the viewer to Sara, who was born with a male body but identifies as female. We can see Sara standing in front of the mirror, scrutinising her reflection. She is represented as Venus, connoting the ideal female body, but also as Narcissus, seduced by the reflection. Sara decides to reclaim her identity through the body. She is portrayed moving to the sounds of sex change surgery; we are introduced to her past and the present, witnessing her transformation.

The mirror invites us to play with presence and absence. It is a hide and seek game between reality and fantasy, the self and the other enabling migrating and travelling – back and forth – through to the other side, into the realm of 'trans'. Mieke Bal suggests that if the mirror is adapted to history seen as reconstruction, it becomes the only medium to read images, to project them or tautologically combine.[35] It incorporates the denaturalised and then pluralised tradition, 'preposteriority';[36] as only then, according to Bal, can transcendence communicate and reiterate the past, and only then are various concepts – myths, tropes, histories – allowed to travel. This new situation, called by Bal the 'renewed authenticity', frames images, put 'forward as beautiful in a culture replete with false claims to an authenticity based on myths of origin and tired of "beauty"'.[37] The mirror was used by Ewa Partum (from Poland) in her 1984 performance *Pirouette* in order to address her past. The artist, wearing skates, walked along a mirror surface installed on the floor, under a fan with an attached nude self-portrait. While the mirror broke, piece by piece, Partum discussed the meaning of a pirouette as a figure, which allows one to look inside the self.

The mirror stage and formation of identity

Rosalind E. Krauss reminds us that with the mirror stage, Lacan emphasises the slippage in how sameness is constituted in relation to the mirror image.[38] According to Lacan, the triad real–symbolic–imaginary originates in the mirror stage, which is rooted in Freud's notion of the Oedipal phase. The Oedipus complex describes the structure of desire and refers to early stages of a child's development and infantile sexuality when unconscious processes are uncovered through language and associations. The boy's desire for mother's exclusivity requires the elimination of the father, of whom the boy is jealous and fearful. The fear originates in the feeling of desire towards the mother that, if discovered by the father, might lead to castration. There also exists the possibility that the boy might identify with the mother and desire the father's attention. The application of this idea to girls is that they initially desire the mother but when they realise they lack a penis, they turn their attention to the father. The desire for possession of a penis cannot be satisfied and they start searching for substitutes.

The Lacanian subjectivity can be traced in his concepts of the mirror stage and the symbolic order and cannot be isolated from and discussed without acknowledging the concept of narcissism. Sigmund Freud, in his paper 'On narcissism: an introduction', declared narcissism to be an intermediate phase between auto-eroticism and object-love. He emphasised its role in sexual development in terms of the link between the ego and the external objects, which resulted in the differentiation between the 'ego-libido' and the 'object-libido'. The 'ego ideal' – an early form of the later established 'super-ego' – and the self-observing agency emerged from those new relations.[39] The term narcissism was introduced by Havelock Ellis in 1898 as 'narcissus-like' – referring to a psychological attitude, and later developed by Paul Näcke in 1899 as 'Narcismus' – describing a position of someone treating his body as a sexual object and hence signifying a sexual perversion. Freud describes narcissism as an ordinary attitude present in human sexual development. Therefore, he allocates it to the libidinal element, not perversion. Freud distinguished a primal and a normal narcissism that in both cases is caused by the libido, which is redirected from the external reality to the ego. He remarks: 'We form the idea of there being an original libidinal *cathexis* of the ego, from which some is later given off to objects, but which fundamentally persists and is related to the object cathexes.'[40] The 'object-cathexes' are the emanation of the libido, which develops a separate 'ego-libido' and 'object-libido' – the libido theory – attached to either ego or objects helping to distinguish between sexual or ego instincts.

Originally, a person has two love objects – him- or herself and the woman who takes care of him or her – resulting in 'primary narcissism' in everyone. Some people later seek themselves as love objects, exhibiting narcissism. It is a point of departure for the development of the love-object. An individual might love what he- or she is, was, would like to be. The narcissistic system implies the 'immortality of the ego',[41] a libidinal *cathexis* in the ego where the primary narcissism is later re-born into object-love. It relies on the formation of an ideal – 'the ideal ego' – that is created by a person in order to measure the ego, and that becomes the goal of self-love. In Freud's account, '[t]he subject's narcissism makes its appearance displaced on to this new ideal ego, which, like the infantile ego, finds itself possessed of every perfection that is of value'.[42] An individual hopes to recover the perfection he remembers from his childhood and projects it as a substitute in the form of 'the ideal ego'. This mechanism increases the human's self-regard, which corresponds with the narcissistic element in love. The return of the libido from external objects and transformation to the ego represents narcissistic love.

The Lacanian concept of the mirror stage, when a child recognises its own image in the mirror as an idealised version of the self,[43] refers to Freudian narcissism and the Oedipus complex, and conceptualises the imaginary body in the mirror's reflection as the male body, a concept that is criticised in feminist discourses. It also uncovers complexities enmeshed in voyeurism and looking, which will be discussed in the following chapters. Narcissism, the mirror image and the ideal self identified in the reflection were central to Lacan's theories of how personality can extend beyond the limits of the body and be inscribed in a social network, and how identity can be constructed or deconstructed when subjected to looking or gazing.

This existence beyond the biological boundaries of the body is appropriated by Rossa and Mavromatti in their performance, where the reflected image of Rossa's body refers to Lacan's register of desire, which articulates the need in demand. It resides in-between signifiers and relies on modification. It also implies a lack of the object of desire where the absent one, the maternal phallus, embodies the Freudian idea of the penis and its lack.

In the context of the Oedipus complex, Lacan argues that the phallus relates to something beyond reach and incarnation (Alice is looking for this indefinable other in her adventures but it seems not to be beyond her reach). If the Oedipal process operates properly, the phallus signifies the missing rather than the imaginary. The male needs to affirm the existence of the symbolic phallus that he does not have. The female either longs for the lost phallus or expects to get it from men, as discussed earlier. The masculine having the phallus is contrasted with the feminine being the phallus; this describes it as the signifier. Hence, the phallus becomes either an imaginary object or a signifier, the object of desire – a reflection – symbolising the satisfaction lost in the Oedipus complex.[44]

In Lacanian theory desire, with its dynamics of the unconscious and the drives – founded on the imaginary confrontation of the ego with the image of the other – relates closely to the mirror phase theory. These are games of presence and absence, loss and phantasy, linking the subject with the object. Hence, the subject assumes an image or a disguise, like some animals or insects in an ethnological mechanism of mimicry – looking like, capturing in the environment – in order to escape predators. These ideas of games and masks are developed by Lacan in the mirror phase theory, describing the imaginary capture of the being in the external image, either the mirror or the other. This new internalised image of the ideal whole self, identified as the 'Imaginary', complements the body, initially lacking and fragmentary. Also, this alienating identification can be aligned with the formation of the ego – the location of narcissism that either exists from the beginning or emerges afterwards. The ego serves as a mediator between the internal and the external. It seems whole, which prevents it from recognising the lack of completeness.[45] In the mirror phase, it maintains the misconception of coherence by projecting an untrue appearance. Lacan argues that the subject initially embodies the real fragmentary body and the alienating image. The mirrored images – located outside and alienated – constitute the ego and hence completeness. In Rossa and Mavromatti's performance the border between the self and the other dissolves and the reflected image becomes stitched to the body.

The subject, besides the 'Imaginary' and the 'Real' (the pre-mirror which cannot be symbolised and which resists representation), also enters the principle of the 'Symbolic' – networks into which we are born, for instance linguistic, social or cultural – preceding birth. Hence, the human being is captured in the image and will be identified and assume signifiers from the parents' language. The linguistic representations, such as, for instance, name, situate the subject in the symbolic universe. This goes beyond the identification with the image into the ideal, understood as the unconscious. In this context, narcissism is both imaginary – as the subject is located in the specular register, where the ego serves as a rationalising medium – and symbolic – as everything has a meaning. The third register of the 'Real' represents the amalgam of the previously mentioned two, relating to objects that lost their meaning and are excluded from reality.[46] In other words when an infant sees a specular image, this is the first time subjectivity encounters spatial relations and an external sense of coherence. The reflected image of the whole self in the mirror (which is contradictory to the primordial sense of the fragmented body as experienced before) becomes the ideal image of completeness that constitutes the ego. This image of coherence, as also suggested by Freud, is formed through an external force, and enables the identification of the internal self with the external realm, which is guided by culturally specific images of coherence, as suggested by Althusserian ideology.[47] The mirror stage provides a model that guides the three orders in which different aspects of subjectivity operate.

The mirror, a border between fixed places – whether the inner and the outer, self and other, female and male, passive or active – creates conditions of violence and further emphasises differences rather than commonalities. The presence of a threshold (in one form or another) empowering or disempowering identity has been noted by many, including Marsha Meskimmon in *Cosmopolitan Imagination*, where she argues:

> If the self and the other, or the domestic and the foreign, are fixed categories, separated by a defined border, that every encounter between them is, by definition, a threshold crossed by violence, a movement from one 'anterior pure' to another.[48]

If we can move beyond the border and adopt the logic of 'trans' or, as Meskimmon suggests, 'the threshold as a transformative state, a process of liminal engagement or a segue', we might be able to rethink subjectivity and make it operational through ethical, aesthetic, social and political agency.[49] As gender is based partly on the psychosexual development of an individual, it is important to consider the possibility of breaking structures such as those embedded in the mirror (childhood experiences enforcing stereotypes concerning femininity and masculinity) propelling gender inequality and disabling the development of subjectivities seen as other. The 'broken' mirror blurs the distinctions between opposites and becomes a locus of possibility and in-between, vacillation of 'and' and 'or' in 'togetherness'.

The imaginary might be seen as inscribed into coherence instead of into what is lacking and might suggest positivity. The *SZ-ZS* performance stitches the borders between the real-imaginary-symbolic. It questions the possibility of visually representing Lacan's triad 'in one gesture'. Rossa explains:

> If the imaginary is the mirror image, and the symbolic is our language-determined social existence, or our actual body, which people see, then the real will be the inconceivable, physically non-existing border between the mirror reflection and the flesh of the artist. The attempt to reify this non-physical connection is painful and infeasible.[50]

In the *SZ-ZS* performance Rossa and Mavromatti were guided by the possibility of crossing from one realm to another that would go beyond the imaginary dimension. The stitching of body parts through the mirror reflects the physical act of connecting the different spaces where the self is produced, consumed and reproduced. It disrupts the barrier between reality and reflection, making the physical unification of mind (what is imagined and conceptualised) and the female body possible. In her symbolic gesture Rossa makes us rethink issues of illusionary borders. Only through the literal stitching with a surgical thread does the physical flesh function in parallel with the mirror and is finally fixed to the illusionary body across the surface.

The title of the performance, *SZ-ZS*, indirectly refers to Dr Josef Mengele, nicknamed 'the Angel of Death' and the series of experiments he performed on twins at Auschwitz during World War II. In one of these studies he supervised an operation in which two boys, Tito and Nino, one of which was hunchbacked, were cut and sewn together to create Siamese twins. The wound became infected and shortly after the operation they died. It is alleged that according to Mengele's orders the twins were tattooed with the letters 'ZW' standing for 'twins' (in German, *Zwillinge*). Rossa and Mavromatti use this story to address mirrorness, issues related to imitation and wholeness, the marking of male and female ('SZ' and 'ZS'), not Mengele or the war itself. It could be argued that a reference to these horrific experiments stresses the conditions of violence created by the mirror and supports what Meskimmon calls the 'threshold', a transformative state. The performance engages with the concept of narcissism and the figure of Alice, but it transgresses them. The mirror, screen, border or barriers renders the unification between the subject and the carrier of the reflection possible. Rossa does not go through the mirror like Alice in order to appear in a different realm where fixation does not allow disconnecting the physical from the mirrored. She stitches *through* the mirror to duplicate her physical body and exist on *both* sides of the border/screen. The real becomes the mirrored illusionary and a locus where a new initial point is set up. This is a new realm of primal wholeness and possibility.

Motility of the look

Kaja Silverman reminds that:

> In his *Écrits*, Lacan writes that 'the mirror-image would seem to be the threshold of the visible world'. He thereby suggests not only that all visual transactions are inflected by narcissism but also that it is only by moving through the mirror stage that one enters the scopic domain.[51]

She proposes to review the field of vision through the mirror stage, which is limiting. It is a threshold and hence a boundary that encapsulates and imprisons. Within its metaphoric dimension Lacan suggests that 'the subject's corporeal reflection constitutes the limit or boundary within which identification may occur'.[52] As such the bodily image includes and excludes other images that are socially and culturally sanctioned for identification. This mirror image cannot be trespassed, as it valorises what is acceptable and what is not.

Yet, Silverman argues that Lacan's theory offers the possibility to address the subject as mobile and hence enabling polymorphous interpretations. This has not been questioned directly and thoroughly so far and yet it lies at the core of Lacan's concept on the mirror stage. The migratory dimension of the subject suggests a range of bodily identifications, what Silverman proposes to call 'the principle of the self-same body'.[53] It is clear that the main concern of discourses around the mirror stage is built upon issues of bodily ego, idealisation and identification. What consequently follows, as Silverman reminds us, is that which constitutes the visual domain, namely 'the gaze, look and screen (or cultural image-repertoire)'. Further, she suggests that 'the look is under cultural pressure to apprehend the world from a preassigned viewing position, and under psychic pressure to see it in ways that protect the ego'.[54] This results in our bodily identifications being subjected to social and psychic constraints, which limit identificatory alignments with anything that is recognised as different.

What is sanctioned as socially valorised guides the forces empowering the look. The question remains how the look can be regulated and restructured to allow us to see beyond limiting assumptions, as Silverman suggests, 'productively and transformatively'.[55] How to circumvent normalising criteria and allow for forms of difference concerning, for example sex, gender and class, among others? How to go beyond idealisation, such as the one encapsulated in the imagined as perfect Venus's body, to acknowledge the existence of bodies that are socially despised and review the female body beyond the male gaze? This does not mean that idealisation needs to be neglected but, as I will argue after Silverman and Irigaray, it should be applied in a way that enables challenging existing ideals precisely by *inviting* the self to identify with monstrosity, grotesque, the ugly, dirty, simply by aligning ourselves with mysteries hidden behind what is considered as terrifying (and petrifying), Medusa's look.

At the same time it is important that ideality is acknowledged and used actively, as it is, for example, by Natalia Lach-Lachowicz (known as Natalia LL; from Poland) in the *Consumer Art* film and photographic series produced between 1972 and 1975, in which naked women are presented in provocative almost pornographic poses, consuming ice-cream, bananas or frankfurters. An innocent activity (eating) acquires an erotic sensual dimension, in which consumption is affiliated with the image of the female body in popular culture and with the booming consumerist culture itself. Paradoxically, the products consumed by the women represented were difficult to obtain in the 1970s in Poland and might be read as objects of need rather than want, or as fetishes of that time, desired to be possessed. The licking and sucking of exotic goods such as bananas, associated with the unreachable West, can be interpreted through the lens of consumerist seduction. Women in Natalia LL's films are active, contrary to the fixed depiction of the passive female body in mass media. Natalia LL reverses the power relations between the male and the female. Here, woman is actively consuming phallic products associated with the male body. She embodies beauty ideals. She is in power and she is controlling her physicality and sexuality, challenging the stereotypical role of women reduced to objects and products to be consumed. Silverman reminds us that

> ideality is the single most powerful inducement of identification; we cannot idealize something without at the same time identifying with it. Idealization is therefore a crucial political tool, which can give us access to a whole range of new psychic relations.[56]

Further, she also stresses that identification follows an externalising rather than an internalising logic, 'that we identify excorporatively rather than incorporatively, and, thereby, respect the otherness of the newly illuminated bodies'.[57] This is important when thinking about tropes of femininity present in contemporary culture that shape our awareness of what is socially acceptable and desired and what is not. Images of femininity such as those embodied in the figure of Venus demonstrate a privileging look that is based on passive idealised female body subjected to the laws of perfection. As I will show later, her fragmentariness and lack is initially unnoticed. Woman serves as the projection of the male ego and the male gaze (as in the case of Natalia LL's *Consumer Art* series) that rejects any identification (but in fact not necessarily) with difference. If we allow for the look to be mobile, and start questioning categories of wholeness and the body in pieces, we might discover the female body does not necessarily have to be idealised *or* revolting. It can simply *be*.

Before I move on in the following chapter to discuss more closely the female body as an object of the desire of the male gaze it is worth mentioning how Silverman expands Lacan's understanding of the mirror stage. She reminds us that it is rooted in Freud's description of the ego as a projection of surface. In Lacan's mirror stage, the ego is formed when the image of the body is recognised by an infant subject within mirror reflection in the form of a mental representation. She says:

> Thus the ego is the representation of a corporeal representation.' So both are visual. 'Not only is the "surface" of which the ego is a "projection" specular, but the cerebral cortex itself also "functions like a mirror". A "site" where "images are integrated"'.[58]

Silverman, quoting Lacan, emphasised the 'fictiveness and exteriority of the image which founds the ego. We are dealing with an artificially constructed image that is projected and within which the subject identifies with sameness. However, it is also possible to associate with otherness, as Lacan emphasises both the 'otherness' and the 'sameness' of the reflection within which the child recognises the self. Silverman reminds us that within the ego is also embedded an aspect that allows the subject to identify with a wider set of constructions that do not align it solely with being a member of a species. It is called the 'moi', the 'belong-to-me', and this is what allows it, within the mirror stage, to identify with what he or she is or is not.

When discussing how the ego can be predicated on both sameness and otherness, Silverman refers to Jean Laplanche and to further elaboration by Paul Schilder and Henri Wallon, who consider the role of sensation in the production of the corporeal ego. The latter understanding of the mirror stage differentiates between the 'sensational' and 'corporeal' ego. In Lacan's reading the encounter between the infant and its specular reflection is a punctual event, whereas in Wallon's account it is an ongoing process that happens between the first encounter and the psychical incorporation of the mirror image. Initially this specular reflection is seen as separate. Slowly the child orients itself towards it, a process that Silverman calls 'identity-at-a-distance', 'condition or quality of being "other"'.[59] Further, Wallon proposes the concept of 'proprioceptivity', which describes the nonvisual emplacement of the body's form defined by gender, sexual preference and race. In other words, in the mirror image the body functions within space, which is associated with the postural function. The muscular sensations, or cutaneous sensations discussed beforehand, are shaped by the interactions between the body and the cultural environment it occupies. The 'gender bending' might suggest the proprioceptive ego may not be compatible with the mirror reflection. However, as Silverman argues:

> Wallon's account of the mirror stage indicates that the proprioceptive ego is *always* initially disjunctive with the visual image, and that and that a unified bodily ego comes into existence only as the result of a laborious stitching together of disparate parts.[60]

This understanding acknowledges difference and fragmentariness. At the same time it demonstrates the dangers of the logic of unity and wholeness, to which I will return in Chapter 3. Once again it becomes clear that the mirror image cannot be detached and requires support from the cultural and social gaze.

Bonds

The trope of the mirror is often adopted by women artists to map issues attached to otherness and difference and gendered identity. In 2011 Anetta Mona Chişa (born in Romania) and Lucia Tkáčová (born in Slovakia) produced a video entitled *Never Odd or Even* in which they bond themselves together in order to create a palindromic entity that in itself is a mirror structure. They wore pale pink costumes and masks with photographic images of the other one's face attached to their heads. The costumes and masks concealed and suppressed their personal traits. The application of a photographic portrait signifying an individual's unique identity visually blends the distinction between 'I' and 'You'. It undermines subjectivity but at the same time enables a closer proximity between 'I' for others beyond 'I' for myself. The self-bondage technique used to attach the bodies together is an erotic practice involving physically restraining oneself for erotic pleasure. Not a power neutral process – combining bondage, dominance, submission and often sadomasochism – it is a challenging practice which is risky and dangerous. It was unusual that Chişa & Tkáčová used this technique to bind themselves *together*. They bound themselves independently and then intermingled the ropes in order to create a structure restrictive to both of them, a structure that resembled a Janus-faced entity. They disabled themselves from free movement. Any physical activity hurt. If one moved, the other felt pain. By applying self-bondage, they inflicted pain on their bodies and subjected themselves to a situation in which they lost their individual freedom and became dependent on one another.

A similar palindromic structure appears in their *Vessel (i aM a venus, A conch, a kiT, a Cat, a Lot)* (2012), a double-head clay vase representing mutual reflection placed on a mirror pedestal. The subtitle is an anagram of artists' names, which demonstrates the principle of their collaboration and which is created from an entity composed from individual selves. The white vase was made by the artists modelling their heads simultaneously, observing each other as if in a mirror reflection. Again, their selves are merged together into temporal oneness, as they say, 'to create an ephemeral I from WE. The mutual reflection crops up as a continuous questioning and mirroring of the self in the other one.'[61]

The works discussed were presented in 2012 at the exhibition in Rotwand gallery in Zurich entitled *i aM a venus, A conch, a kiT, a Cat, a Lot*. Bojana Pejić, writing about the works of Chişa & Tkáčová, argues:

> In his esteemed work, *Politiques de l'amitié*, Jacques Derrida elaborates on the social bonds developed over the course of the Western tradition, which he identifies as forms of loving and desire, quest and promise, consensus and respect for the Other that are not determined by familial ties or ideological solidarity: friendships.[62]

In *The Politics of Friendship*, Derrida suggests that in Western philosophy the representations of friendship were based on the model of brotherhood, in which the figure of the father was absent and the friend was associated with the figure of the brother. This male friendship, even though non-hierarchical, contributes to further extending heteronormative and misogynic frameworks and risks tyranny and totality. This fraternal bond constitutes

> the double exclusion of the feminine … that can be seen at work in all the great ethico-politico-philosophical discourses on friendship, namely, on the one hand, the exclusion of friendship between women, and, on the other hand, the exclusion of friendship between a man and a woman.[63]

This exclusion of the feminine, asserting that woman is capable of love but not friendship, symptomises not only removal from the fraternalist and androcentric discourses but characterises the 'neutralisation of sexual difference'. Derrida's claim to re-evaluate friendship beyond fraternalist restraints resonates with the need to rethink the oppositional structures embedded in sexual difference. It also gives hope for a theoretical framework that would enable revisiting the politics of female friendships.[64]

Chişa & Tkáčová have been collaborating since 2000. They both graduated from the Academy of Fine Arts and Design in Bratislava and currently live and work between Prague and Berlin. The artists represented the Romanian Pavilion in Venice Biennale 2011, which shed light on their practice of challenging gender relations and on the presence of Eastern European women artists in a Western-centric art world. These two women engaged in doing something together evokes, as Pejić suggests, the early 1970s phenomenon of the 'female buddies' in mass media and television, labelled 'bitch media'. In contemporary art practice there are more and more examples of female buddies working together, whether as a broader community or in smaller scale, as in the case of Chişa & Tkáčová, as a pair. Since 2000 they have collaborated in addressing the stereotypical modes of representation that are inherently specific to art from Eastern Europe and consumer expectations when it comes to consuming and producing art. They work across a range of media including performances, videos, textual works and installations, triggering reflections on the different forms of power in post-communist New Europe and revealing society's habits, often paired with concepts of memory and oblivion.

In *Never Odd or Even* and *Vessel (i aM a venus, A conch, a kiT, a Cat, a Lot)* Chişa & Tkáčová are bound together, with ropes or having the casts of their heads attached. These works, similarly to many others they produced before and after, define their friendship and solidify their commitment and bonds. In *Never Odd or Even* they rely on one another and their mutual trust. The work conveys closeness and nearness, their dangers and associated fears, but also a politics of female friendship and, as such, highlights a politics of difference, in particular sexual and gendered difference. The female duo challenges the male dominated art world and teases male sexual phantasies and the scripts inflicted on women by society. They merge (through bonding, gluing, casting) their individual selves into a new entity that negotiates and compromises egocentrism and celebrates otherness and friendship. Pejić argues that their politics of friendship:

> is informed by their feminist positioning, which follows two basic trajectories viewed by Theresa de Lauretis as central to (the history of) feminism. The first is a narcissistic drive for self-representation. This may imply taking on the identity of 'disorderly' and 'unruly women' (Russo), using the strategy of 'womanliness as masquerade', subversion and excess … The other feminist trajectory is the ethics of working together, sharing, and trust.[65]

In *Never Odd or Even*, they wear pale pink suits and masks with photographs of faces of the other, interchanging their identity. Their faces are covered in seductive make-up with red lips and smoky eyes. The self-bondage suggests eroticism and combined with the fashioning (or masquerading) of their bodies, equates to the stereotypical sexual submissive femininity, which is powerless, subjugated and victimised. At the same time, they take control of their bodies, binding them and sharing, and subjecting themselves to being dependent on one another.

What initially might seem a playful stance on Laura Mulvey's 'to-be-looked-at-ness'[66] negotiates complementarity. The technique of bonding rejects the primacy of vision as it relies predominantly on the sense of touch. Chişa & Tkáčová perform Maurice Merleau-Ponty's conceptualisation of 'intercorporiety' and 'the transitivity from one body to another.[67] Meskimmon suggests a shift from object to process, in which the skin becomes 'a threshold of embodied subjectivity. As such, "synergetic" flesh and skin yield to yet another extension of the threshold as process, namely the corporeal constitution of the subject in and through sociality.'[68] The most basic function of the skin is to protect and contain but it also has a communicative function. Silverman emphasises Schilder's account in which cutaneous sensations can become sites of social exchange.[69] Chişa & Tkáčová bring their bodies, selves and identities together into one, immobilise them and subject to physical pain. Similarly to Rossa and Mavromatti, they create a scenario where their politics of friendship articulates another option, a new entity that questions the concept of identity. It is a space of possibility, a 'third' mode of articulation suggested by Marjorie Garber, that challenges 'the idea of one: of identity, self-sufficiency, self-knowledge'.[70] Garber argues that this third dimension might be exemplified by the Lacanian symbolic, 'not a realm apart, but the transference onto the level of the signifying chain of those binary structures that, in the Imaginary dimension, relate everything back to a fictional "one"'.[71] The symbolic order, called by Garber the third mode, involves moving from complementarity to contextualisation, in which duality is questioned. I would argue that this space of possibility challenges the idea of difference by combining the Lacanian triad, as in the case of Rossa and Mavromatti's performance.

Chişa & Tkáčová's act becomes an active rejection of passivity and the formation of subjectivity according to the rules of the mirror stage. It also negotiates the implied narcissism and negates the fraternalistic friendship excluding difference. Pejić sees their work resonating with Mikhail Bakhtin's concept of a 'dialogic work'.[72] Chişa & Tkáčová engage with each other and with other women through their examination of female traditions and histories, 'establishing a kind of female genealogy' and enabling the politics of female friendship.

The swallowed mirror and 'I will not be your mirror'

According to Cixous, women need to confiscate narcissism and the displayed body, implying an eroticised female representation. The patriarchalised image of corporeality, often manifesting a politics of desire, needs to be 'de-paternalised', which might be enabled by adopting the Baudrillardian concept of 'swallowing the mirror', in which the subject is substituted by the object, depriving the sign of meaning and confusing the signifier with the signified. Baudrillard remarks: 'It is as if things had swallowed their mirror.'[73] The reflection of the subject is swallowed and the mirror is broken. This disappearance opens up multiple possibilities for the formation of identity and invites the other, at the same time allowing for a complete oneness with one's Self. Identity can be forged according to ones own preferences and not necessarily through the gaze of the other. It evokes the myth of Narcissus or Hyacinthus,[74] where he perishes in his own reflection in water, unable to recognise himself in the incredibly beautiful image he saw. He wanted to possess and could not. Eventually Narcissus died, and from his blood that soaked the earth a white narcissus grew, whose oils were curative and also narcotic. In another version of the myth, Hyacinthus was an incredibly beautiful young man with whom other gods of the same sex, Apollo amongst others, fell in love. One of them, the West Wind, was so jealous of Apollo that he killed the boy, from whose blood a hyacinth sprang. Apollo mourned greatly, crying over the flower. His tears stained the petals with letters 'ai, ai', symbolising his grief.

What should have been separated seeks to be united. The distance between the real and its double is annihilated in the non-place of reflection. Narcissus is seduced by the surface of water that he cannot transgress. The mirror of water is not a reflection in which the subject establishes his transformation but rather an absorption that seduces. It is not the mirror stage, where the subject finds himself within the imaginary. The mirror of water is an abyss, a non-place, and it is narcissistic in the sense that it allows Narcissus to be first charmed by himself. The myth suggests the idea of the lack of depth, whereas the mirror offers a realm soaked with possibilities. As in Cixous's comparison of woman to an abyss, Narcissus is seduced by otherness. The other version of the myth establishes the existence of Narcissus's twin sister, with whom he was in love. After her death, he visited a spring to see his reflection in the water, which he imagined was his sister's. Henri-Pierre Jeudy, a French philosopher and sociologist, builds on this mimetic relation and introduces the notion of the 'twin refraction',[75] relating to Narcissus, who adopts mimetically the image of his twin, renewed by his own face and so seducing him. This concept reminds one of Chişa & Tkáčová's act, in which the artists reflect each other and are seduced by each other.

In the mirror reflection, everything becomes transparent and hyper visible, stripped of any illusion. Visual existence no longer refers to the subject but to the object of display and reflection that operates the world. 'It is no longer', as Baudrillard observes, 'the subject who operates the world to itself (*I will be your mirror!*)'.[76] The mirror held in front of things is shattered. The object refracts the subject and causes fragmentation and discontinuity. As Baudrillard suggests:

> '*I'll be your mirror*' does not signify '*I'll be your reflection*' but '*I'll be your deception*'. To seduce is to die as reality and reconstitute

> oneself as illusion. It is to be taken in by one's own illusion and move in an enchanted world.[77]

The mirror absorbs by merging presence with absence.

Luce Irigaray plays on the idea of the mirror stage, articulating the female body, seen by Lacan as hole and lack. She questions how to detach the other (woman) from otherness of the sameness. To see woman, it is necessary to look beyond the imposed phallic status of identity and 'her' being either a mirror or the negative of male. Irigaray's concept of the 'speculum' – a mirror used by doctors to examine the internal parts of the body – creates a passage in and through the other.[78] The female body is subjected to the phallocentric structure, where 'woman' can liberate herself from the male aesthetic through the redefinition of the concept of beauty and through production of art.[79] Irigaray implies that '[m]an keeps sight, the gaze, the reflection (Narcissus) for himself and allows woman to keep hearing the echo (Echo). In order to repeat one needs to have first heard.'[80]

The Freudian concept of narcissism was developed by Lacan into the model of the mirror phase, where the subject reappears in an imaginary space of (mis)recognition and identification, creating alienation. However, it can enable completeness. The myth of Narcissus is applied by Cixous in the context of love. She says men led women to hate themselves for their virile needs. She remarks: 'They have made for women an antinarcissism! A narcissism which loves itself only to be loved for what women haven't got! They have constructed the infamous logic of antilove.'[81]

Together with Eros – love – man forbids beauty and bestows on women the fear of Medusa and an abyss. The censorship imposed on the feminine interferes with her embracing of her own sexuality, her body and the possibility of its self-expression. Cixous suggests that women need to write with their bodies, their 'sexts' as a way out, not to fear decapitation or castration and to confiscate narcissism and the displayed body. Through approaching the patriarchalised world and playing with the trope of the mirror, women artists enable various margins – ambiguity, fluidity and the logic of trans – where masculinity can be questioned. Cixous claims that woman is a 'body without end',[82] a whole composed from whole fragments: 'not simple partial objects but a moving, limitlessly changing ensemble, a cosmos tirelessly traversed by Eros, an immense astral space not organised around any one sun that's any more of a star than the others'.[83] Therefore, she suggests: 'Let us dematerpaternalise rather than deny woman … Let us defetishise'[84]

Things have 'swallowed their mirror'. The feminine, often represented through tropes of femininity such as Alice, Venus or Medusa, is falsified by men in order to strengthen their hold onto social status and sexual dominance. According to Baudrillard, Narcissus's image in the mirror is manipulated by the signifier, which has already become the signified. The reflection is swallowed and the mirror is broken.[85] Baudrillard implies:

> 'I'll be your mirror': this is the formula of the subject. 'We shall be your favourite disappearing act!': this is the slogan of the object. Yet that disappearance also has to be the 'appearing act' of the Other. For that is the only way for him to exist.[86]

The mimetic representation in the mirror plays with illusion, terminating reality by reflecting it – multiplying. Finally, Baudrillard suggests: 'Our image in the mirror is not innocent, then. Behind every reflection, every resemblance, every representation, a defeated enemy lies concealed. The Other vanquished, and condemned merely to be the Same … I'll not be your mirror!'[87] The mirror formula allows building a new totality from separate parts.

Look!

Between 2003 and 2008 Katarzyna Kozyra (from Poland) worked on a multimedia project including a series of performance arts in different forms (video, musical, performance) under the overarching title *W sztuce marzenia stają się rzeczywistością* (In Art Dreams Come True). All actions taking place between Warsaw and Berlin were documented on video and resulted in a feature-length film about the project. Kozyra addressed conventional strategies of representing the female body and portrayed them in an artificial world that she created after meeting Gloria Viagra (Michel Gosewisch), a drag queen from Berlin, and Maestro (Grzegorz Pitułej), a professional opera singer and instructor from Warsaw. Both of them assisted the artist with rediscovering herself through her appearance and her voice. The project consisted of a series of performances, *Nightmare* (2004), *Façade Concert* (2005), *Beauty – Pre-view with Gloria Viagra*

(2005) and a pop video *Cheerleader* (2006), among others. In *Il Castrato* (2006) Kozyra re-enacted a one-act Baroque opera during the Gender Bender Gay Culture Festival in Bologna, Italy. Dressed as a drag queen she was 'castrated' of her wig and dress on stage by Gloria Viagra and Maestro. This was an act of reclaiming and rediscovering her androgynous body and of emphasising that gender is just a costume that can be worn. In *In Art Dreams Come True* Kozyra proves on many occasions that she can experiment with femininity and masculinity and transform gender characteristics flexibly.

The most recent film produced under the umbrella of the project is entitled *Summer Tale* (2008). It is a contemporary fairytale that turns into a horror movie. Initially, the viewer follows the tranquil and idyllic life of dwarf women inhabiting a house with a garden. They pluck fruit from the trees, do the gardening, hang out the laundry while the birds are singing, the bees flying and a light wind delicately moves the flowering plants. Then it gets dark and the birds go to sleep. After a full moon rainy night, a giant poisonous toadstool, smelly stinkhorn and white puffball appear in the garden. The dwarves are surprised, yet one of them decides to water the mushrooms, which start morphing. The harmonious life of the women is turned upside down and violated through the interference of unexpected visitors, Gloria Viagra, Maestro and Kozyra, stylised as Alice in Wonderland, who are born out of the mushrooms. The women are first intimidated by the handsome Maestro and beautiful Gloria but they invite them inside their house. The appearance of the unexpected guests disrupts the laws of the fairytale world. The initial openness and kindness of the hostesses is, in fact, underpinned by fear and hatred of otherness. The dwarves do not appreciate Maestro's continuous singing and his stinking socks. The women decide to address the situation, and prepare a brew with disgusting ingredients. They offer it to Maestro, who drinks it, chokes and dies. However, during the funeral, Alice's kiss revives Maestro. The women are devastated. The situation deteriorates as they then discover Gloria is a man and decide to murder her. Subsequently, they also incapacitate Maestro in a fishing net, kill him and hide the two bodies in a cellar. They also catch and imprison Alice who is tied to a chair and forced to observe the dwarves wearing blue foil aprons and chopping the male bodies with axes. After they finish, one of them says: 'Sweetie don't cry. They are evil men. They have to die.' The women go back to their normal daily routine. The viewer observes Alice being freed yet sad and sobbing, and scattering confetti or casting a spell from a balcony over the garden. Then we can see new toadstools. The hostesses have disappeared. The film ends.

Using the medium of a fairytale, Kozyra combines elements of different stories and interweaves aesthetics of Eden and idyllic existence with horror. Even though the viewer might recognise the narrative of *Snow White and the Seven Dwarves*, no particular story is created as the basis for the movie. The artist makes a statement regarding the male element in a bipolar world. Her 'Snow White' is tripled and appears as a man, a woman and a drag queen. Male dwarves turn into she-dwarves. Kozyra feeds the viewer with a moralising parable in which she teaches not to eliminate the other but to embrace it. In her story the other is represented by the male, reversing the usual association of difference and the female. She turns the world upside down and merges femininity and masculinity, blurring gender roles and demonstrating that everything is possible when it comes to identity and gender. She undermines the conventional beliefs and convictions regarding beauty and ugliness, the good and the bad. She is fearless in confronting myths and stereotypes structuring the cultural mirror reflecting society and proposes to go to the other side, break it and contest standards concerning beauty, body, sex and gender. She performs her own identity, becoming a bricolage and mosaic of options, which she eagerly wears and then takes off to try on a new 'dress' or 'mask'. Harald Fricke suggests that the artist opens a space of opportunities. He says: 'Whatever she does, dares, or transforms into can be liberation for each and every one else.'[88]

So, let us have a closer look at the female body, its representational conventions and their deconstruction and, following Kozyra's opening words to her documentary *In Art Dreams Come True* (inspired by Robbie Williams' song of the same title), 'Let me entertain you'.

2

Down the Skin-deep Hole

This chapter takes the reader for a free fall, similar to Alice's journey down the rabbit hole, and explores how the female body is represented by women artists in contemporary art beyond its stereotypical associations with physicality. This chapter questions whether representations of the body are only skin deep and if they can become the means, not just symbols, of production and consumption. I argue that the female practitioners whose work I analyse reach further and portray women as active subjects who challenge Descartes' mind-body dualism and, as a consequence, see the female body as objects. The mind and the body are not separate and are not gendered; man does not equal mind and woman cannot be defined only by her physicality and corporeality. Through theories of embodiment, women artists such as Kozyra, Rossa or Joanna Rajkowska demonstrate that the relationship between the mind and the body is flexible and fluctuating, dependent on but also responsive to the interaction with other bodies and objects.

She is to be looked at

She (woman) is to be looked at, as discussed by Berger in *Ways of Seeing*[1] and she is to be judged by her looks. She is part of what Guy Debord theorised in *The Society of the Spectacle*,[2] in which the image mediates the way people interact and behave. What is considered an 'ideal' image functions as a model, a formula to follow almost religiously and as which to present oneself. Debord says the spectacle is a section of the society that 'concentrates all gazing and all consciousness'. It is 'not a collection of images, but a social relation among people, mediated by images', and he notes that:

> Spectacle cannot be understood as an abuse of the world of vision, as a product of the techniques of mass dissemination of images. It is rather, a *Weltanschauung* which has become actual, materially translated. It is a world vision which has become objectified.[3]

The female body is governed by the rules of this spectacular order and relations in which being turns into having and subsequently into appearing. It is mapped by the commodification and economisation of the gaze.

Baudrillard, by contrast, suggests we are no longer immersed in the society of spectacle[4] that is governed by images shaping reality but in the 'contagion of the virtual'.[5] I would argue that images can no longer be explained or apprehended using the mirror formula to offer a clear distinction between reality and phantasy. Their overwhelming presence in mass media, virtual reality and social networks shapes identities and the perception of the self. However, individuals are not merely passive consumers of these images. They have also become active spectators, interacting with images and using them to perform their identity.

Issues surrounding representation and display have been central concerns of many women artists, including the Factory of the Found Clothes art collective (from Russia), Natalia LL, Dorota Nieznalska (from Poland), Daria (anonymous street artists from Russia) or Sanja Iveković (from Croatia), among many others. They allow experimentation and challenge hegemonic formulae of portraying women, mostly by male artists and 'beauty myths' defined by consumer culture, which builds ideal female images. Women's 'to-be-looked-at-ness' can be used to contest not only issues surrounding unequal representations of gender and the obsessive positioning of the female body as 'lacking' that arises from the Lacanian concept of the 'mirror stage' but also the lack of acknowledgement concerning differences such as race, ethnicity, economic or cultural backgrounds. These subverted representations have the capacity to expand the stereotypical portrayal of women and their subjection to standardised canons of beauty, and offer alternative readings of 'female' representations to those already in play.

Beauty, in the vernacular sense referring to the 'look', is intriguing, not only with regard to external appearances but also in relation to 'the gaze' and opticality. This act of 'looking' generates what is considered normal and abnormal, commonly understood and accepted as beautiful or ugly, abled or disabled. What is particularly interesting is the point of intersection between the inside and the outside, the desirable and the repulsive. I will return to concepts associated with ugliness and the logic of lack in the following chapter but here I would like to focus on myths surrounding the notion of beauty.

She must be beautiful

The works of art that I discuss are modelled on Western standards of beauty, its 'beauty myth' and consumer standards. In the first paragraph of her article 'The ambivalent beauty',[6] Izabela Kowalczyk discusses a performance piece by Marina Abramović (born in Serbia, the former Yugoslavia). In *Art Must Be Beautiful, Artist Must Be Beautiful* (1975) the artist spent an hour brushing her hair, so passionately and violently that her head started bleeding. A simple everyday action, aiming at beautifying, caused pain and anger. Kowalczyk suggests this work is also about 'regimes of beauty and the hidden violence they engender'.[7] Here, an embellishing procedure is not connected with pleasure but with discomfort, pain and, in a sense, according to Kowalczyk, 'a fight against the self'.[8] A ritual to achieve perfect beauty of her own external body fails. It appears that Venus's ideal image interlaces with Medusa's terrifying appearance.

Beauty is also currently defined by popular culture with reference to meanings imposed by Western consumerism, where it is associated with appearance, superficiality, attracting attention and arousing desire. Kowalczyk remarks that Western consumer culture, disseminated by mass media, models body patterns particularly applied to 'woman' who, in order to be 'visible', needs to wear a certain mask and meet certain societal requirements.[9] Beauty can be achieved, but not without sacrifices and often pain, for instance, such as that experienced while undergoing medical procedures, plastic surgeries or other 'rituals' aimed at improving appearance. Beauty has become a commodity, which can be 'bought' and 'exchanged'.[10] Therefore, it is constructed by procedures and processes particular to different cultures. Consumer culture and what Naomi Wolf theorises as the 'beauty myth'[11] defines specifically the standard upon which the ideal woman's image is built. It relies on a perfect representation of various 'beauty myths' – mostly 'looks', attached to the external appearance of the body, which are subjected to the male gaze and the pleasure it incites.

It is fascinating, and at the same time entertaining (if not terrifying), that most magazines, cosmetic brands or television adverts incorporate the notion of beauty. We are bombarded with expressions such as 'Beauty trends', 'Discover your inner beauty' or the names of various cosmetic salons, for instance 'Venus' – suggesting timeless feminine ideals, or 'Plato' – helping one to change appearance and, at the same time, the soul. Beauty saturates the world, focusing on the 'woman' as the signifier of the beautiful and an object of mainstream consumption. 'She' as the body and the figure is sculptured, painted, performed, and appears in movies, photography or magazines.[12] And she must always be beautiful, younger, thinner, with smoother skin and shinier hair.

Beauty

The obsession with beauty – elevating it to an absolute, degrading it, deriding, parodying, beautifying, seducing, simulating, reworking and re-appropriating – is inseparably linked to contemporary attitudes towards the body, gender and sexuality. Women artists such as Orlan, Cindy Sherman and, more recently, Aleksandra Ska or Paulina Ołowska, among others, manipulate their bodies in order to demonstrate how the exterior appearance impacts on cultural images of women seen as inanimate beings. They manipulate the viewer's gaze through asserting their corporeal agency and challenging the objectification of the female body. Saul Ostrow argues that together with the re-invention of the concept of irony in the 1960s, beauty started to be re-appropriated as a cultural and political phenomenon.[13] Rather than being explored as a philosophical discourse, aesthetic judgement and a sign of taste, beauty can be examined, as in the case of the artworks discussed here, as a threshold between a form and a function, the critical and the socio-political that allows investigating various forms of discrimination regarding gender, sexuality and aesthetics. As Araeen Rasheed suggests:

> If art is the expression of beauty … then the meaning of this Beauty must be sought not in the old classics, not in foreign cultures, nor in metaphysics, but in the material reality of our existence as a people and our own cultural life today.[14]

Beauty is associated with classical proportions, symmetry and universal standards of perfect forms, but also with the external look, the ornament and pure decoration. Eleanor Heartney, in the foreword to Peg Zeglin Brand's book *Beauty Matters*, coins the term 'beautocracy', which describes the interest of contemporary Western European and American culture in the concept.[15] Beauty is sometimes traded for the sublime or even ugly. It is also located in gender terms, where the concept is often intertwined with seduction and becomes theatricalised. All those contexts reflect ideas of wholeness and fragmentation, resonating with notions of ugliness and the sublime, prettiness and glamour and enhancing the dichotomy between Venus and Medusa.

In the hands of women artists such as Rajkowska, Kozyra, Ołowska, Ska, Natalia LL and Iveković, among many others, beauty becomes a tool to question the stereotypical representations of the female body that are reliant on ideal images of perfect corporeality. Even though women's bodies are still embedded in social and cultural frameworks that too often situate it in a state of objectification, women artists demonstrate the existence of possibilities of seeing the female body as transitioning and not fixed. They make conscious decisions regarding their bodies, and politicise and activate them to emphasise women's corporeal agency. Dana Benson suggests that political art without beauty is nearing an end.[16] She remarks that the return to and incorporation of the concept of beauty resonates with the current cultural insight model, where art is a method towards exploring the knowledge of culture. Here, a new politically motivated beauty is born, where it no longer refers to values and only appreciating works of art but, more importantly, becomes a politicised voice. In Benson's account:

> The reasons for the current rekindling of interest in beauty are for the most part, it seems to me, superficial and external to art.

> It is really the aestheticisation of the everyday world that is at the basis of this interest. One has to think that art has to keep up with this hyper-aestheticisation or to compete with the easy palatability of the media.[17]

Beauty is confusing, preoccupied with its power and the pleasure it causes. It is complex, even controversial, as it does not relate only to simple prettiness, but it is inscribed into the post-modern framework or beyond. Neal David Benzera and Olga M. Viso remark:

> Notions of absolute beauty are in a current state of collapse as beauty has come to reflect and personify the social and cultural issues of the day. The desire to be multiculturally diverse, to reflect the attractiveness of sexual power while also revealing intellect and experience, and to accommodate the body-morphing potential of cosmetic surgery, biotechnology and prostheses have given way to the alternative forms of beauty that have taken centre stage in 1990s.[18]

In the preface to the exhibition catalogue for *Regarding Beauty: A View of the Late Twentieth Century*, Benezra and Viso also ask what significance the tradition of beauty has for the new centuries. Approaching the concept after the modern aesthetic amnesty, the 'destroying' of the idea and art's experience with formlessness, may seem pointless and frivolous. The divorce between aesthetic value and meaning, the disappearance of form and annihilation of the body also do not implicate the necessary location of beauty within a work of art. However, the notion faces new challenges that refer to situating it not in traditional aesthetics, but, on the contrary, in a cultural context – as a construct that is inherent in contemporary statements towards the body, gender and sex. The misadventures of beauty of the earlier periods caused the allergic reaction of modernism and the fracture between art and beauty that implicated the present attitude of adapting beauty as a nonchalant choice rather than as a way of expression. As Eleanor Heartney suggests: 'Beauty can be a double-edged sword – as capable of destabilizing rigid conventions and restrictive behavioural models as it is of reinforcing them.'[19]

Postmodern ideas of the beautiful were defined by Jean-François Lyotard as sublime, excessive and far from perfection and the ideal.[20] The fragmentary nature of postmodernism resulted in the search for new representations of the phenomenon and caused a paradoxical return of a new beauty – dissected, superficially perfect and symmetrical with a strong political dimension, far from the formalist's conceptions of aesthetics. Beauty became optional. It transformed itself into a post-classical montage, an assemblage of tropes and contexts. This 'bricolage beauty' simulates, copies and replicates. It is defined culturally and politically.

In a Western context, beauty has been associated with the feminine ideal. Paradoxically, the gendering of beauty cannot be linked to Classical Greece. Even though beauty was discussed with reference to gender and sex as far back as Plato's discourses, it did not reflect the fabricated myth of 'woman' by men. Olga Viso suggests that in the Classical period the cult of beauty embodied both sexes, often elevating androgyny to articulate what was considered beautiful. Later, the female as the epitome of beauty dominated Western culture. Since the 1960s, as Viso remarks, feminist theorists:

> asserted the feminine notion of beauty as expressly political. Seeking to reverse the "male gaze" and lift the constraints brought on by the male objectification of woman as sexual objects, the feminist movement declared the female body a "battleground".[21]

Beauty and its connotations became a strongly loaded cultural and political weapon. It addressed the commodification and aestheticisation of the body – predominantly the female one. It demystified not only physical corporeality, but prejudices, repressions, power structures and male dominance. Besides dethroning the control and suppression of the female, beauty also evokes issues regarding women's quest for perfect appearance.

The new beauty seems to be reformed after the mirror gaze, 'merged sexually', as Hélène Cixous suggests, while looking at Medusa's myth. Suzanne Perling Hudson remarks: 'Beauty is … a kind of Trojan horse, capable of smuggling disruptive ideas and concerns into otherwise disinterested institutional spaces.'[22] Recently beauty has become popular, perhaps even fashionable, with numerous texts and exhibitions again tracing the origins of the concept. At the beginning of the 1990s something changed. In a response to the debate during a panel discussion on 'what's happening now', Dave Hickey announced that '[t]he issue of the nineties will be beauty'.[23] He suggested:

> I insisted that beauty was not a *thing* – 'the beautiful' was a thing. In images, I intoned, beauty was an agency that caused visual pleasure in the beholder ... If images don't *do* anything in this culture ... if they haven't *done* anything, then why are we sitting here in the twilight of the twentieth century talking about them? And if they only do things after we have talked about them, then *they* aren't doing them, *we* are ... the efficacy of the images must be the cause of the criticism, and not its consequence ... this is why I direct your attention to the language of visual affect – to the rhetoric of how things look – to the iconography of desire – in a word, to *beauty*![24]

It is interesting that Hickey emphasises the role of visual language and 'iconography of desire'. I will come back to these issues in subsequent chapters. In 1995 Klaus Kertess, curator of the Whitney Biennial, declared that beauty would be 'the issue of the nineties'.[25] In 1996 in the *New York Times Magazine* Peter Schjeldahl said that '[b]eauty is back'.[26] In 2000 the exhibition *Regarding Beauty: A View of the Late Twentieth Century*, organised at the Hirshhorn Museum and Sculpture Garden in Washington and combining different views on beauty in the last four decades of the twentieth century, made the topic re-appear. The examples above are just a few that suggest the comeback of an icon. More exhibitions, publications and conferences have approached the notion, often relating it to ugliness or the sublime. Among theorists reintroducing beauty are Elizabeth Prettejohn, presenting various approaches towards beauty arising from the eighteenth century until the present day, Hal Foster, Dave Beech and Wendy Steiner, placing it in the context of the body and androgyny.

In 2000 Peg Zeglin Brand claimed that '[b]eauty is back in fashion'.[27] Hickey's statement that beauty would dominate the new decade found a reply in Danto's book *The Abuse of Beauty*.[28] The author claims that aestheticians made an error in exploring art only as a construct founded on beauty. The disconnecting of the two spheres began with Duchamp's anti-aesthetic ready-mades. Danto examines the abjuration and abandonment of beauty by the avant-garde, the refusal to make objects that were beautiful in order to seduce viewers. According to Danto that attitude explored the nature of beauty, and thus helped to exclude it from the concept of art as an essential component defining its nature. He notes:

> Beauty could be present or not, and something still be art. The concept of art may require the presence of one or another from a range of features, which includes beauty, but includes a great many others as well, such as sublimity.[29]

Danto examines the psychology of everyday aesthetics, ordinary objects with artistic pretensions and the notion of beauty. According to him, the twentieth century escaped from the idea, commercialising it or simply making it disappear. '"Beautiful!" itself became just an expression of generalized approbation'. Beauty was not connected to form, aesthetics or philosophy, but admiration, 'Wow!';[30] its cognitive meaning was overshadowed by an emotive element. Kirwan asks to what extent the notion exists if it is more often equated with the Kantian definition than the phenomenon itself.[31]

Universal beauty

In 2009 Boryana Rossa and Oleg Mavromatti staged a performance entitled *Vitruvian Body* at *re.act.feminism – Performance Art of the 1960s and 1970s Today*, at the Berlin Akademie der Künste, Germany. In this performance, Rossa undresses, positions her body in a metal structure composed of a round cylinder embedded within a cuboid, and as with the duo's earlier *SZ-ZS* piece, she is stitched to it by Mavromatti. The title of the piece is a reference to Vitruvius *De architectura*, a classical treatise also known as *The Ten Books on Architecture*, written around 15 BC. In Book III of the work, Vitruvius described the human figure as the source of proportion guiding the orders of architecture. This ideal body became recognised as the Vitruvian Man and appeared in Leonardo da Vinci's drawing, accompanied by notes from *c.*1490 known also as *Le proporzioni del corpo umano secondo Vitruvio, Canon of Proportions* or *Proportions of Man*. The construction within which Rossa's body is spread mimics da Vinci's drawing, depicting correlations between human proportions and geometry and the search for universal harmony.

The performance was documented by photography and video, which was projected onto a screen located near the construction. Rossa's naked body was stretched within the circular apparatus with her limbs put

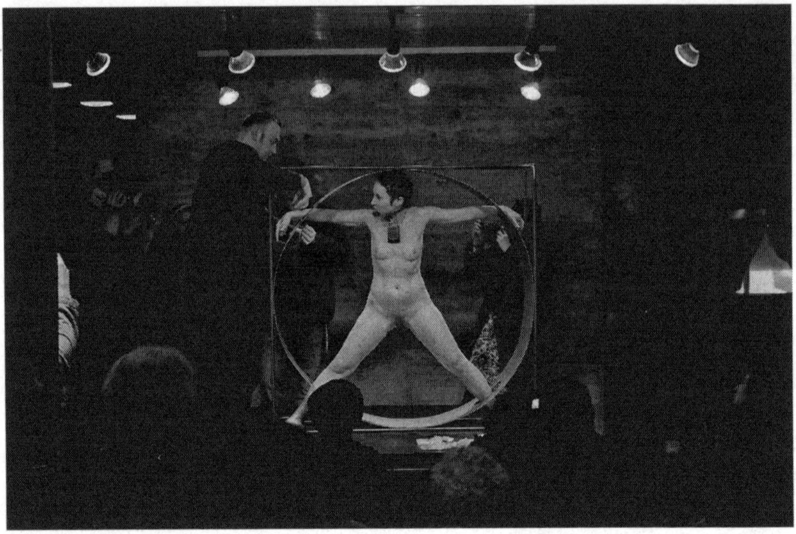

Image 3 Boryana Rossa, *Vitruvian Body*, 2009, together with Oleg Mavromatti, re.act.feminism, Akademie der Künste, Berlin. Photographer: Jan Stradtmann. Courtesy of the artist.

through four cut out holes. While she was explaining the references of the piece to the Vitruvian Man, Mavromatti put on rubber gloves and started slowly stitching up Rossa's body to the structure. Towards the end of the performance the artist asked to have her lips sewn as a protest against censorship. She also allowed the audience to cut her free, which liberated her from visible pain and stopped the blood slowly dripping from her lips.

The tradition of lip-sewing performances calling attention to silencing minorities and denial of hospitality by different states has been used widely by political activists. In the 1980s, David Wojnarowicz (born in Red Bank, New Jersey) protested against the state's neglect of the AIDS crisis in New York by sewing his lips shut with a red thread. He is known for the photograph of a falling buffalo he took in 1988–89, which became a symbol of the AIDS crisis and which was used by the band U2 on the cover of their single *One* (1992). Wojnarowicz, who was abused as a child and had worked as a prostitute in his teenage years, is recognised as a powerful voice of his generation, actively fighting for individual freedom. Mike Parr sewed his lips shut in the performance *Close the Concentration Camps* (2002) in which he addressed the situation of asylum seekers in Australia. In 2010 Mandana Daneshnia, an Iranian asylum seeker who set up a camp in Athens, Greece, sewed her lips together and demanded women's rights. Lip-sewing performances are also linked to the 'voicelessness' of women (exemplified, for example, by the myth of Echo, which is discussed by Luce Irigaray[32]) and a lack of permission for them to speak. Moreover, they are often employed as a re-enactment of the hunger strike. In 2014 Venezuelan students sewed their lips shut to reinforce their hunger strike in the protest against political oppression during President Nicolás Maduro's socialist regime.

The stitching of Rossa's body, similar to the performance discussed in Chapter 1, can also be interpreted as referring to the expanded understanding of Lacan's mirror stage offered by Silverman. She reminds us of Schilder's account, which discusses the relationship between the body and the world of objects that is often embodied by the skin.[33] The cutaneous sensations apart from their physical dimension are sites of social exchange. Silverman says that 'he indicates that the body is not the simple product of physical contact, but that it is also profoundly shaped by the desires which are addressed to it, and by the values which are imprinted on it through touch'.[34] This is also discussed by Meskimmon, as indicated in Chapter 1, in relation to Merleau-Ponty's concept of 'intercorporiety' and 'transitivity from one body to another'.[35]

Rossa's body responds to a whole set of cultural imaginings of the female body, its ideality and role and use. She mobilises issues associated with the passivity of women and their silencing and inscription into male models of perfection. The skin becomes a flexible boundary that can be punctured to challenge social stereotypes and contest relations based on unequal beliefs and laws. It constitutes the subject inscribed into and not outside a net of sociality. This pertains to another concept raised by Meskimmon in relation to identity as a threshold state shaped by embodied exchange. It is conceptualised by Moira Gatens and Genevieve Lloyd as 'transindividuality', which establishes links between the subject as 'corporeal/social and moral and political responsibility'.[36] What is interesting in Meskimmon's reading of 'transindividuality' is her emphasis on collective responsibility as aesthetic, 'premised upon a notion of "response-ability", and that this has important ramifications for exploring the thresholds materialised by works of art'.[37]

Rossa replaces the male body in da Vinci's drawing and engages with the discourse on universal proportions and beauty. A closer reading of Vitruvius suggests that architecture is guided by the ideal human proportions, which are based on the perfect, muscular, white male body. The female body is excluded from the discourse and cannot function as a template for universal proportions and beauty applied in architecture attributed to mental traits. In early philosophy, architecture (known as *technion*) was distinguished from building (*demiorgos*), which is reminiscent of the later division between the mind, often seen as male and the body, considered female. Architecture was associated with order and symmetry and it was guided by a continuous search for perfection inherent in the male body exemplifying the concept of beauty. Rossa is referring to this archetypal image of ideal proportions, and proposes the female body as the ideal. On one hand she challenges the male as the determinant of perfection, and on the other she also draws attention to women's search for perfection within their own bodies. She questions what the perfect body is and how it can be engineered into the perfect human being.

Vitruvian Body embodies the search for ideal proportions and criticises current preoccupations with the ideal body, external appearance and skin-deep beauty, which are projected on women by the mass media and also by history, myths and conceptions that are based on the male genius and patriarchal domination. In many of their performances, Rossa and Mavromatti use the body as a 'site' that determines identity. It is worth mentioning that Mavromatti himself is a performance artist who had to flee Russia after he performed a live crucifixion in 2000, nailing his body to a cross in order to embody the archetype of pain and suffering.

Rossa's work repositions and reconsiders feminist performance art of the 1960s and 1970s and engages with the different archetypes and stereotypes still defining women. *Vitruvian Body* challenges the desire to create the ideal body, which is not anthropocentric but malecentric. Even indirectly, the female body is subjected to the male ideal embedded in the concept of the male gaze. It is often portrayed as passive by men and for the pleasure of men. It is shaped and decorated to conform to circulated Westernised norms of attraction, making women scrutinise themselves. The search for perfection is often painful, as in order for the body to 'fit' the canon and the requirements of the current beauty standards, it needs to be subjected to technological, medical and surgical enhancements. Women have become more aware of their bodies and of representation of their bodies and, as in the case of *Vitruvian Body*, they situate themselves in the centre of their artworks, empowering themselves as objects *and* subjects. Ultrafuturo, established by Rossa and Mavromatti, issued a manifesto in 2004, which reads:

> We declare gender an excessive 'property' of human society, still inherent in human culture and biology, to be overcome completely in nearest future [sic] both morally and physically! We are sure that post-beings of the future will live in total harmony without such rudiments like sexual determination, liberated from intersexual conflicts and miss-communications [sic] ... Woman is the Robot of the world.[38]

The representational exterior

The outside – representation – and the inside – the self – of the object co-exist disproportionately. This 'over-coating' causes a phantasy of the inside implied by the representation. The image – or ornamentation, form, skin-depth, surface – covers the interior. The aforementioned artists provide bastardised images of the female body that emphasise the absurdity of media portrayal of women. Sometimes females are associated with packaging, as in the case of Rajkowska's work, which will be discussed later in this chapter. The female body becomes equated with appearance, the outside. It is a mute and inanimate object of male fantasies. Cousins questions the outside:

> The exterior is the representation of the object for the subject, and therefore included much which is 'inside' the object. The interior is the existence of the object and therefore can include anything on the 'outside' of the object which has not been submitted to a regime of representation. It is in this sense that ugliness arises as and when the interior of the existence of an object exceeds, for a subject, its representational exterior.[39]

The subject exists proportionally to the object when the object still resides in the representation. This causes narcissism of the subject towards the objects, which become a mirror. Beauty and narcissism, understood as the Lacanian 'Imaginary' – an ordinary illusion of reality – are entwined together. Their connection makes it possible for the subject to maintain a coherent experience of the body.

'Ugliness', which similarly to beauty is not universal but culturally derived, on the contrary, refers to a trauma caused when the object's interior explodes through the subject's imagination of the inside. Representation that is external permeates the inside – hidden, empty, unimagined. This subject's phantasy of the object is broken in the moment of ugliness. The unexpected appears and overwhelms the subject as it has no meaning. Cousins argues that excess defines the ugly object.[40] Suddenly, the imperfect body becomes horrible to look at, so it wears various tropes that constitute a provisional whole. The mirror image – or Cousins 'negative world of objects' – creates a reality where there are no shadows – 'there is'; 'there is a "no"'; 'there is no'; 'there is no "no"'[41] – as if in the Baudrillardian concept that 'things have swallowed their mirrors'.

The lack, then, necessitates two various logics, labelled by Cousins 'the ghost' and 'the mask', which evoke Leslie Heywood's ghost bodies. Both are tools used by ugliness to destabilise the subject's immersion in reality. The first plays with the relation between what is visible and hidden and creates a vacuum, a space in between, where we are horrified and haunted. The meaning can be created only if there is any existence. However, the ugliness destroys all forms of representation and so the latter logic, the one of mask, is left. There is no more meaning, as mask is just an addition that cannot contain any significance. Cousins argues: 'It is the cosmetic which always gives on to the horror spread by surgery, to the subcutaneous existence it no longer encases but rather underlines … masks cannot signify.'[42]

In both cases, the threat of becoming ugly paralyses the subject, who fears incoherence. Beauty and the parallel notion of completeness is a weapon against this danger. Cousins argues that beauty and idealisation both help to create an illusion of wholeness; it is 'a narcissistic turning away from ugliness'.[43] He notes that ugliness derives from beauty. Through the metaphor of architecture – the cathedral of Notre-Dame – and the death of the building, Cousins constructs a hybrid, transitional form, which is dissected, amputated and restored. It is like a Babel tower, growing organically by dislocation of limbs and accumulation of 'preposterous histories'.[44]

Its life resides in the irregularity, lack of form, distortion – Quasimodo. His ugliness necessitates vivacity and makes the building alive. His disappearance kills Notre-Dame. The ugly, either as excess or lack, adds value and interest. It often becomes a positive term in contemporary art works, such as in Rossa and Mavromatti's *Vitruvian Body*, which emphasises the connection between the subject and the object on various levels.[45]

The ugly, grotesque, sublime or anorexic are often embodied in Rossa and Mavromatti's works. They combine the extremes – beautiful and ugly – polarising them onto the body, which becomes seductive but at the same time often shocking or repelling. The juxtaposition of paradoxes – seducing and disgusting, life and death, male and female – reflects the blurred border between those concepts and hence completeness.

Venus

Ideals of beauty have changed throughout time and incorporated concepts once considered contradictory – the sublime, ugliness and the logic of lack. The figure of Medusa (the focus of the next chapter), became a signifier of the monstrous and the grotesque and hence, also the fragmented. On the other hand, Venus functions as a signifier of perfection and the female body. Venus is like a magnet, attracting attention. According to Melanie Klein's child development theories, the infant possesses two instinctual drives that are acted out on the mother's body. A child desires either to attack its mother's breast out of frustration or to reunite with it out of gratitude. Peter Fuller incorporates this theory with reference to the interest in Venus's image, which becomes the maternal body or, broadly, the feminine one. It helps restore the primal psychodrama.[46] As Jeffett states: 'The *Venus de Milo*'s enduring attraction lies precisely in the malleability of her identity and her function as fragment … the *The Venus de Milo* is transformed from a symbol of classical clarity to an obscure object of desire.'[47]

In *The Trouble with Beauty*[48] Wendy Steiner introduces Venus – by tracing her birth, existence, exile and entropy – as the embodiment of the concept of beauty opposed to ideas of the sublime, woman and ornament. She examines the twentieth-century trouble with beauty by observing the rejection of the female subject and beauty mainly in modernist art. Modernists abandoned traditional beauty and created a new standard of tough, revolutionary, depraved and perverted beauty. Modernism, modelled on Kantian aesthetics, concentrated on fear and awe, cardinal descriptors of the sublime, in which 'the aesthetic experience is specifically the *non*-recognition of the self in the Other, for the Other is inhuman, chaotic, annihilating'.[49] The nineteenth-century stratification of beauty and goodness motivated the association of beauty with form, fetish, ornament and woman. Since then, culturally implied feminine values, such as allure and love, have slowly disappeared. Ornament was gradually eliminated in favour of pure form and fetish. The avant-garde movement rejected the 'soft aesthetics of the past'[50] associated with the feminine and bourgeois values such as charm, admiration, empathy and sentiment. Steiner suggests that instead of desire, pleasure, ornament and feminine values, beauty was performed, often symbolically, with reference only to form.

Through introduction of exoticism and culturally derived primitivism, the supremacy of the West was discharged and what was earlier considered high and low art and craft started to become blurred. In consequence, images of female beauty were fetishised. Steiner notes: 'Vampire, medusa, gorilla, corpse, mannequin, waste, banality, profanation, and caged animal: for the female subject, these are the alternatives available if "she" is not to be reduced to pure form.'[51] Classical aesthetics' signifiers collapsed. The escape from Kantian separation between charm and beauty were the origin of the idea of the other. This was accompanied by the visible shift in values, from harmony and universality to fascinating horror. The displacement of power and extracting of the primitive and the exotic was the origin for fetishism signalling an error, difference and deviation. It opened up a whole new field to be explored; a sphere that structured distinctions between the 'rational and irrational, civilised and primitive, normal and abnormal, natural and artificial'.[52] The modernist adaptation of the Kantian sublime and its vulgarisation and invulnerability towards the feminine value transformed woman into an abstract form. Leslie Heywood called this reduction of beauty and thus woman to form 'male anorexia'.[53]

The return of the representation that accompanied Pop Art changed the relations of fetish, form, ornament and the feminine subject and made the reinterpretation of beauty necessary. Postmodernism tasted 'more' instead of 'less', ornament instead of purity. Against the paradigmatic presumptions of modernism, postmodernism proclaimed fun, abundance and exuberance. It discovered the semantic deprivation and uniformity in monofunctional modernist architecture. Heterogeneity, intercontextuality and historicism, the carnivalesque and irrationality dominated the postmodern discourse. The status of ornament was restored,[54] but its role changed; it referred now to illusion and humour. And it was expected that the body, gender, together with the female subject would be re-introduced as well in a new perspective, as has been explored by Butler and Irigaray, between sexes, in intergender symbolism. Women artists such as those discussed in this chapter started questioning representations of the female body as presented in the history of art told within white patriarchal academic circles. They critically address popular culture and female-centric topics, which were deemed politically incorrect, such as female sexuality, objectification of women or pornographic imagery applied to the female body. Steiner remarks: 'The 1990s seem like an antic dance in which form, fetish, ornament and woman approach each other and back off, changing partners, appropriating each other's steps.'[55]

This new perspective allows for cohesion and links to the myth of completeness embodied by Eros, who reconstitutes the mirror imago of the whole body. It recreates desire by sexuality. In the most archaic theogonies Eros originated in Chaos. Later, it was believed he was born from the primordial egg – the Night that divided itself into Earth and Sky. Both myths suggest the origin in primal forces, the internal completeness of the cosmos and also the continuity. In cosmology, Eros also represents the procreative force. Alternatively, in psychology, he constitutes a fearful power in human souls and bodies.[56] His genealogy is unclear. The most popular theory implies he was the son of Hermes and Aphrodite. However, various versions of the myth also suggest Anteros – Reciprocal Love, was born to Aphrodite and Ares and the most famous winged god was born to Hermes and Artemis. Eros personifies Love. His power allowed him to play with human hearts – either inflaming them or wounding with his arrows.[57] His opposite – Thanatos or brother of Sleep – Hypnos, personifies Death. According to Freud, there exist two drives – life and death;[58] in post-Freudian thought these are referred to as Eros and Thanatos. The first unites and preserves, while the latter destroys. Even though they oppose each other, they do not function separately. They co-exist, trapping the subject in between, merging sexual and destructive forces – pleasure and death. Hal Foster, while discussing surrealism and the convulsive beauty, locates the struggle of the drives in sexuality – 'erotic binding and thanatonic destruction'.[59] Notwithstanding this dualism, Eros is the liberating and primary faculty, uniting and binding the subject through sexuality. Eros embodies cohesion and the Baudrillardian idea of swallowing the mirror discussed in the first chapter. Silverman argues that love can be used to intervene into conventional representations of the body and identify with images that would otherwise be rejected. Its role is both psychic and political and enables loving and appreciating difference and otherness.[60]

She is the form

Beauty is inflicted on women's bodies, turning them into objects. Some women artists make conscious decisions regarding the presentation of their bodies, which allows them to control their portrayal. Anna Baumgart is a Polish artist who challenges conventional representations of the female body and questions the subject of the other. Her practice includes sculpture, painting, video and installation, and also artistic tattoo. She addresses archetypes of femininity and the different ways in which they are shaped by vision and in particular the male gaze. One of her initial projects, entitled *Let Unrestrained Anger Be Eliminated* (1996), merged technology and the body to portray the resonance between maleness and femaleness. Images of the body were introduced into liquids such as honey, optic and electric devices, which blurred pictured representations of gender distinctions. In *Authentic* (2001) the artist fulfilled her phantasy of locating her body on the other side of the screen. She staged herself as female characters, photographed and digitally edited the images, and placed them in fragments of a Soviet film *The Cranes Are Flying* by Michail Kalatozow and a Polish cult movie *Miś* (*Teddy Bear*) by Stanisław Bareja. She invaded the roles played by the actors to test cultural stereotypes associated with women's submissive roles in their relationships with men. From a passive spectator, she became an active protagonist critiquing the impact of the media on cultural imagination. At the same time she stages herself as an actress becoming a star and an object of male phantasy. She confronts female desire for beauty and attraction and the oppressive regimes imposed on the female body by media imagery. Baumgart emphasises its highly aestheticised reality and points to the saturation of representational structures which diminish women's capacity to become active subjects. Instead, the female body is passively consumed by both men and women. The artist encourages the female audience to re-activate their own bodies and make them political.

Shortly after they met, Anetta Mona Chişa & Lucia Tkáčová produced a video piece *Les Amies* (*Girlfriends*) (2000), which refocuses their preoccupation with the concept of friendship (discussed in Chapter 1) from the bond between themselves onto a relationship between a woman and a huge Barbie doll. This early piece mobilises many issues that they touch on in later works concerning revamped images of femininity that do not conform to standardised images drawn from the authoritative male gaze. Other questions they address entail a critique of commodity and neoliberal capitalism, the consumption of art and the reoccurring enforcement of women into stereotypes. Their work acknowledges earlier feminist artists, for example Judy Chicago, Hannah Wilke, Valie Export or Carolee Schneemann, among others, but Chişa & Tkáčová's response is different. They employ humour and sexual titillation to go beyond the boundaries of the body through the use of props such as make-up or costume. They use popular culture in a celebratory manner and through references to, for example, the Barbie doll, a ubiquitous worldwide symbol of femininity, they interrogate gender roles and widespread representations of femininity in mass media. The fashioning of the body becomes a political statement and this body is not specific. They draw attention to issues concerning every woman.

Chişa & Tkáčová made a short film, *Porn Video* (2004), and a series of posters entitled *Porn* (2004–7) in which they stage typical poses (on top, from behind, suspended), facial expressions (ecstasy, parted lips, half-closed eyes), scenery (classroom, bathroom, lounge, car, lift, bedroom), camera moves (close-ups focusing on genitals, shots from the bottom) from porn movies. The images are on the edge of pornography, simulating the 'porn' atmosphere but both women are fully clothed, and not only clothed but wearing high-necked jumpers, slippers, jeans, pyjamas or tracksuits (apart from more suggestive high heels and red dresses). The everyday clothing suggests the innocence of daily domestic activities (sleeping, cleaning, decorating, taking a bath) that turn into less subtle rituals.

The porn series demonstrates the nature of pornographic images that are based on clichés and stereotypical representations of women embodying erotic pleasure. The playfulness of the images is misleading. The insertion of domesticity within them undermines their scopophilic nature and resonates with the search for identity often guided by ostracising patriarchal stereotypes and conventional attributions of women's roles in the society. The porn series represents a taboo iconosphere soaked with visual representations of typical sexual partnership relations and eroticism from the viewpoint of men's experiences. Chişa & Tkáčová comment on gender identity that goes against compliance with the heteronormative matrix. Their emphasis on the visuality of these images articulates the gaze of the spectator, which establishes the relations of power and possessiveness. The gaze refers not to looking but to staring with a fixed focus on objectified women embodying sexual desire in pornographic shots. The artists ironise depictions of women as sexually attractive, available objects constructed by the conventional male gaze. In the series women are not passive. They actively manipulate the simplifying representations of women saturating the mass media and parody (and deconstruct) male gaze and voyeurism.

A similar topic was addressed by Veronika Bromová from the Czech Republic in the series of digital photographs entitled *Views* (1996), illustrating anatomical details of the female body through cut-outs of different body parts. She also mobilises the issue of pornography and voyeurism, but from a different perspective. Berger suggested that '[n]akedness was created in the mind of the beholder'.[61] Bromová emphasises the manipulation of the body by the male gaze and the violence it inflicts on individual identity. She depicts the physical reality of the female body, its genitals, legs, head or mouth, which is usually seen through its exterior. Bromová de-eroticises it by portraying the female crotch with exposed muscles and tendons. Interiority becomes demystified and unveiled. By deconstructing the female body, the artist also de-objectifies it. Even though the pose of the crotch is similar to the ones seen in porn videos or paintings of the nudes, the rawness of the flesh and internal organs is no longer subjected to the rule of the desiring male gaze. She reminds the viewer that, following Jacques Rancière, '[t]he spectacle is the reign of vision, and vision is exteriority'.[62] In *Views* the female body is no longer the object of male phantasy but it becomes a subject in itself.

Porn Video (2004) and *Porn* (2004–7) by Chişa & Tkáčová can also be seen as what Susan Sontag calls 'Camp', where the serious – as beauty or perfection – is often transformed into the frivolous. Sontag refers to it as 'a certain mode of aestheticism', 'wholly aesthetic', '"style" over "content", "aesthetics" over "morality", "irony" over "tragedy"',[63] stylisation – disengaged and apolitical. Camp is a new sensibility, characterised by exaggeration, close to concepts such as the sublime, ugly or grotesque as it also looks away from beauty. Artists who still make an effort to rehabilitate the notion of beauty risk producing what Anthony Haden-Guest calls 'spiritual kitsch'.[64] Stylisation and artifice rather than beauty describe camp as that which 'preposterously' refers to styles rather than creating its own. It exaggerates and maximises – it worships what Sontag names the 'off' and 'things-being-what-they-are-not',[65] such as in Chişa & Tkáčová's video and porn posters. Camp adores the visual, the make-up, the decoration and glamour at the expense of the content. It indulges itself in mass culture, its replicas and vulgarity. Its canon is described by Sontag as, 'the ultimate Camp statement: it's good *because* it's awful'.[66]

Camp transforms, melting beauty and ugliness together. Moreover, it does not matter what is what, as concepts merge, play with each other, seduce one another, both supplement and mirror their own reflections. Camp is seduced by the androgyne and its exaggeration or attenuation of sexuality. Sontag describes this new sensibility using words such as 'flamboyant female-ness', 'exaggerated he-man-ness', 'triumph of the epicene style'.[67] To enter Camp is as though to go, like Alice, through the 'looking-glass'. Everything adopts different meanings and nothing is what it seems to be. It reminds one of Kozyra's *Summer Tale*, described in Chapter 1, and Alice's Wonderland. A strange surreality of talking creatures, drinks and food extending the body size question all the assumed canons, blurring logic and nonsense. Camp wanders among tropes, transvesting them, putting them in quotation marks and theatricalising.

Perfection is one of the themes in the discussion above and, in Baudrillard's account: 'Though the crime is never perfect, perfection, true to its name, is always criminal. In the perfect crime it is the perfection itself which is the crime.'[68] Perfection and the external form function as seducers. Perfection might in fact offer a metaphor for a critique of consumerism and forces driving the art market. It might even provide a conduit to explore its mechanisms and be useful when exploring the cult and remythologising of the notion of beauty. So perfection is criminal. Perfection seduces. It is inscribed in the concept of the mirror. The Kantian beauty is independent from perfection. In this light, is the perfect image just a costume? Is it inessential Kantian *parerga*,[69] pure 'ornamentation', a drapery or a golden frame?

Perfection, as *parerga*, might function as a form of an exaggerated make-up, playing with the meaning. The addition or the reminder has an exclusively decorative function. Nonetheless, it is not useless. It is required as – according to Jacques Derrida – *ergon* necessitates *parergon*. Derrida, referring to Kant's third *Critique*, questions the frame, the addition, the reminder as not necessarily physical. Therefore, the *parergon* functions not only as peripheral as it directly refers to the lack in the *ergon*. Derrida argues:

> What constitutes them as *parerga* is not simply their exteriority as surplus, it is the internal structural link which rivets them to the lack in the interior of the *ergon*. And this lack would be very constitutive of the very unity of the *ergon*. Without this lack, the *ergon* would have no need of a *parergon*. The *ergon's* lack is the lack of a *parergon*.[70]

Kant juxtaposes the beautiful with the bounded and formed, while the sublime is linked to the formless. Derrida argues that if art enables form by framing, there can exist *parergon* of the beautiful, but it 'seems' there is none for the sublime. The Kantian 'Mathematical Sublime' demanded a conceptual frame: the *parergon*. Derrida refers to the sublime as unable to be located in sensible forms as it resides in the ideas of reason and therefore cannot be presented. However, this unpresentable can be manifested. As the imagination cannot record infinity, it is constrained by reason.[71] The sublime causes pleasure in creating the boundaries, framing itself. Thus, the *ergon* can become *parergon*. The unlimited cannot function without the limited. The sublime can be formed and deformed, can be possible and impossible, because of the *parergon*, the framing effect arising from the lack. It creates a sense of the beyond, which is illusive.

Therefore *parergon* is not peripheral, as it directly intertwines with the internal *ergon* of the artwork. In this context, perfection becomes a camouflage. It is embodied in various forms and is worn as a make-up. It trans-vests; attracting and seducing. It plays – as in Mieke Bal's 'preposterous'[72] version of history – by quoting and referencing. Perfection also functions as a sort of *trompe l'oeil* that cannot be transgressed. It covers the real and changes its dimension by creating an illusion. The real and its double melt, annihilating any distance. Perfection seduces by confusing reflection with absorption. It attracts and deludes with the form as seduction operates by deception.[73]

Use my body, drink me

In 2000, Joanna Rajkowska, one of the most engaging and versatile active contemporary Polish women artists, created *Satisfaction Guaranteed*, a new product brand with a range of consumer products, including cosmetics and six types of soft drinks (cover image) in 0.33 litre cans sold for 19.99 PLN each (approximately £4), under the title *Discreet Return*. Rajkowska works across diverse media, including photography, installation, sculpture, ephemeral actions and drawings, focusing on the relationship between human physicality and psychology and self-knowledge in public and personal space. In a conversation with Artur Żmijewski she explains:

> My attention is focused not so much on group identities, which are the basis of all politics, but more on the *relations* between individuals – between singularities and a place. I focus on what happens between individuals and their locations. Not in us-them relations, but in me-you and me-you-place contexts … My recipe is to propose a vision which relates to the body. This vision sweeps up and revolutionizes human behaviour by subjecting people to powerful shared experiences.[74]

Body is important in her works. She says: 'My body turned out to be an unfailing partner instead and it was always with me.'[75] In 1994 she proposed the concept of 'body as sculpture' to reflect this connection between the outside and the inside sphere. She is known mostly for her political urban interventions but her practice is also rooted in processes of embodiment. These concerns meet in *Satisfaction Guaranteed*, which brings together issues of the private and the public, communal consumption and the female body. It was presented for the first time at the Centre for

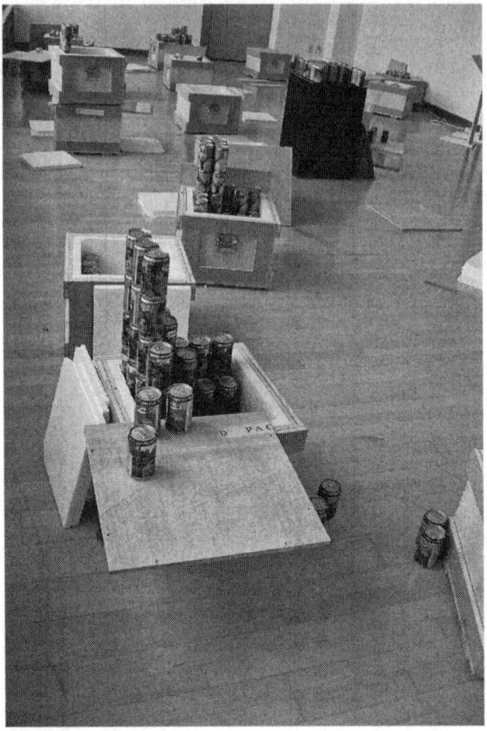

Image 4 Joanna Rajkowska, *Satisfaction Guaranteed*, 2000, aluminium cans, flavoured fizzy drinks; 0,33l; © Joanna Rajkowska, courtesy MOCAK The Museum of Contemporary Art in Kraków, Poland; photo: Joanna Rajkowska. Courtesy of the artist.

Contemporary Art, Ujazdowski Castle, in Warsaw, Poland at an exhibition curated by Ewa Gorządek. The exhibited objects were accompanied by an exhibition catalogue in the form of a promotional leaflet and illustrations displayed on 400 billboards all over the country, being part of an Outdoor Gallery, an art project led and sponsored by AMS (Art Marketing Syndicate SA) that grants billboards to convey messages to the public. Rajkowska calls to the audience:

> Listen up.
> Utilize my body. Make a series of canned drinks, cosmetics and frozen food from it. Use a fresh body, it's the best kind. First, you have to remove the skin and divide up the body.

> Puree some of the innards, leaving others fresh. Some of the organs, glands and bodily fluids must be saved. Don't forget about the neurons and the fat. On the base of these ingredients prepare carbonated beverages of different properties, later soap, Vaseline and perfumes, finally frozen food. When you've gone through all this, sell it for good money.[76]

Satisfaction Guaranteed, which initially seemed to be just a very well designed marketing campaign, was radical, eccentric and provocative, particularly on Polish art scene at the turn of the millennium. Rajkowska noticed that products carry information that she used to deliver her own message. Stach Stabłowski recalls her words that a mass consumer product 'is an "information bite", a "gene" that can be cloned into the image of the contemporary world. It can also reconstruct contemporary ways of thinking'.[77] Rajkowska's objects were manufactured in large quantities using industrial methods of mass production and following the dictates of product marketing framework and branding with carefully designed packaging and logo. They were made under the brand 'Satisfaction Guaranteed', which is a common pledge given by companies to ensure their customers of quality and performance of their products that guarantee 100 per cent satisfaction. It is also a phrase which is a popular marketing slogan, implying that a service or product is reliable and of quality. Even if it fails to deliver what it promises, the customers will be offered another form of satisfaction, for example compensation or a refund to meet their expectations.

The range of consumer products manufactured by Rajkowska were functional and included soft drinks in six flavours that could be drunk, two types of soap, petroleum jelly and perfume that all could be used. However, even though manufactured in an impersonal manner through mass production, these products were highly personal. Szabłowski noticed that at the first encounter with the packaging and the list of ingredients 'the consumer's routine is twisted', as 'the ingredient used to produce the products of Joanna Rajkowska is … Joanna Rajkowska herself'.[78] The content of the packaging included intimate components such as fluids, essences and secretions collected from the artist's body. The drinks were made of extracts from the mammary gland, vaginal mucus, DNA, cornea, endorphins and grey brain matter, mixed with water, preservatives and carbon dioxide.

The petroleum jelly incorporated the artist's saliva, the perfume was composed from pheromones and the soap was produced from her body fat. By using ingredients of herself to produce the products, Rajkowska deliberately brought the internal and the external together. She externalised the internal and offered it to her audience in order to interact with other bodies. She consciously wanted to be consumed and by doing so she both empowered her audience by inviting it to engage with her body and disempowered it by making them 'chew' and 'drink' her. This embodiment is mediated through intercorporeality, the interaction between the mind and the body. Rajkowska portrayed the exterior objectification of the female body that conforms to Western femininity and turns into a product. Her products remind me of the cake prepared by Marian in Margaret Atwood's *The Edible Woman*.[79] It was shaped into a woman wearing a pink dress with a floral design. When she finished preparing it, Marian said to the woman made of cake, 'You look delicious ... very appetizing. And that's what will happen to you; that's what you get for being food', Next, she served the cake to her fiancé, Peter, saying,

> You've been trying to destroy me, haven't you ... You've been trying to assimilate me. But I've made you a substitute, something you'll like much better. This is what you really wanted all along, isn't it? I'll get you a fork.[80]

By preparing the cake, Marian finally addresses her subjectivity and starts thinking about herself in the first person. She is no longer an object to be consumed by men. She is no longer a product but a human being with desires and needs. She reclaims her 'I', her subjectivity and her 'self'. Rajkowska's drinks, soaps, perfumes and food are substitutes for woman. They epitomise external femininity seen through male eyes, which is to be embraced and conformed to by women for the pleasure of their men.

The packaging of Rajkowska's products was personalised. She used photographs of herself and her intimate body parts and other images from her family albums, including some portraying her childhood. The soap packaging is embellished with a photograph of herself with her mother, her husband appears on the packet with the perfume and the petroleum jelly shows herself with her father. Apart from visual material, the containers included a short description of the advertised effects each product was supposed to trigger, which replaced the traditional information provided by manufacturers concerning nutritional values or dangers of allergic reactions. For example, the drinks were refreshing but they also induced erotic sensations or relieved pain. The packaging of Kok was embellished with an adolescent crotch and a text explaining it contains coconut nectar that evokes erotic stimulation. The can, Cold Eyes, informs us it is made of retina and it tastes of watermelon. It sharpens vision. Orgasm is mango flavoured and has an effect on the central nervous system. All cans include a short text saying that all rights to the composition of ingredients are reserved and that the formula is restricted. Other sodas soothe a sense of loss and uselessness (pear flavoured Mental) and transform the genotype (Do you want?). There is also a mint-flavoured Timelessness which is refreshing. Cosmetics offer another set of sensations. Petroleum jelly evokes 'immediate relief' but it could also cause 'degeneration of the reproductive instinct', 'aversion to animals' and a 'feeling of embarassment'. Users of the Family Life soap could expect to experience 'a fear of family life and watching TV together'. A possible side effect included masturbation. The perfume promised to 'liquidate blood connections and produce a sense of absolute individuality' but with the potential to experience desire to 'suddenly board a bus to go somewhere and meet someone'.[81]

In *Satisfaction Guaranteed*, Rajkowska speaks the language of production, the market and consumption.[82] She says the language of labels carries a myriad of information and meanings. When used in a private context, it becomes very powerful.[83] The exhibition catalogue was published in the form of the sort of leaflet with offers typically distributed by stores. The front page or cover announces a special offer on page 13, a promotion (exhibition opening) on 26 June 2000 at 6 pm and promises satisfaction guaranteed in large red (in Polish) and green (in English) letters. There is also a green sign on top of the page reminiscent of a recycling symbol except that between the green arrows we notice a female body on four legs. We can also see two products, a drink can 'Chcesz?' (meaning – 'Do you want?') at 19.99 PLN and Vaseline at 9.50 PLN. On page 13 there are more products reduced by 10 per cent while stock lasts, including soap based on human fat. The back of the brochure is filled with information about exhibition sponsors and there is an advert for Norcool, a supplier of cold rooms, fridges and wine cellars.

Rajkowska produced commercial merchandise literally from her body, her life and herself. It is an intimate self-portrait, a personalised autobiography turned into commercial products for sale. She said: 'Listen up. Utilize my body.' And then, 'sell it for good money'. The objects were intended for others to use. She invited active participation from the audience, whom she asked to purchase and drink and apply her merchandise. Rajkowska says she desires a close contact with another human being. This project allows a utopian closeness.[84] She offers herself to be tasted, drunk, lathered and applied onto other bodies; this collapses the border between the private and the public. She is generous in sharing her body and hospitable in creating a sense of bonding. She is also open for contact with another person, against the rules of consumerism and mass production that is anonymous and depersonalised. The most basic activities of drinking and washing are applied here to make contact with the other, which is now often lost in virtual reality governed by electronic communication, lack of time for another human being and loosening of interpersonal honest and generous relationships, which, paradoxically, were more common under communist rule in Poland. Szabłowski argues that the project involves what he terms 'the mechanism for the distribution of existence in the contemporary world', which Rajkowska uses 'juxtaposing intuition and a nasty laugh.'[85]

The artist claims that this project did not critique consumption but her place as an artist in contemporary society, and was born out of frustration. She hates selling herself while doing commissions so decided to sell herself literally, in the form of merchandise (she also produced *Woman Shaped in Balls. With a Distinct Salty Taste* (2000), frozen food). She says: 'I decided to sell myself as cheap as I could – to give out my own body for sale in the coolest of ways – as a canned drink.'[86] Rajkowska could price herself and wanted to be available cheaply and on a massive scale. This cynically demonstrates that, following the rules of marketing and branding, anything can be sold, even physiology and the most intimate parts of the self. The products included bits of her body but also her traumas, problems, disappointments and fragments of biography. The labels provided information about ingredients but also her personal issues related to family.[87]

At the same time *Satisfaction Guaranteed* unmasks the mechanisms of cultural consumption, which blurs the boundary between consumers and products. It victimises women in particular, who themselves passively become objects to be consumed and digested visually. Their bodies are subjected to the rules established by the male gaze, materialism and norms induced by social stereotypes. In *Satisfaction Guaranteed* Rajkowska willingly offers herself to be consumed, similarly to Marian's cake, demonstrating full awareness of the exploitation of the female body. She exposes the norms and values that are established and dictated by the capitalist society and manipulated onto the consumer, who follows them religiously. She also admits there are aspects, even if it is an afterthought, referring to Catholicism in her work ('capitalist Catholicism'). She says, it encompasses the idea of body transformation, 'to become I have to vanish', so she literally melts in people's mouths.[88] Szabłowski suggests that her strategy follows the magical rituals of primitive cultures and the mentality of cannibals who believe that consuming parts of other humans will give them the strength and possessions of the victim. This also emphasises the affinities that exist between 'primitive' tribal cultures and contemporary society that perceives the world in a skewed manner derivative from media imagery and advertising slogans.[89] Consumerist culture incites our desire for material objects and we never have enough. We want more, beyond our needs, and we are never satisfied even if the versatility and range of products on offer is continuously growing. Finally, we start consuming ourselves.

Rajkowska's products were displayed in the same way merchandise is showcased in stores. The cans were placed in refrigerators borrowed from Norcool and labelled as 'Do you want?', 'Mental', 'Kok', 'Afternoon timelessness', 'Orgasm' and 'Cold eyes', which reflected the effect they were supposed to induce, namely (respectively) intensifying the feeling of absurdity, release from boredom and a sense of lack, erotic stimulation, regeneration and refreshment, and finally influencing the central nervous system and sharpening vision. Initially, Rajkowska approached Coca-Cola with a request to use their refrigerated cases but the request was denied. The artist warns, or perhaps promises, that 'after consumption, you will be able to experience my life', which resonates with the advertising slogans we encounter on an everyday basis. We are continuously promised a better, healthier life, a whiter shirt, a younger-looking skin or a sexier appeal if we use specific perfumes or buy a particular car. We are told our family life will be saved if we start using appropriate cereals or clean our bathroom with limescale remover. At the same time humans are becoming products themselves. We can insure our breasts or other body parts and our needs can be taken care of if we are ready to pay for them. Rajkowska plays the game of consumerism and invites us to join in. She offers a potential to challenge the vicious cycle of production and consumption. She manipulates the rules to serve her own purpose and raise awareness of the dangers of brainless consumption. Her manufactured range demonstrates that our existence is governed by the rules of fast tasteless food, fast unethical fashion, fast physical love and fast meaningless encounters on practically every level of our existence. We ourselves are disposable waste that is noticed only through surface looks, ignoring emotions and personalities that are lost in the chain of quick utilisation in a world where 'want' is superior to 'need'. Rajkowska offers us a fiction (none of the ingredients of the products are her actual bodily secretions) in which consumption is total and overwhelming, starting from the fundamentals, the body, through biography and emotions. She simply wants to communicate with the other and to talk.

Rajkowska's products were manufactured in post-1989 Poland, when artists were more aware of the female body as a site of consumption and objectification and when a new type of consumer was born, wallowing in free market economy, the democratic system and enjoying the new found abundance of goods on shop shelves not known under the communist dictatorship. The year 1989 initiated privatisation and the commercialisation of the national economy. The market was provided with appropriate legal grounds to ensure a free flow of merchandise and became competitive by the end of 1990s. Consumerism brought by Western globalisation directly translated into politics and also concerned the body, which became entangled in cycles of manipulation and consumption. Communist systems restrained the individual and denied individuality. The fall of Communism was welcomed with the hope for a less constrained identity. Paradoxically, consumerism further isolated the individual, focusing on material possessions and values dictated by consumption and the power of one's economic status.

Other women artists in Poland such as Natalia LL, Maria Pinińska-Bereś and Ewa Partum, among others, questioned the dangers of consumption, which were often neglected and overshadowed by the instant gratification that all sorts of goods at last freely available provided. They also recognised the particular risks to which women were exposed as their bodies have continuously been subjected to the laws of the male gaze, the cultural canons of beauty and scopophilic invigilance. Often women themselves participated in consumerism, desiring what they were told they should be desiring through images, advertising slogans and magazine articles.

Rajkowska does just that. She uses products women desire to attract their attention and demonstrate issues that should be digested beyond consumption of goods. These derive from the phallocentricality that elevates the symbolic male organ to the universal power structure, at the same time extinguishing and othering the female. She applies language, branding and marketing to mimic tactics governing consumerism and, as such, she is subverting conventions. In *Satisfaction Guaranteed* she uses the masculine system of representation hostile to the female body to disrupt its otherness. This strategy has an affinity with Luce Irigaray's concept of mimesis which she theorises in *The Sex Which Is Not One*[90] and which serves here as a very powerful feminist tool to imitate conventions but also to resist them. Irigaray's mimesis subjects women to stereotypes of themselves and at the same time erodes them from within. It is one of the methods she uses to challenge thinking about female bodies in contemporary culture. Irigaray departs from Lacan's thought in *Speculum of the Other Woman*[91] and argues for a female subject position that should be separate and autonomous, independent from male subjectivity and disconnected from the restraining association with nature and matter. This critique emphasises the absence of sexual difference in Western culture and proposes novel language and strategic essentialism that engage with categories used historically to oppress women as a tool to disenchantment. The process of mimesis is a tool that allows us to demystify and contest such stereotypical harmful views in which women are seen as illogical or lacking, dispersed, 'nothing to see', slaves and other, contrary to men who are logical, unified (such as in the Phallus), masters and subjects. Mimicking negative associations demonstrates that women are other than what and how they are typically represented. Only through revisiting Western oppressive formulation of sexual difference it is possible to see female subjectivity in its own right, not a mere deformed derivative of male identity. By preparing different products, similarly to Marian, Rajkowska deliberately and consciously places her body at the centre of her practice and speaks about herself in the first person.

Although Irigaray questions Lacan's theories, she remains committed to the methodology of psychoanalysis that enables harmful representations of women to be overcome through exposing them, asking after the other and emphasising that subjectivity has changed yet male dominance is still sustained. Similarly, Rajkowska reveals the repressed position of women fabricated into objects and invisible as subjects, and demonstrates that they have been silenced and excluded. Her cans and cosmetics reveal the position of women as physical bodies who are denied autonomous subjectivity. At the same time her pledge to listen to her, drink her and use her forces a shift in female subjectivity and the body. She is speaking in the voice of the oppressor, but not in order to perpetuate normativity. The various levels of interpretation of *Satisfaction Guaranteed* manifest the complexity of seeing the female body as lacking that is no longer solely a symbol but also a means of production and consumption. This resonates with Roland Barthes's: 'I am neither subject not object but a subject who feels he is becoming as object.'[92] Rajkowska wants to emancipate the spectator and make visible certain issues around feminine roles. She challenges Pollock's observation that: 'Indeed woman is just a sign, a fiction, a confection of meanings and fantasties,'[93] She is, following Irigaray, inverting subordination into affirmation, in order to reclaim sites of woman's exploitation. She is also aware that, after Baudrillard, an object needs to first become a sign to then become an object of consumption.[94] It is also worth referring to Rancière when summarising Rajkowska's project: 'It is a complex set of relations between the visible and the invisible, the visible and the speech, the said and the unsaid.'[95]

3

White and Red Queens, or Venus and Medusa

This chapter is concerned with dualism. Once again I refer to Alice (in *Through the Looking Glass*). With reference to 'playing' and the game of chess to which the Red Queen introduces Alice, I play with the trope of the White and the Red queens by substituting Venus and Medusa to dismantle the objectification surrounding the representation of the female body. The discussion explores theories informing narratives of beauty and ugliness, completeness and incompleteness, and analyses them in relation to specific art projects.

Manipulating the look and addressing difference

In Baudrillard's words: 'The Medusa represents an otherness so radical that one cannot look at her and live.'[1] The figure of Medusa (the Gorgon who turned all who looked at her to stone) is associated with monstrosity, ugliness, something that is distorted, fragmented, wrong and lacking. She is the opposite of Venus (the Roman goddess of love), who connotes perfection and unity. According to Baudrillard: 'Desire is always the desire for that alien perfection, at the same time as it is the desire perhaps to shatter it, to break it down.'[2] To challenge perfection and idealisations of the body is to challenge the conceptualisation of wholeness and unity, which, as I propose below, is possible through the deconstruction of the figures of Venus and Medusa.

Venus imposes a positive association of the body with perfection while Medusa imposes negative connotations, with the idea of lack. On one hand the body is defined by parameters of narcissism; on the other it is described as unattractive and incomplete. I propose merging these two perspectives and suggest that wholeness of the stereotypically beautiful body, deliberately used by artists to challenge the objectification of women, as discussed in Chapter 2, does not automatically mean fragmenting a conventionally unattractive body. What is culturally defined as lacking or incomplete, inciting unease and sometimes disgust, does not need to be considered as the opposite to beautiful. Differences in exteriority, capability and otherness do not equate with forbidden subjects. Women artists consciously use narcissism and attractiveness in terms of Western standards of desirability but also vulnerability, irregularity and bodily abjection to address difference and demonstrate that in fact the border between beauty and ugliness can be crossed. They suggest that 'excorporative' or 'heteropathic' identification[3] and continuous alignment with what is culturally defined as ideality is impossible and can be contested through identification within 'incorporative logic' that enables heterogeneity. The representation of the female body, guided by narratives of completeness and fragmentariness and subjected to the cultural gaze, can be reimagined. The theory that follows provides a framework used to analyse Alicja Żebrowska's video installation, *Grzech Pierworodny* (Original Sin) (1993/4). In this work, the artist uses cultural associations with Venus and Medusa to challenge conventional interpretations of female sexuality.

Baudrillard separates 'the erotic body' – where the signs of desire are replaced and the function of this exchange is superior – from 'the body as a site of fantasy', where desire is predominant. In such an understanding, the erotic becomes equated with the functional. The body begins to function as pure flesh, so it slowly disintegrates into pieces, where each part of the body is in 'a gigantic process of sublimation'.[4] The body as a whole slowly vanishes. In Baudrillard's account:

> Irregularity or ugliness would bring out a meaning again: they are excluded. For beauty here is wholly in abstraction, in emptiness, in ecstatic absence and transparency. This embodiment is

> ultimately capsulated in the gaze … Medusa eyes, eyes themselves turned to stone, pure signs.[5]

Silverman also proposes it is possible to address difference through a cultural gaze. She suggests incorporative logic and reminds us that '[t]he aspiration to wholeness and unity not only has tragic personal consequences, but also calamitous social effects, since it represents one of the most important psychic manifestations of "difference"'.[6] Silverman states that Lacan's premise of 'the screen' is conceptualised in relation to the gaze. He suggests that subjects depend on external representation to define a visual identity which he theorises as a screen, not a mirror image. However, as Silverman argues: 'In order to emerge within the field of vision, the subject must not only align him- herself identificatorily within the screen, but also must be apprehended in that guise by the gaze.'[7] I suggest that Venus and Medusa (or the White and Red queens) are such images and permit the subject to incorporate difference through reworking and revisioning figures that are culturally heavily loaded.

Further, Silverman notes that Lacan theorises the screen as nonreflecting and also differentiates the gaze from the look in terms of the gaze possessing the visual authority. 'He thereby suggests that what is determinative for each of us is not how we see or would like to see ourselves, but how we are perceived by the cultural gaze.'[8] This suggests that we cannot choose how we are seen. We might be able collectively to substitute the existing screen but we will not be able to set up a new one that would allow different visualisations. Individually, we might try to transform the normative image through which we are seen or, on the contrary, deform it. All these scenarios involve acknowledgement that the subject apprehends visual identity through images that are culturally constructed. Lacan also detaches the gaze from the look and denaturalises the relation between the subject and the screen. However, Silverman suggests we think of 'the screen as repertoire of representations by means of which our culture figures all of those many varieties of "difference" through which social identity is inscribed'. Every idealising attribution, e.g. whiteness, masculinity, heterosexuality implies its opposite and:

> imposition of all of these forms of difference depends upon imaginary alignment of certain subjects with what is negative rather than ideal, the images through which the subject is culturally apprehended do not always facilitate the production of a lovable bodily ego.[9]

Silverman's incorporative logic seizes upon the excorporative identification, which enables the undoing of 'the delusory unity and presence of the bodily ego'.[10] In Lacan's mirror stage the child is implicitly gendered masculine and other differences beyond sexual ones are also not present. Anything negating identification that leads to narcissistic gratification is excluded. Lacan argues that the subject's alignment with the image is a guide towards unity and wholeness. It is impossible, however, to constantly identify with ideality, which in turn causes bodily fragmentation – what he called the *corps morcelé*, the body-in-pieces or 'the fragmented body'.[11] Silverman refers to Schilder's account of the mirror stage, in which this identification is beneficent and 'it is the precondition for change, what must transpire if the ego is to form anew'.[12]

Heterogeneity is mobilised by the ways in which difference is identified by physicality beyond the psychic paradigm central to Lacan's thought and becomes incorporated in identity. This requires the negation of images with which one can easily be aligned and being curious about what is different. The cultural gaze projects certain representations on bodies; these are guided by the presence or absence of a penis and this structures power relations. These distinctions lead to the skewed relations between males and females and, as Freud suggests, the 'horror of the mutilated creature', or 'triumphant contempt for her'.[13] Silverman proposes the principle of 'the self-same body', which is at the core of differences such as gender, race, class or sexual preference. She argues:

> Reluctance on the part of the sexually, racially, or economically privileged subject to identify outside of the bodily coordinates that confer that status upon him or her, to form imaginary alignments which would threaten the coherence and ideality of his or her corporeal ego. Typically, this subject either refuses 'alien' identifications altogether, or forms them only on the basis of an idiopathic or assimilative model.

She then comments on the ego that it 'maintains itself by repudiating whatever it cannot swallow – by refusing to live in and through alien corporalities. This is what I will henceforward refer to as the principle of the "self-same body".'[14]

Following this logic, Venus and Medusa, symbolising beauty and ugliness, in fact complement each other, as I will discuss below. The implosion of these tropes enables a new image of the female body to emerge, in which fragmentation or otherness does not necessarily have to be seen in negative terms, and I will argue that Venus's tradition is, in fact, founded on castration and mutilation, commonly associated with the Medusa myth, and is also closely connected to the politics of vision and the male gaze.

The politics of vision

Several of the women artists discussed in this book use their bodies to question the cultural norms defining the female body as beautiful or ugly. They celebrate difference by continuing the legacy of Western feminist art (for example, Chicago, Schneemann, Valie Export, Sherman) and demanding social change. Aleksandra Ska (from Poland) uses corporeality to question what is considered ideal. In the video *Fat Love* (2009), viewers are confronted by the naked torso of a young woman wearing an exquisite necklace made of sausages, some of which are dipped in mustard. In 2009 the video was projected in a butcher's shop, 'Prosiaczek' ('Piglet'), during the *Urban Legend* festival of public art in Poznań, Poland. The store had gained recognition after being awarded certificates for its white sausages in 2008. On a large screen behind the counter displaying sausages, hams and other meats, a chubby woman tenderly caresses the 'beads' of the necklace. She smells them smiling, licks them and sucks them gently. Then she bites into the meat and eats the beads with enjoyment, licking her fingers and slowly chewing the meat. Ska pays homage to the legendary delicious white sausage from the region of Wielkopolska (Greater Poland in west-central Poland with Poznań as the chief city) and the audience watching Ska's video were offered samples of the sausage to taste. There is nothing vulgar in the woman's eating actions – she simply eats the sausages – and yet some of the clients of the store asked for the video to be switched off as they found it disturbing and disgusting.

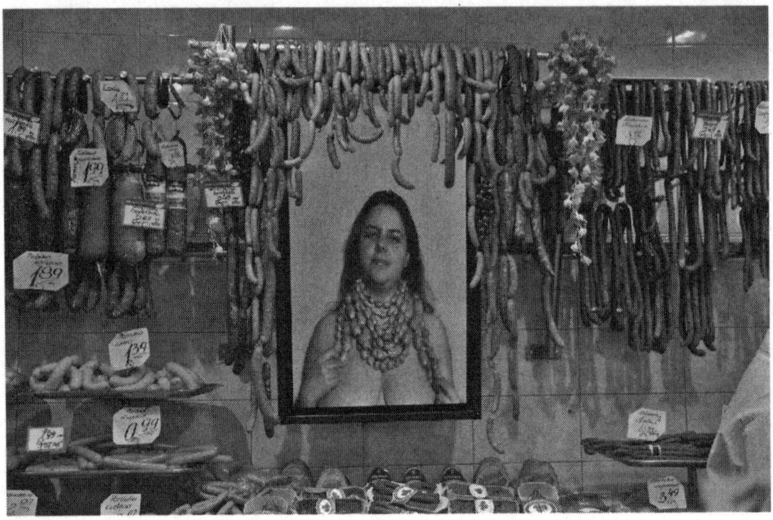

Image 5 Aleksandra Ska, *Fat Love* (2009), video installation, video still. Courtesy of the artist.

The portrayed woman is chubby so why is she taking pleasure in eating? Shouldn't she refuse any food and aspire to conform to the thin stereotypes promoted by the mass media? She isn't seen as beautiful. She is not a Venus. Her flesh is juxtaposed with meat.

Food has often been associated with sexuality. Countless magazine and web-based articles describe what to eat before, during or after sex; what food to consume to have better or more sex, or to attract a partner. There is a Polish saying, 'przez żołądek do serca' ('the way to a man's heart is through his stomach' is the English equivalent), that emphasises this relationship. Food is employed to seduce (oysters and chocolate are considered aphrodisiacs in Western cultures). Lollipops are a sexual metaphor; whipped cream may be used for sexual titillation. Some foods are symbolic and are associated with body parts (bananas and cucumbers have phallic shapes, and melons connote breasts). The other side of the coin is that the relationship between women and food brings up issues around eating disorders.

In the video, the sensuality of consumption emphasises woman's sexuality. As a woman the portrayed female should control her desires and harness her appetite for food and sex. She is a seductress and a temptress;

and she shouldn't be. Ska portrays unapologetic female pleasure and deliciousness of the female body. The woman in the video is self-assured, and confident about her body, sexuality and her beauty, which does not need to conform to ideals imagined by the mass media. She is the goddess of consumption and insatiability.

In her 2012 performance entitled *Osobisty Akt Artystyczny* (*Personal Artistic Act*) in Łódź, Ska becomes an edible woman, similar to Atwood's Marian, Rajkowska's female body packaged as products to be consumed, Natalia LL's *Consumer Art* or the female body in the works of Elżbieta Jabłońska, Zuzanna Janin or Grupa Sędzia Główny. Wearing a voluptuous, green, baroque-like dress that is turned into a table in the waist area, the artist is a food provider and she is the food. The upper part of her body is entwined in scrolls of sausages, which are served on her chest and neck and on the dress-table. She holds a big knife and offers the sausage to the viewers. The woman as a waitress or caterer and a table is tempting with her body, and the touch, smell and taste of meat/flesh. She resembles a Dutch Golden Age still life painting depicting expensive and exotic objects. Here, Ska offers the pleasure of herself. She is an active 'master' of the ceremony, deciding who will participate in the feast. She is conscious of her body and her sexuality and she is in control. Even though her image is monstrous and might cause fear or anxiety reminiscent of the Medusa figure, she is seductive and beautiful.

The female body, which historically was inscribed into patriarchal and heteronormative discourses and canons ascribing roles to women, has been subjected to different representational transformations. The body, as a congregate of identities, becomes a space of or for metamorphosis and reversal. It turns into a changeable construct in a constant fluid state, which is addressed by women artists such as Rajkowska, Sherman, Partum, Abramović or Natalia LL to challenge and subvert rigid structures. Postmodernism opened up the possibility of exclusions, and 'neither/nor' narratives. Lyotard's discourse allows for vision and the visible. It introduces the concept of 'anamorphosis',[15] a distorted projection that allows difference, the inclusion of possibilities, not only detachments and pluralism, where everything becomes gradually indifferent. What he calls anamorphic is 'in the different kinds of continuities, distortions and motivations produced by a point of view',[16] inviting the co-presence of mixed meanings and fighting nostalgia for completeness. Lyotard proposes: 'Let us wage a war on totality; let us be witness to the unpresentable; let us activate the differences and save the honour of the name.'[17] Such an account enables us to see the female body beyond beauty myths and patriarchal regimes, and the emergence of hybrids such as beauty with all its implications, including the ugly or the sublime; grotesque or ironised; and the logic of 'trans'. This transitory displacement and collage of meanings is embodied in the trope of the mirror, which enables transformations of the binary systems.

The politics of looking and the gaze are also evoked by the act of quotation. The mirror – the looking back – never ends as the reflection always has to reiterate itself and Bal suggests:

> If looking … consists of embedding or adapting that which is there to see outside of us into our stock of unconscious memories, then these are self-memories, and looking is self-looking; looking 'through' or 'with' self-images from the past that we carry with us, and which we have filled with illusionary fulfilment.[18]

The act of looking also implies such ideas as focalisation, performativity or iconicity. Combining different shades of gaze articulates the movement – travelling between the visual and the narrative. Bal suggests that this might empower the object of looking – disobjectifying and discolonising it and allowing for various cultural, temporal and spatial frames. The envisioning process can become more mobile and dynamic.

In the context of the gaze, Bal evokes the concept of iconophobia and gynophobia.[19] The latter refers to the fear of woman – *horror feminae* (illustrated by Ska's *Osobisty Akt Artystyczny*) – that is best embodied in the myth of Medusa, who murdered by petrifaction everyone who dared to look at her. Her own gaze reflected in the mirror of Perseus's shield finally killed her. The myth embodies both participants in looking – the observer and the observed. It also encapsulates the metaphor of the mirror and the myth of Narcissus – both as the emergence of subjectivity and as a simple reflection. Medusa becomes *femme fatale*, a contemporary Venus, irrevocably connected to vision on two levels. Firstly, she died because of the visual and secondly, she killed by her gaze – it was enough just to look or be looked at by her. Myths of Venus and Medusa are precisely about looking, in a very broad sense. Medusa's and women's eyes in many artworks are bound, empty or averted. Medusa is often portrayed as though she is looking away, petrified by her monstrosity or perhaps even femininity, or the male gaze. As Venus, she might seduce and attract but would be imprisoned in the masculine projection of femininity represented by the Venus. Craig Owens suggested that woman, as the subject of representation, had been excluded from power. 'She' appeared as an object, but was absent within culture. In postmodernism 'woman' returned as a figure for the unpresentable, such as the sublime or the truth. The only way for the 'woman' to speak seems to be by assuming the masculine role, which often leads to her false representation.[20]

The female body as representation embodying the Medusa myth, the observer and the observed is portrayed in Aleksandra Ska's *Ska I Hate You* (2011) videos. Viewers are confronted by an image of a woman wearing skin-tone panties and pink stilettos lying (served?) on a table between exotic fruit and vegetables cut into fantastical shapes. She looks bored and annoyed. The scene is opulent, with an abundance of fruit and the beautiful woman placed among decoratively arranged watermelons, pineapples and carrots, and other fruits and vegetables. The table starts rotating and we are presented with a view of the body and the table from all sides. After each rotation, the table stops and the woman says 'Ska I hate you.' Her face reveals resignation, disgust and annoyance. The table starts rotating again and so the vicious circle continues. Here it is the artist herself confessing hatred towards the self, but in other two artworks from the series women are represented in the same manner (they wear different colour stilettos and their hair is styled in a different way). They all say, fiercely looking at the camera (and the viewer) 'Ska I hate you'.

The videos portray a patriarchal vision of the female body – beautifully spread on a serving table, ready to be consumed, literally or figuratively by the male gaze. The women are silent and passive up to a point when they spit the words 'Ska I hate you'. They become active through their hostility. They hate the artist, as does Ska when representing herself in one of the videos. Does she hate herself because of the way she depicts her own body – immobile and inactive in between exuberant, ripe, fresh and exotic fruit and vegetables, ready to be consumed? Do the other two women hate the artist because their bodies are portrayed as conforming to patriarchal, art-historical canons of the female nude? Do they hate their 'self', unclaimed and subjected to patriarchal power structures, also concerning the gaze and the look? Are they unable to establish a deliberate and self-conscious 'I'?

Ska creates a new iconography of abundance and venom. The women in the video remind one of Medusa, staring provocatively at the viewer. They seduce and lure with their beauty but they take control of the feast at which they are served by repeating the title phrase. The artist deconstructs the Western art history canon of representing the passive naked female body by breaking the silence and speaking up. She intervenes in one of the most recognised images of the female body portrayed by male artists and disturbs it, enabling subject formation. Here, women are no longer excluded from the system of power. They affirm their 'self' and reject the 'self' created by others. They are no longer imprisoned in the masculine projection of femininity. They desire to be liberated from beauty canons and from oppressive patriarchal manipulation of their 'I'.

The act of looking embodies not only gynophobia but, I would suggest, caligynephobia or venustraphobia – the fear of 'beautiful' women or even beauty. Nonetheless, as Bal reminds us, beauty is already embedded in the mirror stage, which inaugurates its existence and the need for it. The subject is attracted by the image seen in the reflection. It projects its own beauty onto the other, forming itself – as does, for instance, Narcissus. Narcissus died as the image's erogenic effect seduced him, not allowing him to create the self. The mirror embodies the space that the body of the observer occupies, without existing there. It is just the beginning of the formation of the new self. The boundary of the mirror thus creates the body, making it visible for the self and for others. Its frame constitutes a duplicated image of the body – of the self and its reflection. In the figure of Narcissus, the representation is so beautiful that it can no longer function as a simple icon. It becomes what Bal calls 'mirroring *as* a mirror', not a simulacrum, but a metaphoric substitution.[21]

The mirror encapsulates the threshold of the visible and the fictional, 'preposterousness' and pastness. This kind of historicising look functions as a layer, and it is useful to reiterate Bal's argument on Narcissus:

> With any luck, the mirror that reflects the contemporary baroque [or classical] body in conjunction with the baroque [or classical]

> body, cracks but does not shatter, thus leaving us with a fragmentation that we can live with. Only within these cracks, and if we are mindful of them, can a conversation take place.[22]

The male gaze

The act of looking with reference to erotic and sexual difference is investigated in Laura Mulvey's article, 'Visual pleasure and narrative cinema'.[23] Mulvey examines the consequences of the male gaze for the 'woman' and her image, as a lack and a castrated being in patriarchal culture. Woman signifies the male other, a silent container of meaning in contrast to man who produces meaning. This phallocentrism also affects various ways of seeing and the pleasure taken in looking. The assumptions – aesthetic and political – are fed by the omnipresence of the figure of ideal woman, Venus, who manipulates visual pleasure. The patriarchal order is structured around formal beauty and implied erotic codes. It needs to be broken and it needs 'transcending outworn and oppressive forms, or daring to break with normal pleasurable expectations in order to conceive a new language of desire'.[24]

The gaze – which in Lacan's theories refers to the subject who observes the image reflected in the mirror, confronting the exterior 'other' – implies the idea of staring back (as in Ska's videos, in which women stare back at the viewer). The male gaze objectifying 'woman' proposed by Mulvey is deconstructed and developed beyond heterosexual connotations. Other theorists rely on lesbian, queer or transgender perspectives; Nalini Paul and Eva-Maria Jacobsson, among others, elaborated Mulvey's concept by promoting the idea of the 'female gaze'. The male gaze was complicated further by including Lebensztejn's 'blank gaze', Stein's 'lesbian gaze', hooks' 'oppositional gaze' or Pratt's 'colonial gaze'.[25]

Bracha Ettinger, who proposed the thinking apparatus of matrixial sexual difference and the concept of the 'matrixial gaze', offered yet another possibility in the focus on the subject/object relation.[26] Ettinger refers to the Lacanian subject but deconstructs it and offers a new feminine difference with the 'matrixial gaze', building upon co-emergence and 'trans-subjectivity'. She critiques the phallic structure to discuss female/male differentiation. The 'matrixial' realm offers a shareable dimension, where meanings, images and objects are seen before any opposition.[27] Ettinger proposes the rethinking of femininity outside of the binary differentiation of the male and the female, by using co-emergence. This trans-subjective dimension is called the matrixial realm and can be accessed by a new vocabulary, namely 'matrix', 'metamorphosis', 'mamalangue', 'borderlinking' and 'borderspacing'. In the introduction to *The Matrixial Borderspace*, Griselda Pollock argues:

> The Matrix as a signifier offers a means of realigning subjectivity in tune with the possibility of a multileveled (re-) inscription of difference in the relation with the specificity of the humanized/ humanizing female body-subject, which thus becomes a transformational potentiality for intersubjective transactions.[28]

The Oedipus complex discussed in Chapter 1 is closely linked to another term associated with the gaze, scopophilia, discussed by Freud and being part of structuring desire. Scopophilia refers to the pleasure arising from looking and seeing (the Greek word *scopos* means looking and *philia* is associated with love of something). In psychoanalytic terms it is connected to repressed desire and is often not acknowledged consciously. John Berger, discussed earlier, emphasises the power associated with looking and the positions of men and women as viewing subjects within patriarchal society in his book *Ways of Seeing*.[29]

The pleasure of looking – Freudian 'scopophilia' associated with a curious gaze and voyeurism – is later developed in a narcissistic form.[30] Woman is looked at as a passive object subjected to the male gaze, and her representation is stolen, quoted and becomes extended by the phallocentric order in the illusion of a perfect body – for instance of Venus.[31] Her image is reworked, inducing fetishistic and voyeuristic processes. Mulvey suggests that 'far beyond highlighting a woman's to-be-looked-at-ness, cinema builds the way she is to be looked at into the spectacle itself'.[32] Woman functions as an illusion re-appropriated to the male gaze and the measure of desire, becoming 'a one-dimensional fetish', 'subordinated to the neurotic needs of the male ego'.[33]

The Lacanian themes are part of discourse concerning, among other things, representation, functions of the gaze and mediation of perception performed by the ego and the logic of wholeness and fragmentation. These are materialised by Mulvey in her psychoanalytic approach to the cinema, in which she refers to the symbolic structure and the phallic function that embodies the Lacanian mirror stage. The male spectator, desiring the female-other, identifies with the male hero representing ego ideals on the screen/the mirror. The male protagonist is active and possesses narrative and visual power. His screen image becomes internalised as an ideal.

The Lacanian 'split' entity of the subject is composed from the gaze corresponding with a desire for self-completion, which can be achieved through the other. The gaze, is defined by Barthes as a visual tool that makes time endless. By means of the gaze one is sustained and 'appears in an eternal state of suspension'.[34] This ahistorical time is characterised according to the Foucault's heterotopias,[35] which were discussed in Chapter 1.

The contemporary figure of Venus, embodying the female ideal, is a quotation from the past. Her representation functions as a mirror image, which is more complete and perfect than the real experience. She is a structure to be looked at as another person, with pleasure, as in scopophilia or as self-identification, as in narcissism. Neither mechanism generates meaning, but idealises and eroticises, complementing the ego and the libido with their fantasy. The female 'form' is determined by the active male gaze projecting his own caprices onto her. The 'woman' is at the same time displayed as an object, one being looked at, making her a visual passive, a desired accessory to the patriarchal imaginary. However, this mirroring of males' own fantasies also reminds us that 'woman', as lacking the phallus, implies the idea of castration, and looking at her might be difficult. Therefore, as Mulvey suggests: 'Hence the look, pleasurable in form, can be threatening in content, and it is woman as representation/image that crystallizes this paradox.'[36] Venus seems 'perfect' but her figure also carries associations with fragmentation or 'disability', which are initially unnoticed and, once noticed, are considered threatening.

Ability and disability

Culturally, the body is split into two categories – complete and incomplete, abled and disabled, hallucinated or imagined as whole. This binary implies the idea of the fragmented and disabled body. The splitting derives from myths of beauty and ugliness that laid the foundations for what has been considered 'normal' and abled. The embodiment of beauty and desire is connected to the embodiment of ugliness and repulsion – Venus versus Medusa. These two mythological figures and tropes, the perfect Venus body and the disabled Medusa body, are necessary in the dialectic of beauty and ugliness, wholeness and fragmentation.

Myths of beauty and ugliness have created the dialectic of the 'ideal', 'normalcy' or the 'disabled'. Tropes of femininity such as Venus represent the dualism between the desired and the repulsive. The classical, immaculate body, exemplified by the 'perfect' figures of Venus, refers to concepts of proportion, harmony, symmetry and the idea of wholeness. The Greco-Roman Classical model highlighted the corporeal as a passive object in opposition to the active mind or the soul. After the Cartesian separation between mind and body, consciousness was elevated above corporeality. In the light of this, it is interesting to consider the image of a classical *body* as a frame and question why it implies the idea of wholeness, even though the *Venus de Milo* (or *Aphrodite de Milos*, created between 130 and 100 BC) is now visibly impaired and we only imagine the figure as a whole. *Venus de Milo* is perceived as a complete body, contrary to its visibly mutilated, fragmentary, disabled form. It is noteworthy that *Venus de Milo* was chosen as a symbol for the American Society of Plastic Surgeons (ASPS) and appeared on its emblem. The figure was selected to represent both the scientific and artistic aspects of reconstructive surgery. Combining beauty and healing, it proclaimed a bridging of the gap between normalcy and what was considered abnormal and often disabling.

Disability implies a disruption in the visual or aural field, relating to the gaze, that should somehow be regulated, rationalised. As Lennard Davis argues:

> We can begin by accounting for the desire to split bodies into two immutable categories: whole and incomplete, abled and disabled, normal and abnormal, functional and dysfunctional. In the most general sense, cultures perform an act of splitting ('Spaltung' to use Freud's term).[37]

Culture divides bodies into normal and abnormal, good and bad. It even encodes its parts, labelling them. For example, today in the West a good body is thin and tall; a bad one is fat. Lips or eyes are categorised as accepted parts; sexual organs are distasteful. These divisions create categories of abled and disabled, where the fragmented body becomes the repressed one, especially if the impairment is considerable rather than limited. Paradoxically, an armless figure of Venus with a 'scarred' face is considered one of the most beautiful female statues in the world. It inspires, attracts and seduces. The disabled Venus still functions as the ideal of Western beauty and eroticism, far removed from the horror and pity that impairment usually evoke.

Disability implies concepts of deficiency and prosthesis. According to Marquard Smith, disability is defined negatively, evoking associations with 'non-integrity', 'deficiency, incompletion, inadequacy' or 'incapability' both physical and of identity. Consequently, the body becomes also socially and politically inappropriate and Marquard argues that 'dismantling and assembling are inseparable' and the 'prosthetic body' testifies to this inextricable connection.[38] Prosthesis implies original incompleteness, and it articulates the corporeal as a heterogeneous assemblage, always in a state of flux. It is not an addition to the body, which – as I will argue further with reference to Lacan's *corps morcelé*, developed further by Davis – is already fragmented.

Davis's model of disability can be used to illustrate the differentiation between Venus and Medusa, where Medusa's fear originates in the horror that is induced by confronting the lack. Smith argues that we need to see that there is no deficiency and the body is already in pieces. He suggests that the eroticisation is inscribed in the concept of the absence of the gap in the body, not in the disguise generated by art history, which, by imagining the whole, invokes 'an apotemnophile, someone interested in the desire to have a limb removed'.[39] A disabled body seems too real or even too corporeal, yet also too little, lacking something. In both cases the disabled body is not enough and functions as a threat for the culturally implied ideal of the pure, complete body. Despite this, the incomplete, obscene or perverse body often appears in art works.

Disability within culture mobilises various negative metaphors. It denotes more than a medical condition or difference; it introduces narratives of dependency and deformation intersected by physicality. Apart from this, disability is strongly contextualised in stigmatised social conditions founded upon gender, sexuality, race and class. It serves as physical evidence for the damaged and the wrong, simultaneously functioning as a transgressive and subversive condition, understood in a broader context. It possesses various identities associated with ideas of the complete and the incomplete, the imaginary whole and the neutral, coupled with the other and the monstrous.[40] Disability suggests inferiority and a negative form of embodiment. Disability rhetoric is identified by feminist scholars such as bell hooks.[41] Nonetheless, when read from a disability studies perspective many issues are often ignored, such as the effects of language on the marginalisation of disabled people. Disability implies a monstrous other, disablement, a figure of negativity and a displaced individual. It suggests yet another 'other' that is not recognised.

The body as a material and an identity – fragmented, deprived of vision or enhanced by prosthesis – embodies what is culturally and socially assumed as normal and abnormal. Disability becomes a social narrative, represented by cultural and female tropes, embodying various meanings, stereotypes and mythologies. In the face of the social construction of the category and its various definitions – such as limitation, physicality, lacking, monstrosity, incapacity – the incomplete might function as a threat to the desire of wholeness and the deceptive conception of the body as a non-fragmented entity.

According to Martha L. Edwards, disability can be approached either in medical terms, when it refers to physical impairments, or relating to the community when the limitation is considered socially. She remarks: 'The community model presents physical disability as a cultural construct in which "physical disability" has no inherent meaning but is defined by any given community's understanding of people's roles.'[42] In this model, the degree of one's impairment is described according to one's ability to execute particular responsibilities in the community. This structure was applied predominantly in Ancient Greece, where a precise definition of a physical disability was non-existent. The body was perceived as complete, while contemporarily it is investigated as an aggregate of fragments. Historically, disability has set standards of what is considered normal in various fields – medicine, sexuality, psychoanalysis, even criminology. 'Irregular people', as Anita Silvers calls individuals whose bodies do not fit the commonly agreeable canons of beauty, are marginalised as partial.[43] Disability functions in representations of the body and it also appears in the absence of representation, as in Butler's or Irigaray's discourses, where the body is materialised only partially or in the anorexic logic. Disability metaphors, conveying the damaged, abject, other or incomplete body, can be powerful in exploring practices of othering but they also make narratives of cultural and historical disability visible. Written into artistic practices and representational strategies, they may help dismiss metaphors of damaged and stigmatised bodies, which are not valued culturally and socially. Disability narratives and experiences may reshape debates about exclusions and invite wider participation of bodies and identities marginalised as different, impaired, incomplete or disembodied.

Considered as a unified construct, the body can be identified by its individual parts – limbs, organs, cells. In fact, Venus functions as disabled female in art, culturally signifying how we perceive the body by imagining the whole (by seeing 'phantom limbs') as defence against incompleteness, castration or the Bakhtinian 'grotesque body',[44] and on the other hand by analysing the fragmentary nature of parts of the body. Venus is seen as a figure rather than a person. Still, she is a strong cultural symbol and a signifier of a range of discourses discussing the female body, the ideal or completeness.

The story of Zeuxis, who painted a perfect picture of Helen of Troy by collecting various models' most beautiful features, illustrates the fragmentary nature of the body as assemblage, bringing together parts into a beautiful unity. It embraces the ideal of completeness that can only be fully comprehended by adding the parts, and summing up fragments imaginatively, even if they are physically missing. It also refers to the Lacanian notion of the first experience of the body, which is, paradoxically, fragmentary. For a child, a body is an assemblage of various parts, Lacan's 'imagos', referring to instincts. Building the self requires unifying these fragments by imagining the whole. At the 'mirror stage' the child misrecognises an image of the self, the identity of the whole that is given as armour against the fragmentary chaotic body. Thus the disabled body is the 'imago' of the fragmented, repressed body. It is a mirror phase that has gone wrong. The self is also threatened with the disruption and incompleteness of its structure, reminders of the very first experience.

Venus and the politics of the fragment

The Venus tradition, implying aesthetics of beauty and wholeness, seems to explain itself through constant presence in the common imaginary, with continuous associations and referrals. Suzanne Ramljak, introducing Venus as the emblem of feminine beauty, questions the origins of her fame. Venus has become a brand and a pin-up girl – she has appeared in advertising and commercial merchandise[45] and her bust served as salt and pepper shakers made in the 1960s. She appeared in The Simpsons' episode 'Homer Badman' (1994, episode 9, season 6) in which Homer was beguiled by a Gummi Venus he saw in a candy booth during the Springfield Candy Convention. After he learnt that the Gummi Venus was extremely rare and was carved by Gummi artisans who specialised in working in this medium, he stole it. Back at home, the Gummi Venus was lost, only to be found stuck to the back of the jeans of the babysitter, a feminist graduate student, Ashley, whom Homer was driving home. After Homer grabbed the candy (and Ashley's butt), he was accused of sexual harassment. Finally, Homer blissfully ate the Gummi Venus (which reminds one of Rajkowska's products to be consumed and Marian's cake discussed in Chapter 2). Venus's figure was also promoted as a prototype for a Venus Ninja toy, and her silhouette appears on the covers of books, magazines, CDs or is shaped into the form of a table lamp or a vase. Likewise, the history of the *Venus de Milo* arouses interest among researchers, collectors or curators.[46] Venus has inspired artists since antiquity, not only in Western culture but also trespassing cultural boundaries in the works of artists such as Yayoi Kusama in *Nets and Venus/Infinity Nets with Venus* (1997). Rodin, Man Ray, Salvador Dalì, Robert Graham, Katharina Fritsch, Judith Page, Jim Dine and Arman, among others, refer to her sexuality with an almost fetishistic obsession examining body parts as separate elements – flesh, surface, identity. Venus has re-opened the debate on notions of beauty, gender, perfection, eroticism and seduction.

Venus – or Aphrodite[47] – symbolises love and beauty. However, according to Plato, the goddess possessed two natures. She appeared either as the embodiment of pure, spiritual love – Aphrodite Urania, or as the incarnation of sex and lust – Aphrodite Pandemos.[48] There exist two versions of Venus's origins – she was the daughter of Zeus and Dione or of Uranus, whose severed genitals fell in the sea and gave birth to Aphrodite who rose up from the sea foam. The goddess was entangled in many affairs and had many children, among them Hermaphroditus, Eros and Harmonia. Venus was represented in sculpture in various poses, usually nude,[49] sometimes with drapery around her hips, and sometimes emerging from sea foam. The *Venus de Milo* is one of the most famous representations of the goddess, continuously reworked and re-appropriated. René Magritte made four modifications to plasters of the figure between 1931 and 1936, applying paint to her replica, claiming that this 'restores to the Venus an unexpected life'.[50] He also asked his friend André Breton to invent a title for the work, and *The Copper Handcuffs* refers metaphorically to restrained desire although the figure is armless and unable to wear handcuffs. Salvador Dalí recloned Venus in a variety of ways; artists such as Jim Dine return obsessively to the statue, repainting and resculpting her; Clive Barker portrays a tongue stuck in her cheek – *Venus with Tongue in Cheek* (1990). As a trope and an ideologically loaded figure Venus is destabilised, recomposed and revolutionised. Venus embraces opposing paradigms of the perfect female figure and of an armless representation of the past. She symbolises a lover and a prostitute. Venus and Medusa (like the Red and White queens) complement each other, constituting a hybrid of parodied, ironised or subverted and contested iconic conventions concerning the female body.

The classical suggests the concept of the fragment, which is often used in contemporary art with reference to incompleteness. It abandons direct historical references and converts them into their opposites. The fragment has developed into a structural instrument, which recognises differences. It functions as a collage of narratives and myths, sampling history and ideologies, having an affinity to the 'ruin'. It is disruptive and therefore it becomes political, subverting past traditions.

In the past, fragments offered a 'wonderful idea', embodying power and control. The discovery and excavation of the ancient Roman cities of Pompeii and Herculaneum in the 1730s significantly influenced the neoclassical use of the fragment. Neoclassicism aspired to liberate itself from tradition by replacing restoration with the appreciation of the fragment,[51] and antique parts of sculptures were re-appropriated and copied as homages to Greek and Roman style and a longing for lost magnitude and order.

Neoclassicism marks a point in the eighteenth century when fragments began to be incorporated in artworks as signifiers.

The rediscovery of ancient sculpture is discussed in many theoretical texts, such as Johann Joachim Wincklemann's *Reflections on Imitation of Greek Works in Painting and Sculpture* (1755), Gotthold Ephraim Lessing's *Laocoön* (1766), Johann Gottfried Herder's *Plastik* (1778) and Adolf von Hildebrand's *The Problem of Form in Painting and Sculpture* (1893). In the eighteenth and nineteenth centuries the re-use of the classical was strongly connected to the concept of touch, evoking tactile sensuality, often embodied in the portrayal of wet drapery.[52] The perfect appearance of the 'bodies' and their immaculate execution was connected to the idea of beauty, which, according to Burke, implied smoothness.[53] The 'clean' surfaces led to almost two-dimensional sculptures that evoked painting. Later, the obsession with surfaces turned into the modernist appreciation of holes and cuts, and in postmodernism fragments become signifiers of chaos and hybridity, incorporating the poststructuralist theories of Jacques Derrida, Jean Baudrillard, Michel Foucault and feminist discourses.

Modernists' anti-classical attitude targeted the *Venus de Milo* as a ridiculous icon,[54] no longer serving as the symbol of beauty but rather as one of derision. Perhaps this suppression of the common model, together with the re-emergence of Venus in avant-garde movements and surrealist representations, helped with re-imagining not only of her form and the ideal canon, but also of notions of perfection, beauty, wholeness and their fragmentary, paradoxical, imperfect nature.

The Surrealists' interest in eroticisation, the psyche and desire liberated the subject from the constraints of reason. Representations of the female catalysed social change and woman became the emblem of sexual arousal confined by the male or subjected to masculine libidinal needs. Bondage, *emballage* and packaging made Venus an object to play with within the psychic field. In the *Vénus Restaurée* (1936) or *Full Concealment of Venus* (1934) Man Ray divided and cut her. Juxtaposing her with other symbolic items, he re-appropriated this iconic object of desire. Salvador Dalí explored Venus's feminine powers by cutting and fragmenting the body and in *The Secret Life of Salvador Dalí* remarked that: 'Nothing is more appropriate to a perfect beauty than a stupid expression. The *Venus de Milo* is the most obvious example of this.'[55]

Dalí's Venuses embodied Wilhelm Jensen's female figure from the novel *Gradiva.*[56] Freud and the Surrealists were fascinated by *Gradiva*, believing it served as an archaeological metaphor for the study of subdued desire. The *Venus de Milo*, as an archaeological artefact, became an ideal through fragmentation representing the psyche's ideal object. *Gradiva* functioned as a metaphor for a therapeutic process curing neurosis and Venus, symbolising the psyche's ideal object of desire, represents the impossible, becoming the Freudian fetish, a displaced object.[57]

Venus is also one of the most popular tropes in visual culture. Pop Art in the 1950s and Nouveau Réalisme in the 1960s made her into a product of mass culture. She appeared to be a perfect combination of high and low culture, the supposedly supreme classical art image and a form of popular commodity. By the end of the 1960s Venus was transformed as a sex symbol in commercial advertising.[58] Arman fragmented the figure and recombined her in various options – for example, as a statue of liberty in *Le phantome de la liberte* (2001) or covered in clocks in *Untitled* (1998) or painted in various colours and stabbed with sticks in *Untitled* (2001). In contrast with this glorification, Judith Page, in a series on the marriage of Venus and Mars, animalised and bastardised her. She created eight various incarnations of Venus, all aggressive, as in *Beast* (1990), where the female head is substituted with an animal one, and each version is immune and resistant to Mars's godly powers. In Betty Tompkins's painting *Popular Brands* (1993) the figure serves as a logo of female beauty, branded with cattle marks. These examples illustrate the wide appropriation of Venus's figure in art and popular culture and demonstrate that the figure of Venus is conflicted and might be confused with the figure of Medusa.

Medusa and the incomplete complete body

Medusa, one of the three Gorgon sisters and the only one who was immortal, was once a beautiful goddess who suffered because of men. Different gods abused her. The sisters – Stheino, the strong one; Euryale, the wide-roaming one; and Medusa, the cunning one – are surrogates for the moon goddess,[59] whose face was called the Gorgon's head by the Orphics. Athena turned Medusa into a repulsive creature after her sexual intercourse with Poseidon in one of Athena's temples, the monster with snakes writhing in her hair and a killing gaze, turning people into stone by looking at them. Eventually, Medusa was decapitated by Perseus, who managed to do so by looking at her reflection in his shield, which neutralised her gaze. Some myths say that each drop of blood from Medusa's neck became a snake; others suggest that the winged horse, Pegasus, and giant, Chrysaor, sprang from the blood leaking from Medusa's wound. In another version, two brothers were born from the Earth or sea foam soaked with Medusa's blood.[60] This is reminiscent of the birth of Aphrodite and explains why Pegasus is associated not only with inspiration, knowledge and speed but also symbolises the birth of beauty, originating paradoxically from ugliness.

Athena embellished her own shield with Medusa's head and skin. She extinguished the difference and otherness embodied by Medusa, that after the decapitation had appeared only as a sign of warning on various magic wallets. Athena's rationality and control of the disabled Medusa's body transformed it so that it could no longer terrorise. Hence, Medusa signifies the double, desire and repulsion, beauty and ugliness; the disabled woman in contrast to the complete Venus's body. A contemporary dissected body offers a possibility of combining the monstrous image of Medusa with Venus's seemingly coherent body to bridge the gap between what is culturally defined as beautiful or ugly. (In Chapter 5, I return to the figure of Medusa in the context of female sexuality.)

The popular myth of Medusa, where she is represented as a monstrous woman, implies the image of an ugly, terrifying, bound body. Fragmentation refers both to imperfection and disability and to completion. It is not only the melding together or bonding of consequent parts that creates wholeness. The missing portion or organ can be substituted by a prosthesis or a mask,[61] creating prosthetic beauty. During World War I, reconstructive plastic surgery led to the establishment of the Masks for Facial Disfigurement Department at the 3rd London General Hospital in Wandsworth, South London, and Francis Derwent Wood created facial prostheses (metallic masks) based on pre-war portraits of the injured wearers.[62]

The body functions as a reminder that the 'normal' body is fragmented and should not be conceptualised as other if it does not conform to stereotypes of normalcy. The missing parts point to missing functions. Idealised conventions relating to how a body ought to look like result in disability or mutilation but are not registered or acknowledged and Davis argues that: 'The disabled body is corrected by the wholeness of the constructed body of the nude. But … the emphasis on wholeness never entirely erases the foundation of the Venus tradition in the idea of mutilation, fragmented bodies, decapitation, amputation.'[63] This disabled body, besides being the physical body of a group of people, serves predominantly as the Lacanian concept of everyone's body, referring to the first infant's instincts existing in the realm of the 'Real'. The so-called 'normal body' – considered complete in Western aesthetics – conceals the primal form and appears later, in the realm of the 'Imaginary'.[64] As Susan Sontag once argued, 'only "fragments" are possible ….'[65]

The sublime and the ugly

The sublime is often opposed to beauty, but it might be seen as inscribed within the notion of beauty, although no longer in relation to perfection, harmony and wholeness. The debate on the sublime, which is a very complex concept, has shifted from attributing its cause either to nature or to ideas in mind. Platonic discourse, and subsequently Neoplatonic and Christian theories, link it with a pure, timeless 'Idea'. It is also explored in linguistics as a concept disconnected from the natural world and therefore entering language, where it gains transformational power. Philip Shaw remarks:

> If the beautiful relates to notions of unity and harmony, then the sublime refers to fragmentation and disharmony, to the moment when thought trembles on the edge of extinction. … The beautiful, that is, only attains its 'proper' quality when it is deranged by the sublime.[66]

Sublimity was often understood as signifying what was beyond reason and comprehension. It stood for the divine or the grandiose in nature. Edmund Burke associated it with the 'authority of a father', whereas beauty resided in the realm of the mother and thus the feminine.[67] The Burkean sublime concentrated on terror and the psychological effects, embodying ideas of sexuality and gender, which resulted in a shift of discourse on the concept and relocation of it from nature to the mind. Kant, juxtaposing Descartes' rationalism and Hume's empiricism, defined the sublime as formless, disunified and limitless, situated in objects of nature.[68] It referred to a struggle between the perception of reason and the senses as the sublime could elicit both pleasure and repulsion.[69]

Following the introduction of the Kantian subjectivist sublime, empiricist and naturalistic theories were substituted by a focus on consciousness. Western abstract art also concentrated on the sublime. The pictorial surface became the subject matter, substituting the earlier reverse order, which focused on creating the illusion of reality.[70] In postmodern discourse, the sublime still referred to what was vast, unlimited and immanent, but not postulated only through explorations of transcendence as in earlier writings. It became an illusion in a new reality, the unpresentable and the other.[71] Theodor Adorno proposed a closure to discussion on the sublime and beauty as 'the term has been corrupted beyond recognition by the mumbo jumbo of the high priests of art religion'[72] but Lyotard and Derrida continued to work in the Kantian tradition, questioning the structure and the meaning, emphasising transformations within linguistics. According to Lyotard, the sublime is without limits, shocking, misleading, and creating a sense of otherness.[73] His discussion in *The Postmodern Condition: A Report on Knowledge* indicates that the sublime constitutes a disruption in events and leads towards lack and contradiction.[74]

The Poststructuralists' sublime operates within the realm of language. The Post-Freudian sublime, on the other hand, relocated the concept to psychology, despite earlier Kantian thoughts on the limitations of this approach. In gendered discourse, the sublime was usually regarded as a masculine faculty while the beautiful resided in the feminine; this was debated in feminist discourse.[75]

The contemporary interpretation of the sublime has led to the concept of the 'other', the mirror stage and desire. The postmodern sublime no longer referred to the unknown and powerful force, as in Burke's writings, but started acting as 'beautiful'. This falsification became a way of deceiving the viewer. In the context of the discourse of non-entity and fragmentariness of the body, the sublime becomes an attempt to reread certain traditions and concepts without referring to the classical Greek notion of beauty. It allows irony, paradox and subversion of narratives and tropes. McEvilley calls it the 'post-sublime',[76] admitting otherness. Jeremy Gilbert-Rolfe considers the 'technocapitalist sublime', citing cyber-reality, technological marvels and consumer objects.[77] Wendy Steiner talks about 'the sublime shudder',[78] a mix of humility and triumph, monstrous and convulsive beauty, dehumanising woman. Therefore, the sublime, rather than resisting the notion of beauty, as it has since Burke's 'terror-sublime',[79] becomes incorporated within beauty, as an opposing element.

The gendered distinction between the sublime and the beautiful requires closure. Here, reference to the fusion of the two concepts in the Greek lyric poet Sappho's comparison of the concept to love is relevant. Eros imposes the idea of unity and merging of identities. Therefore, Sappho's sublime is neither whole nor fragmentary. It causes a tension between assembled bodies: opposite but not separated.[80]

When it comes to beauty and the idea of wholeness and perfection, in addition to sublimity they all incorporate ugliness. The term 'ugly' has been extended to forms, beings and morality since Plato's and Thomas Aquinas's discourses. It referred to the disproportionate, hybridised or fragmented but it would be an oversimplification to assume ugliness as the opposite of beauty. Karl Rosenkrantz defined it in the nineteenth century as the 'hell of beauty',[81] drawing on its similarities to the negation it implies. He discussed various forms of incorrectness in form, art, nature and spirituality that did not oppose ugliness to beauty, apprehended as harmony, completeness and symmetry.

Ugliness has been manifested in different ways, either formally, as a lack of proportions, or in itself, showing scars, wounds or causing disgust, for instance. In the eighteenth century, theorists focused on beauty and, rather than considering its formal qualities, they debated the effects it produced. The explorations of the reactions it evoked rediscovered the sublime and also moved perception towards the concept of ugliness. Besides still being equated with the grotesque and the deformed, it was transformed into an idea associated with the interesting and the individual. Victor Hugo's Quasimodo, Mary Shelley's monster or Oscar Wilde's Dorian Gray are ugly and tragic, devoid of beauty but constantly revealing the new.[82] They are seductive and, as Charles Baudelaire wrote in *A Selection of Consoling Maxims on Love* (1846):

> For certain more curious and disenchanted spirits, the pleasure of ugliness comes from an even more mysterious sentiment, which is a thirst of the unknown and a taste for the horrible.[83]

In a series of articles entitled 'The ugly'[84] Mark Cousins discusses the negativity attached to ugliness since antiquity. The dichotomy between beauty and ugliness relies not only on a simple negation but also on the mode of representing the truth. The latter is associated with distortion, error, contingency and, as mentioned before, with individuality, and Cousins remarks: 'At a logical level, ugliness is the negation of beauty; at the level of perception, ugliness is the opposite of beauty.'[85] It could even be said that it functions on an utterly different level. Since antiquity, what was beautiful needed to embody ideas of totality and completeness. Therefore, the ugly referred to everything that resisted wholeness. Thus, it can be regarded as a certain type of beauty that does not necessarily deform it, but, on the contrary, strengthens it.

Cousins argues that the inquiry into ugliness ought to be detached from aesthetics, which describes beauty and the subject's relation to it. Ugliness is not an aesthetic experience and cannot be preferred or hierarchised as a certain set of attributes. It functions as a space between the subject and the object. Ugliness constitutes the object that is in a wrong place, contaminated and stained. Cousins indicates that '[a]n economy of dirt is therefore one way of opening up the question of ugliness'.[86] It needs to be purified but not aesthetically, as the stain is not ugly and does not require beautification, but it is out of place and thus needs relocation. The ugly can spread and contaminate what is around it, crossing boundaries and flooding the space where it should not appear. In a sense, it demonstrates it is larger than its representation and can consume the entire zone between the subject and itself. Cousins suggests that '[c]ontemporary aesthetics has established the beauty of ugliness, reclaiming for art everything in human experience that artistic representation had previously rejected'.[87]

Drawing on the Freudian concept of reality as a hindrance to desire, Cousins frames desire as both capturing and rejecting pleasure. The ugly

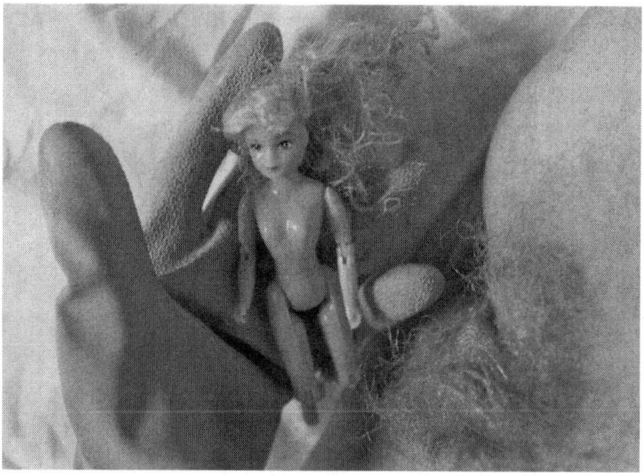

Image 6 Alicja Żebrowska, *Grzech Pierworodny* (*Original Sin*), 1993/4, video installation, photography, video still. Courtesy of the artist.

object constitutes an obstacle; it should not be there.[88] This obstacle – the ugly – becomes a punitive force, threatening the subject as an excess, not lack of beauty. The only way out is, as Cousins suggests, is for the subject to disappear. Therefore, ugliness implies not looking, but turning away. At the same time, ugliness connotes pleasure. According to Cousins: 'It is an account of the ecstasy which the unconscious enjoys in all that is dirty, horrifying and disgusting – that is, of ugliness as an unbearable pleasure.'[89] This pleasure is embodied by the figure of Medusa.

Original sin

This affinity between beauty and ugliness, Venus and Medusa (and the game-playing of the Red and White queens in *Alice*) can be illustrated by Alicja Żebrowska's 3.08-minute video installation, *Grzech Pierworodny* (*Original Sin*) (1993/4), in which Venus is embodied by a Barbie doll and Medusa is metaphorically represented through the image of a vagina. The video was accompanied by a series of photographs, *Narodziny Barbie* (*Birth of a Barbie*). The film starts with words 'the presumed project of virtual reality' and follows with a series of zooms in on a vagina, which throughout the duration of the video is stimulated with touch, masturbation with a dildo, medical irrigation and insertion of different objects. Once again Żebrowska is preoccupied with symbolic beginnings, a realm of the new female body that opposes the negative connotations ascribed to it by men according to which female sexuality is the origin of evil (as illustrated in the myth of Medusa).

She emphasises that this is a virtual reality, which might refer to the artificiality of all ideologies, in this case constructing the female body in visual culture. The imagery is visceral and corporeal. Female genitals are shown as though through a magnifying glass. They are subjected to sexual experiences, medical examination, experiments and labour. The final footage pictures the birth of a Barbie doll. In the video Żebrowska mobilises the issue of female sexuality often considered shameful, sinful and sinister, in particular in Catholic interpretation. In the title of her work, she refers to the Book of Genesis, in which Eve succumbed to the serpent's temptation and ate forbidden fruit. Since then, Eve has been blamed for original sin and punished by being subordinated to man and having to endure the pain of labour. She has also served as a testimonial to woman's 'true' nature: evil, disloyalty, decisiveness, seduction, disobedience and guilelessness, which have been used to support the measures taken to curtail the rights and status of women. In the Book of Genesis, Żebrowska sees the origin of the identification of female sexuality with guilt and shame as well as social stigmas, all of which is disproportionate when compared to male sexuality. She challenges this through direct imagery of a fully exposed vagina which is emancipated and can take pleasure to fulfil its own needs and desires, not those of a male.

The first screening of the video took place in a room infused with an apple aroma, which also alluded to the Garden of Eden and original sin. The moment the fruit was tasted, morality in the West was established. Apples, as forbidden fruit, represent sinful sexuality, interlaced in the video with religion, the female body and consumption epitomised by the Barbie doll. This in turn alludes to beauty myths and ideals of the female body, embodied in the figure of Venus. By employing Barbie, a well-known image of stereotypical femininity widespread in visual culture, Żebrowska unmasks the male images of female bodies enslaved under the dictatorship of beauty. She juxtaposes it with Christian patriarchy and points to the beginnings associated with original sin, where female beauty leads to the condemnation of women (as in the figure of Medusa) and initiates her being seen as inferior to men.

Religious imagery has a long tradition of representing the female body as split between sexuality, epitomised by the figure of Venus, and purity, symbolised by the Virgin Mary. This is an almost schizophrenic portrayal of desirable and yet sinful flesh subjected to the tyranny of the male gaze and fetishisation. The female body is portrayed as wrong, shameless and disgusting. In *Original Sin*, Żebrowska reverses this cultural code of sinful woman and questions the degradation of the female body and the male fear of the vagina. The imagery she adopts might be seen as physical, disgusting or even arousing by some, but it emphasises her iconoclasm and concern about Christian portrayals of the female body directly translating into beliefs of how the body should behave and subjugate itself to a superior male order.

The video was created in a particular moment in Polish history. In 1993, the Polish government signed a concordat with the Vatican, which was heavily criticised, mostly in terms of the restriction of the country's sovereignty and the violation of the principle separating the church and the state, leading in turn to the breach of equality between faiths. It was signed before the country's new constitution was finalised, which further clericalised public life in Poland. Another contentious point of the concordat concerns the tax voucher system, according to which part of income tax revenues can be transferred to religious bodies. It also grants financial concessions to the Church. This means the state directly subsidises the Catholic Church by paying into the Church Fund. Another obligation of the concordat for the state is to provide Catholic religious education in state schools. The state also regulates the organisations run by the Church, for example universities or university departments. Finally, with the signing of the concordat, the power of the governing bodies is ceded to an international organisation, of which the Polish Catholic Church is a part. Canon Law, which is foreign, became included in the Polish legal system and is independent from the Polish authorities. Also, Canon Law marriage (practically indissoluble as the bride and groom are obliged to sign a promise not to divorce) became possible, in which the priest takes over the role of a state registrar. All this indicates a limitation of the sovereignty of the state in certain cases and the strong, if not privileged, social and political role of Catholicism in Poland. The year 1993 was important for another reason. It was the year when an anti-abortion law was enacted in Poland, abortion having, paradoxically, been legal under communist rule. The Polish act became one of the most restrictive anti-abortion laws in Europe. Abortion is still illegal in Poland unless pregnancy endangers woman's life or health, or the foetus is seriously malformed, which needs to be verified by a physician, or it is a result of criminal act, which needs to be certified by a prosecutor.

In light of the power given to the Church, women's rights and female autonomy have been denigrated even further by disregarding a woman's right to her body. The female body was repressed and subjugated to Christian morality proclaiming chastity and godliness, also imposing on it myths of motherhood and budding life. Żebrowska counters these discourses by positioning the female body alongside religious symbolism. She refers directly to the abject body and Medusa image through combining physiological and religious language. She opposes repressed corporeality and celebrates female sexuality, equating physical ecstasy to spiritual excitement. The images that appear in her video are almost medical. They pay tribute to the specificity of the female body, which is not a sexless womb destined to deliver children following a divine act of god. It is an autonomous body challenging the cultural ideologies built around the feminine. The stimulation of the vagina through touch and masturbation portrayed in the video takes control of the body, opposing manipulatory practices of the Church and the state and the religious sexophobia still present in Poland. The close-ups showing irrigation of the vagina and insertion of different objects often cause disgust, if not repulsion. Some viewers feel offended by zoomed-in frontal exposure of the female genitals. Żebrowska brings together the female body and religion, and diagnoses the suffering and other psychological consequences the Church and its totalitarian and often anti-democratic values imposed on women's lives in Poland. The anti-abortion law caused women to fear their bodies and sexuality, and generated anxiety about unwanted pregnancies. The law also caused the emergence of underground abortion clinics, which are unsafe and too often not affordable to most women. All this is camouflaged by the state elevating maternity, family values and pro-life rationales as key virtues sought in women.

Żebrowska depicts female rebellion against sexuality being seen as sinful and shameful. She uncovers the paradox of representing women as Venuses, idealised and sublimate, and simultaneously arousing desire. She also points to the marginalisation of female imagery in a pornographic sphere that suggests the female body belongs to unofficial narratives which are dirty, forbidden and wrong. The close-ups of female genitals can be shocking to those who equate them with what is private, closed and invisible. Żebrowska refers to peripheral vision and includes images of female private parts in her artworks that are not part of the mainstream vision. They are not positioned centrally in the visual field and usually function outside the centre of the cultural gaze. Rather than eliciting voyeuristic pleasure through looking, staring and fantasising about the female body, her video is unsettling. Female genitals become Medusa, at whom one cannot stare.

Original Sin is concerned with dualism and juxtaposes beauty and the holy birth with monstrosity, lust and filthy labour. The artist combines tropes of Venus and Medusa, femininity responding to the male gaze and subjected to patriarchal structures with femininity, which is considered sinful, ugly and which can provide pleasure to women. The vagina is a site of original sin and sins associated with culturally created images that skew representations of the female body and subject it to the tyranny of perfection and idealisation. Żebrowska does not want the viewer to turn his or her gaze away. She challenges the stereotypical representation of the female body and demonstrates that there is nothing distorted, dirty or out of place even though such erroneous interpretations were enforced when discussing the female organ and female sexuality. She proposes to refocus the gaze, scrutinising the female body through the 'economy of dirt'. Her video accommodates contesting narratives and refocuses the cultural gaze that has for far too long been guided by bipolar 'Red and White queen' identifications, excluding difference and defining the female body as lacking.

4

The Cheshire Cat and the Disappearing Appearances

This chapter adopts the metaphor of the Cheshire Cat (from *Alice's Adventures in Wonderland*) to demonstrate that representation is fluid and, through using different strategies of embodiment, it can become flexible. It discusses theories informing narratives of presence and absence, appearance and disappearance enabling the undoing of gender. These theories are used to analyse artworks, articulating issues around multiple identities.

The origin of species deconstructed

Many misunderstandings and misinterpretations concerning women and the female body exist, often perpetuated by gossip and social beliefs based on binary views. They validate and manipulate stereotypes that are inscribed into rigidly defined categories of, for example, male and female. These representations are so rooted in the cultural gaze that they do not allow the body they portray to be transformed beyond the cemented incarnations and beyond its physicality. The Lacanian mirror stage, explained earlier, offers one the possibility of forming individual identity beyond representation. It is a phase in which the child recognises that the representation of the self through images and/or sounds does not equal the self. Identity is in flux and it is split, which enables negotiation of similarities and differences and of hierarchised gender designations. The traditional identifications and appearances can be challenged and subverted through the body in the recognition of difference and a refusal to conform to conventional binary cultural stereotypes. The body is both seen and felt. It can become a subject, not just an object manipulated into passivity or activity, always considered as secondary to consciousness. Similarly to the Cheshire Cat, who appeared and disappeared, the body exists and disappears, to appear again. It is presentable and representable, same and different, active and passive because of the dynamics of the mirror. It does not only contain and protect but also communicates and problematises the separation between the mind and the body towards subjectivity and objectivity, and the different perceptions of the self. Embodiment demonstrates the possession of the self through resonating with the mirror, which cuts through myths of wholeness and completeness inscribed in the previously discussed figure of Venus (see Chapter 3). The metaphor of the Cheshire Cat allows me to negotiate the space in between (also symbolised by the hole and the looking-glass reality) in relation to identity. I argue that the acceptance of difference happens and it is a site of 'into' and 'out of' presentation and representation, eclipsing the logic of either/or. The structural aspect of appearing and disappearing is useful in dismantling stereotypes concerning the female body.

Women artists – for example, Anastasia Vepreva (from Russia), Anna-Stina Treumund (from Estonia) or Natalie Maximova (from Russia), among others – often speak about the inadequacies and asymmetries concerning the female body. They feel it is their responsibility to process and interpret these unequal representations and communicate them to a wider audience. In 2010 Anetta Mona Chişa & Lucia Tkáčová produced a 35-minute video entitled *The Descent of Man, and Selection in Relation to Sex*, which challenges gender stereotypes and the repressive dichotomies of male/female structures.

The Descent of Man, and Selection in Relation to Sex refers to Charles Darwin's theory of evolution, which is regulated by means of natural selection and is considered fundamental when discussing the origins of mankind.[1] The video depicts blonde women sitting in a line, whispering and passing a message between them. Their action is reminiscent of the Chinese Whispers or Telephone game, in which one person quietly confides a message to another, which is then whispered along a line of

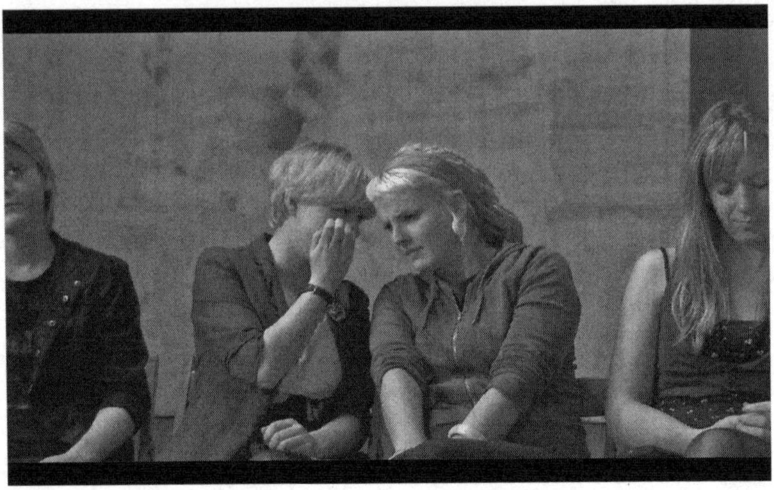

Image 7 Anetta Mona Chişa & Lucia Tkáčová, *The Descent of Man, and Selection in Relation to Sex*, 2010, video still. Courtesy of the artist.

individuals until it reaches the last person. When it does, the message is spoken out loud. Often, in the process of retelling, the statement changes its initial meaning and differs from the first one. The game depicts a cumulative error caused by inaccuracies, erroneous corrections, purposeful alterations of the message, impatience, gossip spread or unreliability of human recollection. This error is discernible when comparing the initial and final information but also when examining the intermediate changes to the original meaning during the passing. The game illustrates the truths that are passed on and their corruption caused by inadequate communication, which often has harmful effects. In another version of this game, called Rumours, the initial message is deliberately altered by the players.

Chişa & Tkáčová say their video depicts a 'corporeal translation'[2] of Darwin's nineteenth-century text, in which he describes the sexual, physical and psychical origins of mankind, as well as cultural and racial differences, and processes of natural selection that determine the superiority of humanity. His theory of evolution is based on the premise that all life has descended from a common ancestor and that complex creatures evolve gradually over time. In the process of natural selection, the beneficial mutations associated with organism's genetic code are passed on between generations, leading to variations in the original creature. Natural selection preserves members of the species best adapted to their environment, gradually eliminating those not equipped, or less well-equipped with the functional advantages that enable successful competition in the wild. Darwin's theory of evolution demonstrates a complex process of numerous and successive modifications. Currently, researchers critically evaluate the theory in the light of technological and scientific advances that allow for its focus to be re-adjusted towards an appreciation of differences and correction of aberrations.

In *The Descent of Man, and Selection in Relation to Sex*, the message passed in a chain from one individual to another concerns the theory of evolution. The process of retelling the information alters its meaning through individualisation. It also evokes the principle of the theory in demonstrating how change is generated between the past and the future and reveals an opportunity for a more fluid approach to the body and identity. Gender roles and patriarchy, considered a natural order, have often been discussed in relation to biological tropes, Darwin's *On the Origin of Species* and in various sociobiological theories. These are counterbalanced by social constructionist theories emphasising culture as structuring gender roles. According to Darwin, natural selection governs culture, mind, language and memory, generating criteria of superiority, survival and attractiveness. It is associated with individual variation and the proliferation of species. For example, some sounds and bright colours are perceived as beautiful, which suggests that sexual selection is enriched by aesthetic factors and becomes personalised depending on individuals' desires and preferences. In Chişa & Tkáčová's video, the message changes its original meaning in the process of being passed on. The act of whispering and confiding the message opens up the possibility of alterations. The initial meaning is lost through a cumulative error in between whispers and a new meaning is created. In light of what has been lost in translation, one can either go to the origin of the message or start from the hybridised final announcement. Whichever option one chooses, an opportunity arises to transform and metamorphose a canon subjected to many inaccuracies, asymmetrical structures and corrections. For example, the female body can be seen beyond the dialectic of beauty inscribed in the male gaze.

Possibility for transformation

Many tensions are associated with tropes of femininity such as Venus or Medusa. Following Bal's 'narratology', trope – as opposed to metaphor or allegory – is a figure seen in semiotic terms and a connotative element, which generates imagery and offers different perspectives on *how* rather than *what* things are represented.[3] Also, as a figure of speech, a trope suggests transparency, which anaesthetises users as to how culturally available tropes, such as tropes of femininity, act as anchors for dominant and shared assumptions about the female body. Transformation allows for the exposure and denaturalisation of some common representations.

Modification and transformation of the body includes complex ideas touching upon issues of gender, subjectivity and its embodiment in the gaze of the other. The body is seen either as female or male, and less often as fluid. The female body is portrayed in figures of Venus and Medusa, which opens up the possibility for modification and appropriation and also generates a new perspective where the body is seen as a hybrid, in constant flux, shifting identities and gender, perhaps as a 'trans-body'.[4] Some of the women's practices discussed in this chapter offer an opportunity for testing disappearing appearances and mapping 'trans' as a new agenda for identity politics that goes through the mirror and subverts binary orders. This is a space of the 'looking-glass', where everything is turned upside down – Venus into Medusa and the body into trans-body – and where presence and absence are possible. When talking to the Cheshire Cat, Alice asks: 'Would you tell me, please, which way I ought to go from here?' The Cat replies:

> 'That depends a good deal on where you want to get to.' 'I don't much care where,' said Alice. 'Then it doesn't matter which way you go,' said the Cat. 'So long as I get SOMEWHERE,' Alice added as an explanation. 'Oh, you're sure to do that,' said the Cat, 'if you only walk long enough.'[5]

Baudrillard argues that the dichotomous structure of the female/male marks individuals and semiologically reduces the symbolic, annulling the possibility of other identities.[6] Therefore, 'symbolic exchange' needs to be incorporated into the thinking about the body, as we are indeed currently experiencing what Judith Butler called 'gender trouble'.[7] Furthermore, Baudrillardian symbolic exchange is a cyclical process, reversing the binary logic (not opposing it), making presence and absence ambivalent. He reminds us that we are now in the era of the economic and the semiological, where the subject is fetishised by the law of value and where sexual politics is situated in simulation and gender politics. This is a phase of the collapse of the imaginary and the real into appearances, make-up and play allowing transformations. Baudrillard proposes a solution of multiplicity and hybridity – what I would call 'trans' – which expands gender and sexuality into hybridisations of identity and intersubjectivity. To quote visual artist and cultural producer Volcano Del LaGrace:

> It is the "play of looks" that I want to explore, within the framework of desire and its visual representations. By unearthing some of psychical, social and sexual processes involved in representations of desire we can begin hopefully to examine the dynamic of desire present in the relationship between the photographer [and here I would add mirror], the photographed [Narcissus or self] and you.[8]

'Trans' encompasses a space in between, into and out of, a threshold where everything develops into ambiguity. In Lyotard's account, representation is displaced and its limits are extended in an aesthetic response that allows otherness.

The logic of lack

The logic of trans when scrutinising corporeal tensions necessitates thinking about the body in pieces as theorised by Lacan (explained in Chapter 1). Concepts of fragmentation and completeness contextualised within the notion of beauty discussed in the previous chapter evoke Leslie Heywood's notion of 'anorexic logic', which she discusses in *Dedication to Hunger. The Anorexic Aesthetic in Modern Culture.*[9] It also refers to Wendy Steiner's idea of gender readjustment, forgetting the feminine subject, the idea of androgyny and codifying of the body, explored in her book *The Trouble with Beauty.*[10] Indirectly, anorexic aesthetics can be identified as a current concern within Western aesthetic artistic practice and androgyny as an attempt at and nostalgia for wholeness. The phenomenon is located primarily in a Western philosophical context; Freudian psychoanalysis, post-modernist and post-feminist discourses and contemporary consumer culture. The anorexic body, similarly to narratives on disability, concerns figures of abjection based on figuration and body image, which is culturally specific and encoded through mainstream narratives. An anorexic body reproduces tropes of vulnerability, difference, incompleteness and inferiority.

According to Heywood the body is not only a biological construct but primarily cultural. Its constructedness allows the reconfiguring of gender relations, articulating an alternative, other space. Its negativity or even an idealised mirror reflection become objects of fascination in the age of uncertainty and lack or flux of boundaries. Anorexia derives from 'hysteria'; a disease that emerged from the lack based on physical and psychical grounds. It developed into anorexia, a process of vanishing and elimination. Heywood remarks:

> Anorexia has emerged as a point of convergence between the literal and the figurative; between the artificiality of gender constructions that mark an unstable cultural system and a medical discourse that appeals to the essential 'truth' of the body to shore up weaknesses in the cultural model of gender. Like anorexia, medical discourse is an attempt to establish control that simultaneously demonstrates a lack of control.[11]

'Exploding the body of a reincarnated slave', fragmenting it, disfiguring, locating masculine over feminine, mind over body, the falling apart of the idea of wholeness, is what Heywood calls 'anorexic logic'.[12] According to Heywood, this is one of the determining aesthetics of recent times, embodying ideas of otherness and the binary between the female and the male. It is a set of assumptions referring to disfiguration and falling apart, originating in a gendered context. A sense of fragmentation and a symptom of keeping different pieces together defines not only psychic and bodily disorders. The 'anorexic logic' embraces various layers of cultural contexts, including art. It marks an ungendered space within which the body disappears. At the same time it is where the notion of the body, gender and fragmentation intersect, enabling difference and seeing the female body as a whole. Heywood's 'anorexic logic' is an escape from the cultural construction of the female body and it enables to revise cultural and social roles, and genders.

Anorexia was first mentioned by Plato in *Symposium*, where women's bodies were equated with commodity and physicality. The males transcended materiality, which situated them outside plurality and temporality and subordinated them to universal 'Forms'[13] or 'Ideas'. Plato's dualism clearly divided the female, associated with the transient material, from the male, universal and atemporal spirit. This equation structured paradigms of gender and discourses on the body. The phenomena of the world of senses were feminine, deceptive and unreal, as in the subsequent Cartesian theory. To get to the 'truth', the mind had to transcend the body by love – a link between the material and eternal world. In the Platonic ladder – describing the hierarchy of thought over senses, mind over body, male over female – love elevated ideas, from physical to universal, moral beauty.[14] This ladder is the first articulation in Western philosophy towards subordination and sacrificing of the feminine in order to free oneself from bonds of senses, materiality and particularity.

Descartes discussed 'philosophical anorexia' as the excess of the mind that is masculine, over flesh associated with the feminine and deceitful.[15] This Cartesian anorexic logic embraced Western literary and philosophical tradition. The female was also sacrificed in the idealist tradition. In *The Phenomenology of Spirit*, Hegel described love as an intertwinement of the female, the body and the family.[16] The masculine, on the other hand, was associated with the mind and the state. In order to become self-conscious, the male needed to subordinate the female and be situated outside of the family. The Hegelian dialectic shows that both genders are in ethical opposition. Maleness is presented as superior and individual. It unifies with its negative – the female – into a union of male consciousness and its satellite – female dependence. Hegel attributed sexual difference to the mind – the man's was conceptual and abstract, active and independent while woman's was emotional and concrete, passive and dependent. Therefore the feminine embodied nonbeing, cultured devaluation and subordination. Women attempted to attain the mind in order to exist. They developed into a form of emptiness, or as Hegel called it, 'impotent shadows'.[17]

Freud, in contrast to Plato and Hegel, did not oppose the feminine to the masculine, but rather showed that, according to the psychoanalytic model, woman could define herself against man.[18] His theory of sublimation and relation with the body was defined by the anorexic structure. The male Oedipus complex and the female castration complex transformed each other and sublimated the object love generating the super-ego, which situated the individual in society. The super-ego was created by rejecting the loving Oedipal wishes. For the female, the castration complex creates its feminine version instead of destroying the Oedipus complex. The super-ego does not form and thus woman is excluded from culture and society. She wants to participate in 'civilisation'; hence she either resigns from sexuality, wants to be a man, or plays her role, loving her father and family. These aspects, as in Hegel's theory, are predicated on the body described as lack – of Hegelian consciousness or of Freudian male genitalia. The female tries to exit the body in order to finally 'be', to get out of the non-existence, nothingness, to be something other than passive physicality, flesh and sexuality. Paradoxically, by becoming anorexic and accessing subjectivity through adopting the male identification, women become Hegel's 'impotent shadows'. In order to access the mind, woman renounces the body, defining herself as lack, emptiness and a black hole. The disembodiment is a form of a reduplication of male subjectivity that results in the dehumanising of the female and a gender schizophrenia, a 'schizophrenic liberation' as Heywood calls it,[19] that ironically destroys the body. Perfecting the body, striving for the ideal, creates a culture of assumptions regarding gender, identity and subjectivity. The logic of fragmentation is born out of articulating 'the perfect', 'the desirable', 'the required' and 'the expected'.

The split of the subject, the changing of the polarities of cultural construction of body and gender created a dialectic of lack, annihilation and disappearance. The horizon of 'anorexic logic' developed further in the polarity of the feminine and the masculine and the 'third space' – the idea of androgyny and escaping from gender. Anorexic aesthetics is a logic of negation, elimination and escape from gender. It consists of 'the ghost body' that defines the way we perceive our bodies; 'the real body', the biological one; and 'the ideal body', the one we desire.[20] The idealisation and deceiving of reality creates a ghost body. Anorexic aesthetics explores an alternative space that is multidimensional, focusing not just on the masculine or the feminine, heterosexual or homosexual, high or low. It is born out of uncertainty of the culture of its own boundaries and polarities.

Ungendered body

Heywood's 'anorexic logic' is a trope of rewriting roles, genders and cultural ambivalences. Once unquestionable categories such as the body are destabilised and need to be restructured. Anorexia is an experience of embodiment, an agency of negation, and an escape from gender through the reification of anorexic ideals. But it is also a façade that hides a paradigmatic Cartesian subject of nonbeing, forgetting and fragmenting the body and the idea of cutting the subject into pieces and creating a heterogeneous discourse.

Disunification is a construct that can be controlled or even repaired by separation from the body. In Western thought, the mind is believed to be masculine and the senses – deceptive and fragmented – are gendered feminine. 'Woman' functions as the embodiment of deception and physicality that becomes empty and unimportant. The body situates the feminine within the temporal, fragmented world. She is devalued and subordinated because of her physical being. Therefore she dehumanises herself, trying to create an ungendered space. She attempts to replace the physical body with the textual sign. This 'schizophrenic liberation' is a form of 'gender schizophrenia',[21] as Heywood calls it. The feminine functions as an equivalent of emptiness or lack in the context of cultural assumptions, where the male is associated with the mind and being, and the female with the body and nonbeing.

Anorexic logic is deeply seated in the social context, and anorexic behaviour is the reaction to and shaping of that context. Therefore the concept of androgyny, discussed by Steiner – and also Luce Irigaray, Judith Butler and Bracha Ettinger, among others, whose ideas will be developed in discussing about Cixous's bisexuality in the next chapter – becomes a space where the differences unite or rather complete each other, creating an amalgam of Venus and Medusa – wholeness and fragmentation. In Steiner's understanding of androgyny, the body functions as a postponement of the choice between the masculine and the feminine. It is an ungendered space where logic is recoded in a way that is unified and incorporative rather than exclusionary.

In 2004 Boryanna Rossa performed a piece entitled *The Last Valve* in her apartment in Sofia. Wearing a red satin chemise, the artist sewed her vagina closed with surgical thread and needle. The act was videotaped and photographed. Rossa says the piece 'is a manifesto of a future of free gender distinctions.'[22] It refers to point five of Ultrafuturo's manifesto from 2004 (cited in Chapter 2) and which points to gender as 'an excessive "property" of human society' that needs to be challenged in order to achieve harmony and completeness. The manifesto states that sexual determination distracts from unity and causes miscommunications.[23]

In the performance Rossa deliberately violates and inflicts pain on her body. For women in particular, it is hard to understand why a woman would decide, with premeditation, to subject her body to such a horrific procedure. However, I suggest that Rossa's performance does not belong to a category of actions that intend only to shock by featuring the wholly naked violated body. The artist is sewing her intimate parts closed in a politicised gesture that emphasises a number of issues. The artist uses her body as a vehicle for delivering a politicised action in the area of sexual politics. The act of suturing is radical and has many connotations, some of which were mentioned in Chapter 2 where I discussed practices involving lips being sewn closed.

Practices concerning women's bodies are culturally specific and raise a number of complex issues that may be subject to debate beyond the culture of origin, such as female genital mutilation. As a result, when watching Rossa's performance it is difficult to avoid the recollection of alternative possible meanings to that intended by Rossa's public sewing of her vagina. She voluntarily enacts female genital mutilation, something of concern to Western culture, where it has never been practised, and global culture where efforts are being made to change the female mutilation undertaken in conservative, patriarchal societies. Female genital mutilation comprises procedures that are not medically justified, and in which external female genitalia are partially or totally removed in painful and degrading circumstances. Rossa's performance is not a direct social commentary on female genital mutilation but the artist certainly problematises the issue of the abuse of and assault on the female body. In patriarchal cultures women, subjected to and acting in line with male originated rituals and conventions, undergo this horrific procedure, which causes bleeding, infections or even death. The way in which it is practised, in particular in backward rural communities, including severe cutting and damaging of healthy genital tissue, stitching with dirty horns or crude twining and lack of hygiene, is culturally justified and accepted.[24] Female genital mutilation is a violation of women's and girls' human rights and demonstrates extreme inequality between sexes. It interferes with the female body and also breaches the right to security, health, physical integrity and life as acknowledged by United Nations.[25] The practice is socially, religiously and culturally sanctioned and is considered an essential part of preparing girls for their adult life. It is deeply rooted in beliefs concerning female modesty, which result in restraining female sexuality and severing parts of the female body that are considered shameful and unclean. The United Nations and World Health Organization condemn this horrific cultural tradition and advocate for its abandonment.

By sewing her vagina shut, Rossa also emphasises the urgency of overcoming gender distinctions mentioned in Ultrafuturo's manifesto. Similarly, in 1976 Marina Abramović and Ulay (Frank Uwe Laysiepen; born in Germany) challenged fixed gender identity in their performance *Talking about Similarity*, in which Ulay sewed his lips together, depriving himself of the ability to speak. In consequence, Abramović responded to questions from the public, imagining what he would have said if he could have spoken. This action problematises the mirror stage and introduces the importance of sound and language in the formation of ones' identity. It also demonstrates that the actual mirror is not in fact needed in the process of shaping the self. The performance illustrates the dynamic between two identities, his and hers, which interchange. Lip-stitching also emphasises that language can be restricting and can repress identity, as it often maintains traditional gendered identifications, which are based on gendered rights of possession. The mirror, however, as unterritorialised space, offers a non-gendered concept of sameness and difference in which identity can be shaped by rendering gender identifications ambiguous. The position of Abramović, speaking for Ulay from a place of difference, acknowledges and challenges the reliance of identity formation on the body seen as an object and/or subject.

Rossa in her performance closes the last valve that will lead to a new species and gender revolution. It is worth recalling that the title of the performance refers to an article with the same title written by Vladimir Ilyich Lenin.[26] It was published in 1912 and described the Stolypin and the Narodnik agrarian programmes departure from the medieval landownership in Russia. In 1905 Pyotr Stolypin, the prime minister of Russia at the time, passed what came to be known as the Stylopin reform. Lenin argued that this populist reform was aimed at solving the problem of medievalism and feudalism in Russian agriculture by 'giving a new lease of life' to 'peasant' and enforcing capitalist-oriented private ownership. Lenin suggests that this opened 'another valve' to 'let off some of the steam', releasing tension and delaying the Bolshevik Revolution of 1917. Lenin returned to Russia from exile and joined the Bolshevik Party, which overthrew the Provisional Government in order to construct the socialist order under the motto 'All power to the Soviets!'

Similarly, Rossa symbolically closes the last valve, the vagina, to allow for a revolution to happen. A valve is a device that regulates the flow of a fluid by controlling passageways. When it is open, the fluid flows freely from higher to lower pressure. When the last valve is closed, the process it controls is disrupted. Rossa's closure of the vagina alludes to how gender operates in culture and society. She envisages a new ungendered species and a new class of cyborg beings, described in the manifesto. These creatures are not gender specific and as a result gender is not founded on a bipolar structure that results in oppositions and tensions. The artist takes inspiration from the animal world, where there are transgender models of sexuality.[27] She proposes hybrid bodies that escape gender determinations and heteronormative models and embrace diversity and difference. Her definition of gender is more fluid and open towards otherness. Stitching up the vagina is a symbolic gesture that annuls the lack delineating the female body, which becomes sexually undefined. There are no genitals that would suggest sex and the vagina associated with an abyss, hole and fragmentariness is erased. There is also another, more tongue in the cheek dimension to Rossa's performance. She is referring to the Bulgarian expression 'stitched up cunt' that describes women not willing to have sex at any time or be subject to male desire.[28]

Seeing through lack

At one point Alice says: 'Oh, how I wish I could shut up like a telescope! I think I could, if I only knew how to begin.'[29] This seemingly innocent statement points towards many complexities attached to the female body functioning in a society that privileges Western-centrism, whiteness, thinness, maleness, heteronormative and bipolar structures, and so on. When analysed with reference to the mirror stage, it becomes obvious that identity is formed in line with the different idealisations imposed on the body. The question arises whether the subject has to succumb to these idealisations and slowly 'shut up', or if an opportunity exists to form a coherent identity that is not obliged to identify with socially and culturally preferred images. Alice's point about 'shutting up like a telescope' brings forward another issue, namely narratives concerning the disappearing body, and the lack and fragmentation that is also associated with the Lacanian concept of the mirror stage and identity formation. Alice does not know where to begin, which might suggest that an alternative option can emerge for the female body that can be subjected to corporeal redefinition.

The images of the female body that can be observed practically on a daily basis – promoting thinness, blondeness, whiteness, passiveness – become not only representations to which women aspire but eventually materialise into their mirror reflection. This results in the female body being seen through these images. The dynamics among the image, the subject and the cultural gaze is emphasised here and it becomes obvious they are interconnected, and images of, in this case, the female body, are subjected to the scrutinising collective cultural look. Women seeing themselves through this look discover their inadequacies, defects and flaws. They wish to shut up, disappear, annihilate or transform their bodies. They review their corporeality, which mobilises the dynamics among what Silverman calls the gaze, the look and the screen. She explains it well when analysing negritude.

> The gaze turns out to be unlocalizable and 'unapprehensible', at the same time everywhere and nowhere. If, from a distance, the white look is able to assume powers which it does not in fact possess, that is only because of the screen, which intervenes not

> just between the gaze and the subject, but also between the subject and the gaze. The mediating agency often aligns the gaze with both the male and the white look.[30]

The oscillation between the look, the gaze and the screen results in the subject fluctuating between closing and maintaining the distance between the visual imago and the proprioceptive body. It is drawn to idealisation (or de-idealisation) and forced into it due to prevalent cultural ideals and social pressure. The subject identifies with and is seen through these images which leads to its fragmentation and a violent dispersal into pieces. This disintegrated body portrays Alice's fantasy to shut up like a telescope. It is not Schilder's positive account of fragmentation, which was discussed in Chapter 3. Here the body desires to identify with perfection and ideals and reject any difference or marginalisation that would disintegrate it further. What is normative is safe and helps form the corporeal ego.

Silverman reminds us that the body is a cultural structure that does not exist before its construction and, in consequence, is in fact not present to the subject. She says: 'Indeed, "presence" is itself only an imaginary effect of the integration of the visual imago and the sensational ego.'[31] This might cause the female subject to embody the cultural mirror of the representation of the idealised female body. Yet, it has a close relation to the real body. Silverman points to a Freudian account that, because of this direct connection, allows the female subject to accommodate heterogeneous corporeal identifications. She refers to Freud's essays, 'Femininity' and 'Female sexuality',[32] in which he questions the sensational and proprioceptive body in relation to the female subject and its corporeal activity and passivity. In the cultural model, the female castration crisis results in passivity, which can be experienced as normative femininity, 'sexual anaesthesia' and 'the refusal to register gender at the site of the sensational body' or 'the so-called masculinity complex, a retreat to the negative Oedipus complex'.[33] Freud also suggests that in the negative Oedipus complex, the girl identifies with the mother, who is the lovable image. The moment of transformation occurs when the female subject distances herself from the maternal imago and identifies with the cultural repertoire of images (governed by patriarchal power) in which her body is seen as lacking and insufficient. In consequence it is prompted to aspire towards perfection, beauty and exceptionality that would help erase any reminders of castration. Silverman reminds us that '[s]he must thus embody both lack and its opposite: lack, so that the male subject's phallic attributes can be oppositionally articulated; plenitude, so that she can become adequate to his desire', which in turn, leads to a 'double bind'.[34]

This reading proposed by Silverman, and the narcissistic object-choice, allow for the female subject to reject her identification with lack. The love of women is directed towards distanced desired images of ideal femininity, yet it is not self-love but, as Silverman suggests, the impossibility of loving the self.[35] The narcissistic object-choice prompts self-love but also love for 'the one who is able to love the subject in a way that compensates for the impossibility of self-love'. In 'On narcissism' Freud suggests that the crisis of femininity can result in passive or active positions. In the first scenario, the subject becomes a love object desirous of being loved. In the second option, the subject breaks from the double bind described by Silverman and replaces her ego-ideal with a man, the ideal she wishes to become.[36] Both scenarios can result in subordination and dependency but they can also be used to the female subject's advantage. The different body images that arise from the organisation of the ego, the ego-ideal and the proprioceptive body, allow for identificatory flexibility, being in flux and crossing gender lines. Silverman proposes that the female spectator can identify more freely than the male one.[37] It seems the female body can also adopt different strategies to challenge subject-positions and function at thresholds of gender and libidinal identifications, becoming active and adopting values that might conventionally be associated with the male body or actions. This aligns with contesting the male viewing position described by Laura Mulvey in 'Visual pleasure and narrative cinema' and further elaborated by Theresa de Lauretis in *Alice Doesn't: Feminism, Semiotics, Cinema*.[38] The female body, even if defined as lacking, can access corporeal imagos to disrupt and rework gender and reconfigure forms of difference. It can adopt images of masculinity as screen to identify with them, use the body as an agency to access otherness or to deconstruct them and manipulate into camp images that are worn. This corporeal travesty and the trans logic helps achieve imaginary coherence that is based on fantasising gender.

Aleksandra Kubiak and Karolina Wiktor (both from Poland) constituted an artistic duo under the name Grupa Sędzia Główny (Chief Judge

Group). Between 2001 and 2010 in their performances (which they call chapters, often divided into episodes if a performance evolves, not necessarily chronologically numbered) they pushed the boundaries of gender roles by playing with their audiences and employing cruelty, masochism, role-playing and perversion to test not only the pleasure but also the responsibility that comes with power. They contest gender stereotyping and violate social norms by employing contemporary visual and media culture with which their audience is familiar. In 2010, owing to Wiktor's serious illness, the activity of the group was suspended and, in 2013, the group disbanded. Since then Kubiak has continued her individual career.

Grupa Sędzia Główny exploited narratives of reality shows, tabloids, television and phone sex lines to perform awareness of and politicise the position of women in the cultural mirror. They borrowed themes from mass culture and critique clichéd notions of gender and social and cultural stratifications. Much of their practice was influenced by private experiences and traumas. They said there exists an element of 'tabloidisation' of feelings and that even if some actions are deeply personal, it is not always obvious to the viewers.[39] They always performed as a duo and their double actions, referring to the dynamics between their own bodies but also between their bodies and the audience, embodied the friendship, mutuality, sisterhood and generosity discussed in earlier chapters. Their activities were often shocking and exposed personal mythologies and fixations, fears but also fantasies. Grupa Sędzia Główny animated and manipulated the viewer by playing with feminine appearances. They said that the way they look is important. They created a conscious image of looking perfect in high heels, wigs and dresses specifically designed for them, made by a dressmaker with whom they collaborated. They demonstrated the oppressiveness of these images of femininity forced upon women by male expectations and imagination.[40] They also revealed the impact they have on society and cultural mechanisms guiding representations of the female body. The initial apparent affirmation is, in fact, a critique and deconstruction. The two women often handed power over their bodies to the audience who could use them as medium to project their dreams about female bodies.

Grupa Sędzia Główny was popular, particularly among the male audience. Most often they were described as 'young, pretty and eager to strip'.[41] They toyed with the audience, reclaiming their bodies to seduce and awe though titillating performances. They were usually naked, wearing high heels and sometimes sexy lingerie. They licked vodka off the floor, stripped and laid eggs in front of the puzzled viewers, who criticised their actions but could not stop looking, driven by desire and curiosity. They were hypnotised by the parted lips and thighs and initially did not notice they were confronted *through* the nudity and some easily recognisable sexual codes attached to the female body and its functioning in contemporary visual culture, as a commodity and an object. The nakedness of the artists was a provocation. Kubiak and Wiktor said that, instead of being undressed by the male gaze, they would do it themselves.

> We'll do it for art, in order to show how hypocritical we are and what sanctimonious poses we take. And it's not only for men. Women aren't better. Nobody forces them but still they let treat themselves like a 'product' [sic]. They reduce their value to parading with naked belly buttons and showing their buts [sic] and breasts in tight clothes. The season has just started.[42]

Grupa Sędzia Główny used their bodies as tools to first lure, subject themselves to public judgement and then provoke. They were for the male and the female gaze but they also took pleasure from looking at the audience and observing their actions. It might seem they were the victims, scrutinised by the gaze and judged. The female body has often been victimised through being naked and exposed to male looking. Here the situation was reversed. The two women played the roles of a master and slave in active performance and it was not obvious if the viewers were not the victims. The name of the group refers to the highest-ranking judge in a court, who remains in charge of all criminal cases. A judge should be impartial and issue rulings (following a trial in open court) based on the interpretation of the law and judgement. The performances of Grupa Sędzia Główny were public, as though in an open court and subject to different interpretations. Yet, even if literally offering their bodies temporarily to the audience as material to be examined, they were in charge of the final verdict. They were the ones ruling and issuing judgments.

Kubiak and Wiktor made visible instances in which the representation of the female body is conventionalised and sought to reformulate it.

Their actions might be described as performances of the look and the gaze through the cultural screen. Silverman conceptualises the look as emplaced within the spectacle, the body, temporality and desire and, even if limiting, it can circumvent the limits to enable seeing in other ways. This is what distinguishes the look from the gaze. Silverman also proposes the concept of 'the productive look', inscribing otherness in the field of vision. It derives from (and expands on) Lacan's gaze based on lack and acknowledges the void. Silverman locates a space in the field of vision that can be occupied by the subjective agency, which, in her account, depends on the lack.[43] Kubiak and Wiktor looked at each other *and* the audience, subjecting their bodies to the gaze of the viewers that is shaped by cultural tropes and clichés. The audience looked at them through their own experiences and socialisations *and* exchanged the looks with bystanders. The dynamics of looking is at least three-directional. The travelling of the gaze happens on many levels that are directed by the overarching scrutinising cultural eye of dubious morality and ethics. Sometimes the performances were staged in such a way that the looks were divided. For example, in *Chapter III* (2002) they lay in front of mirrors on two sides of a wall, one of them wearing white, the other black lingerie and trousers pulled down. They saw their own reflection in the mirror and that of the viewers passing by but they could not see each other. The rhythm of the personal relationship was expressed in a different way. Although parted by the inability to see each other, they became reunited through sound. Seeing was replaced by the presence of artists' voices as they told each other stories, including *Alice in Wonderland*. In other instances, the audience looked at them from the same level, from above or from below. The artists staged their own physical position and directed the look to contest the gaze and the representation of the female body. They played a game with the viewer and they also empowered themselves with the look, gazing at the audience.

Multiplicity of female desire

Luce Irigaray discusses female sexuality and the female subject functioning as a hole that is juxtaposed with the male subject taking on the privileged position of superiority. Male identity is associated with unity, defined by oneness of the male sexual organ. Such logic denies acknowledgement of female sexual organs that are always plural and multiple, for example vaginal lips. She establishes that the male discourse is associated with the 'specularisable', the visible, the mirror reflection, that which can be visible as the penile erection.[44] This is further elaborated in her other publications. In *This Sex Which is Not One* and *Speculum of the Other Woman*, Irigaray proposes language that is diffused and more fluid and, as such, adequate to describe female sexuality.[45] She builds upon Derrida's critique developed in his essay 'La question du style'[46] and adopts his deconstructive philosophy to demonstrate the phallocentrism of Lacanian discourse. Irigaray rejects the definition of femininity as lack supplementing male desire. She refers to Derrida's double centrism, which infuses logocentrism, characterising Western philosophy and referring to nostalgia for a lost presence, with the phallus replacing the central position of the logos as the core signifier. Carolyn Burke argues that the phallus allows for the representation of sexual difference and desire. In this light Derridean, phallogocentrism 'declares the inextricable collusion of phallocentrism with logocentrism ... and unites feminism and deconstructive, grammatological philosophy in their opposition to a common enemy'.[47] According to Gayatri Chakravorty Spivak, Irigaray sees this as an opportunity to challenge oppositional structure and bring to light the inequality and oppression lying at its core. She proposes replacing phallogocentrism with 'vulval' or 'vaginal' narrative that privileges female sexual sufficiency in the creation of meaning and emphasises its multiplicity.[48] It is interesting to note that Derrida also uses feminine terms such as 'virginity' and 'hymen' as metaphors and tropes. They do not replace masculine terms but function in parallel, to enable multiplicity rather than moving from one binary to another. He uses them to talk about textuality and writing.[49] Spivak suggests this might be seen as a feminist gesture, deconstructing binary logic and indicates a new sexual fable, which is contrary to 'phallocentric fable of meaning. She calls it 'hymeneal', and argues that it accounts for 'sexual union forever deferred', allowing for fusion and abolition of differences.[50]

In *This Sex Which is Not One*, Irigaray goes 'underground', 'down the hole' in search of a space where women can learn anew to speak. In her preface she refers to a review of a Swiss film, *The Surveyors*, in which the main protagonist (Alice) finds herself in a new dwelling, as though on the other side of the looking-glass, where she goes against the different systems of oppression imposed on her (or women in general). The review is entitled 'The looking glass, from the other side' and Irigaray uses it to emphasise some tropes and figures related to female desire in order to sketch a new geography governed by opposition to these systems of oppression trusted upon the female as a concept.[51] Irigaray joins Alice in her journey to the other side, which she conceptualises as a realm beyond the law of the logos and one that disrupts the phallogocentric order. She writes: 'Alice's eyes are blue. And red. She opened them while going through the mirror. Except for that, she still seems to be exempt from violence. She lives alone, in her house. She prefers it that way, her mother says.'[52] Irigaray argues that women are located on the other side, in a new psychic space beyond the patriarchy. She conceptualises a new realm in which woman is no longer seen as lack and male negative. It is not an inverted space but a site where polarities are dissolved, which might be described as pre-oedipal or postpatriarchal.

This Sex Which is Not One begins with Alice's journey. Throughout the book, Alice turns into Alices for whom Irigaray offers an open structure, allowing for the redefinition of their identity and sexuality, and plurality and multiplicity. She is rescued from the Oedipus complex and her body is enabled to oppose absence and lack, questioning the privileging positions of phallogocentrism. Irigaray argues,

> Must this multiplicity of female desire and female language be understood as shards, scattered remnants of a violated sexuality? A sexuality denied? The question has no simple answer. The rejection, the exclusion of a female imaginary certainly puts woman in the position of experiencing herself only fragmentarily, in the little-structured margins of a dominant ideology, as waste, or excess, what is left of a mirror invested by the (masculine) 'subject' to reflect himself, to copy himself. Moreover, the role of 'femininity' is prescribed by this masculine specula(riza)-tion and corresponds scarcely at all to woman's desire, which may be recovered only in secret, in hiding, with anxiety and guilt.[53]

She elaborates, noting that the female imaginary can overcome this logic of fragmentariness if it employs the logic of 'a phallic maternal' and rejects the 'masquerades of femininity'.

The judging controlling female gaze

Women can redefine their identity and sexuality *through* female imagery and through toying with figures of femininity. Grupa Sędzia Główny played with beauty and monstrosity and repulsion. They fully embodied the dialectic of Venus and Medusa, destroying the image of the female body either by negating its attractiveness or by inflicting pain on it. The visual language they used directly speaks about and *through* femininity. In their performances, the female bodies were first presented as seductive phallic femininity with the male gaze mapped onto their corporeality. They responded to cultural demands and, even if in pain, realised fantasies of the mostly male viewers. Slowly, as time passed by and the gaze consumed their bodies, femininity turned into repulsion. In *Chapter XXIII* from 2004, subtitled *Pretty? About Prettiness…*, Kubiak and Wiktor – wearing black wigs, black dresses and stilettos – were imprisoned in a wired cage that separated them from the audience (at the same time confining them within the viewers' gaze). They employed erotic poses and climbed the table. Subsequently, on all fours, they drank beer from the same bowl, impersonating 'hot' and 'sexy' femininity. Suddenly, the sexual turned into monstrous when they started vomiting and urinating. This was again ruptured and they returned to their erotic poses. In *Chapter XXX* (2005) they performed in a pub during *Interactions* International Art in Action Festival in Piotrów Trybunalski in Poland. Wearing black dresses, black wigs, stockings and high heels, they played darts with the audience. The winner was promised a prize of having the artists available for 24 hours, which was regulated by a contract. After the competition, a fight initiated by the loser took place and the performance finished before the winner signed the agreement. In *Chapter LXI, Women's Day* (2007) repulsion was also affirmative, not negative. They sprayed the gallery floor with vodka from their mouths and then, on all fours, licked it seductively. They were wearing red dresses with white polka dots, black wigs and high heels. The kneeling position was literal and sexual. After they emptied the bottle, the artists sat next to each other, pulled up their dresses and spread their legs wide, revealing that they were not wearing pants. They kept staring provocatively at the audience.

The actions of Grupa Sędzia Główny were political. They fought for women's right to their bodies. Although this did not result in any change in legislation, this form of activism is needed in a country with a history of oppression and a burden of complicated relations, with Russia and Germany in particular. The shifting borders and transformation to a Soviet-style regime subjected Poland to communist dominance, which was challenged during numerous riots and political struggles mainly during 1980s. Activists, from the Solidarity Movement for example, were violently oppressed by the state forces. However this did not discourage the opposition from acting. After the collapse of the Soviet Union, the disbanding of the Warsaw Pact in 1991, and a subsequent absence of socialist system regulating political, economic and cultural realms, Poland underwent numerous transformations, which brought it closer to the Western world. These led to the country joining NATO in 1999 and its entrance into the European Union in 2004. Such a complicated history of oppression and socialist patterns also impacted women, making them a politically, culturally and economically disadvantaged group.

Some of the artworks I discuss in this book might be seen as repeating women's practices that had occurred in the West as feminist art practice gained momentum. Representations of women were challenged in feminist art of 1960s and 1970s through using the body (by, for example, Carolee Schneemann and Judy Chicago), but this was not a common practice in Eastern and Central European countries, which were subjected to oppressive communist rule. However, after the fall of the Berlin Wall in 1989, feminist and gendered debates in Eastern and Central European nations gave voice to women. Using their bodies, they could interpret mechanisms of the post-dependent and post-transformational condition of Central and Eastern Europe and its relationship to the West. They also problematise the situation of women who, even though granted constitutional equality and freedom during communist rule, were and still are associated with the private realm and rarely acknowledged as full members of society. Gender equality was established under Communism and women did not need to fight for the right to their bodies. Theoretically, there was no need for a women's movement. For example abortion, which is now illegal in Poland, was allowed but it was instrumentalised and had nothing to do with women's or human rights. Its current position is a direct result of this needs-based approach, Polish cultural traditions privileging family and society and the power of the Catholic Church. These cherished cultural values necessitate self-sacrifice from women, who are responsible for reproduction and serving others (and the nation), and are not seen as individuals. This position then allows the female body to become a site of political activism for many women artists.

Grupa Sędzia Główny responded to the social and cultural issues shaping the position of women in Poland. One of their performances, entitled *Chapter XI, Bacchanalia – Night of the Solstice* (2003), coincided with the arrival (or rather denied mooring) of the floating abortion clinic, *Langenort*, in Gdańsk.[54] In response to women's expected social and cultural role to reproduce with no right to decide on what happens to their bodies, the artists, wearing long black skirts, laid hard-boiled eggs and offered them to the audience. This act symbolised giving birth. At the same time, the egg, being an epitome of life and revival, here was 'dead' and boiled. They responded to people's reaction to the floating clinic, which had had eggs thrown at it. They also said the use of eggs was inspired by a Japanese pornographic film *Empire of Passion* in which a couple of lovers make love until they die. In one of the scenes, the male lover inserts an egg into his partner's vagina. She then gives birth to it and he eats it.[55] They wanted to emphasise the circulation of pornographic images within the more official and mainstream narratives and their role in shaping social behaviours.

Grupa Sędzia Główny's performances were based on the principle of self-sameness and twin likeness. By looking alike, they also represented the average women's experience and addressed the collective female subject born out of socialisation and patriarchal culture. It seems they were interested in the process of becoming and their playing with clichés of femininity narrated the female body and inscribed it into different situations, allowing it to experience what Irigaray defines as plurality and multiplicity. Their twin likeness also embodied the concept of the mirror reflection in which one conforms to cultural norms. Both women were aware of the similarity and advanced it. They said they 'made an inventory of things' they intended to do to their bodies to become more alike.[56] Similarly, in their performances they did the same actions and dressed identically. This synchronisation was also reversed in instances when they 'swapped' bodies, becoming a symmetric oneness and a hybrid, as for example in the performance *Chapter XXV* in 2005 when they connected their mouths and vaginas through plastic pipes and turned into a unified creature. In

Chapter V, from 2002, their naked bodies were wrapped in transparent foil and imprisoned in a transparent tube. A pipe connecting their mouths carried air breathed from and in between one another between their bodies. In *Chapter X* (2003) they embodied Botticelli's *The Birth of Venus* by standing together and kissing, and touching each other, in a shell illuminated by a strobe light. The bodies were pricked with needles that held pipes attaching them to one another. They then came out of the shell and mingled with the viewers, kissing some of them. Their initial inaccessibility was broken when they reached the audience. They were no longer objects to be looked at but bodies to be touched and interacted with. This experience of bonding and duplicating the self resonates with the notion of intimacy, the politics of friendship and the concept of the mirror, which embodies their constituting themselves in one another. It also points to emotional dependency, at the same time distancing the female body from the subjection to male economic or physical reliance and building upon the concept of love. Kubiak and Wiktor created a symmetric position where the power is exchanged and did not belong to just one agent. They built a symbiotic relation in which narcissism was no longer situated in the affirming male gaze but was based on love through oneself towards the other.

In 2005 Grupa Sędzia Główny invited the viewers of TVP Kultura, a Polish cultural TV channel, to participate in *Chapter XL*, entitled *Telegame*. The artists were in a television studio and people were asked to call in and request them to fulfil their orders. When asked why they decided to do this, Karolina Wiktor said:

> We were told that we were doing something wrong, that we should have done something in different way. … So we have said with deliberation: 'If you know just do it. And experience us.' This title is perverse, because in Polish 'Experience me' can mean 'teach me' but also 'Experience me, Karolina, and check out who I am.'[57]

On the night, Paulina Reiter introduced them:

> We are at the studio of The Night of Artists. Tonight we have The Chief Judge Group: Aleksandra Kubiak and Karolina Wiktor. This programme won't succeed without the viewers, without your participation. I ask you to call the studio and the

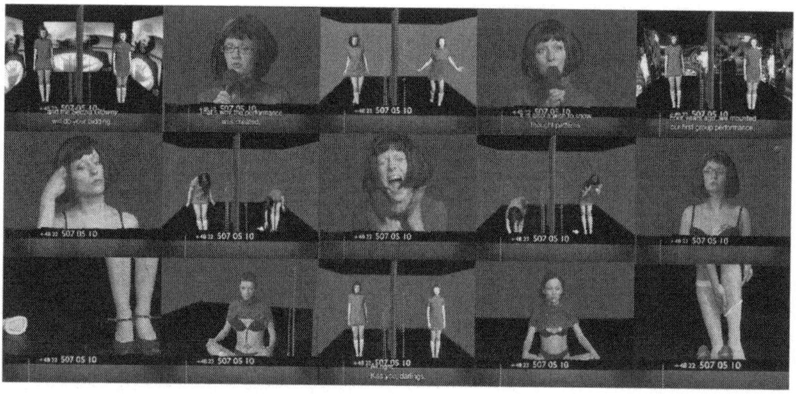

Image 8 Grupa Sędzia Główny (Chief Judge Group): Aleksandra Kubiak and Karolina Wiktor, *Chapter XL, Telegame* (2005), on Public Television TVP Kultura. Courtesy of the artist.

> Chief Judge, performance group, will carry out your every command, every wish and every order.[58]

Kubiak and Wiktor were waiting in the television studio for the calls and the orders they were ready to fulfil. They wore the same clothes and looked alike but they could not see each other as there was a curtain separating them. This border differentiated the way in which they responded to the instructions. They interpreted the tasks differently but even though their responses were not identical it was obvious they were considering how the other one was reacting to the viewers' wishes. Their actions were recorded and projected to the audience watching the programme. Their request to call them and they would fulfil every order brought people's fantasies into the spotlight. Some, the majority men, took the bait. The artists were asked not only to bow, come closer to the camera, take their wigs off, turn around, recite the first verse of the Polish national anthem but also to sit cross-legged and lift their dresses, uncover their breasts and take their panties off. Then they were asked to get dressed and, again, take their stocking off. Kubiak and Wiktor patiently, passively and obediently followed the orders. The viewers were aware the artists were not acting of their own free will and would meet their demands. Most of the male callers abused their power and wanted to satisfy their desires. The action made the drives hidden deep in people's minds visible and confronted them, challenging both social and double moral standards. The performance was recorded by TVP Kultura. Its viewers are believed to be interested in artistic practice and critique, yet most of the callers asked the artists to simply undress and succumb to their insatiable gaze, seeking to make the female body subject itself to the gaze.

Kubiak and Wiktor created a bond with the audience but it differed from their other actions. Here the notion of intimacy had another dimension. Usually, it had been employed by Kubiak and Wiktor to define their relationship. It was an overarching concept representative of being together, openness and sexuality. Piotr Rypson points to the etymology of the word 'intimacy', which derives from Latin *intimare*, meaning 'to announce, to make known'. He suggests that the performances of Grupa Sędzia Główny described the intimacy, in the sense of interpersonal relationships, between the artists and also between them and the audience, touching upon issues of sexuality, seduction and repulsion that were brought to light. Rypson notes the actions often employed the figure of the doll. Kubiak and Wiktor dressed up, applied make-up and became available for public scrutiny. They turned themselves into fetish objects and subjected themselves to the viewers' control. In fact, they were curious about what would happen during their actions, how the audience would react and were flexible when it came to the course of their performances. They engaged in a follow-up assessment of what emerged from their work in order to prepare the next performance. Rypson suggests intimacy in this case might refer to a legal term of 'intimation', ordering and imposing authority.[59] This reading offers an interesting perspective in which the viewers become challenged and forced to rethink their own feelings and experiences. Grupa Sędzia Główny transgressed the boundaries of their own and others privacy and intimacy through female corporeality.

In 2007/2008 Kubiak and Wiktor started a new series of performances under the title *Beznadziejnik*, which can be translated literally as 'trash bash', meaning a person subjecting themself to ridicule. This new cycle was no longer numbered with Roman numerals but with Arabic, which suggested a rupture from previous provocative actions. With *Beznadziejnik*, the artists entertained and annoyed, even staging a diary of a hopeless woman. They ridiculed themselves and bored viewers, drawing upon the aesthetics of gossip tabloids and music TV channels. The first action, a film shot at the University of Physical Education in Warsaw, Poland, was entitled *Chapter 0. Furies*, or *Trash Bash Rejectamenta 0*, and brought the two narratives together. The artists played the Roman goddesses Furies, also known as Greek Erinyes. These deities, the three sisters – Alecto (the angry), Megaera (the grudging and jealous) and Tisiphone (the avenger) – symbolised vengeance and cruelty. Their hair was interwoven with serpents, poisonous blood dripped from their eyes and their breath was burning. They persecuted various crimes and injustices, which refers to the name of Kubiak and Wiktor's group. Ludwisiak suggests the performance portrays the essence of art creating a dialogue with *Controversiae* by Seneca the Elder, which describes the torturing of a model by Parrhasius of Ephesus who, in order to depict the bound Prometheus realistically, allowed the model to die.[60] In *Furies* Kubiak and Wiktor were strong and dominant. They were assisted by their friend, Weronika Pilarczyk, the third Fury. The artists' pronouncement read: 'Ladies and Gentleman, exercising our prerogatives and jurisdictions Chief Judge now decides to award a prize to the best artist of the Spojrzenia 2007 Exhibition.'[61] They reached for the matriarchal routes of the judiciary and took over the power. All women wore tight red jumpsuits and were surrounded by half-naked men who carried them on their shoulders. They were also assisted by a police cordon. With whips in their hands, embodying dominatrices, the women tamed the men, subverting the power and challenging conventional relations between sexes. Here the women were in control and passing the sentence.

Grupa Sędzia Główny played with the audience and became their toys in the guise of femme fatales, call girls, Lolitas, whores, naked objects or dominatrices. They made visible human desires and fantasies and they simulated situations in which they could deconstruct the image of the female body beyond the lack and inferiority imposed on it through social conventions and the cultural mirror. They played with clichés and stereotypes and the social role of women through direct connotations with pornographic imagery. Their bodies became tools that they shared with the audience in the hope that the viewer would look beyond the body towards a social system that needed rethinking (and continues to do so).

Alice's 'shutting up like a telescope' points towards culturally constructed images of femininity, which often promote the disappearing body and the lack. Anorexic embodiment is associated with discourses of representation and positioning of subjects as others who are denied a voice. In both cases it is through the body that the excluded subjects can speak. Merleau-Ponty argues that the body is the primary site of encountering the world. It is the origin of any signification and orients us in space, which discharges Cartesian dualism and negates the abjecting of the body.[62] The negation of this binary, whether demonstrated by the Venus/Medusa logic or the dichotomy between completeness and incompleteness, locates bodily identity within the possibilities of the body and what it can do. In terms of anorexic embodiment, associated with narratives of representation and power but also spectacle (both seducing and repellent), the body becomes animated through destabilisation of the historically marginalised bodies.

Grupa Sędzia Główny, Boryanna Rossa and Anetta Mona Chişa & Lucia Tkáčová demonstrate through their artworks that the privileging of certain body images or valorisation of wholeness imprisons the subject in limiting and restricting images that do not allow for difference. Depreciation of insufficiency and narratives of lack lessen opportunities for transformative looks at the body. Culturally defined norms cannot be narrow and allow only for ideal and perfect images that depreciate difference and restrict subjects that are seen as unworthy of love. Silverman comments: 'We need to learn how to idealize oppositionally and provisionally.' She also says it is important 'to idealize outside the corporeal parameters of the self'. This can be achieved through moving from 'aspiration to perfection' towards 'the experience of corporeal fragmentation'. This also means 'consolidating oneself as a subject of lack' and identifying with bodies that 'we would otherwise phobically avoid, to facilitate our leap out of "difference" and into bodily otherness'.[63]

5

A Rose Garden

This chapter analyses artworks that present a world beyond gender divisions, inviting multiple gazes and sexual identities. It explains theoretical underpinnings building towards the concept of genderland. Theories of seduction and desire are introduced in relation to the identification with difference. They are embodied in the metaphor of the rose garden in *Alice in Wonderland*. The chapter explores the rose garden as a site of transformation and possibility, in which the female body becomes a powerful subject *and* object, challenging myths that imprisoned woman.

Genderland

In her project *Onone. The World after the World* (1995–99) Alicja Żebrowska created Onone, an androgynous fantasy, where gender binaries do not exist and androgynous beings leave their primary sexual identity in order to embrace transhuman existence. These hermaphrodite beings depict corporeality and life forms that are in constant flux and are subjected to metamorphosis. Bodies are in continuous configuration, moulding and modifying matter. The project starts with a 3.30-minute video entitled *Onone - Assimilatio*, produced in 1995. It is accompanied by electronic music composed by Dariusz Baster. The word *Onone*

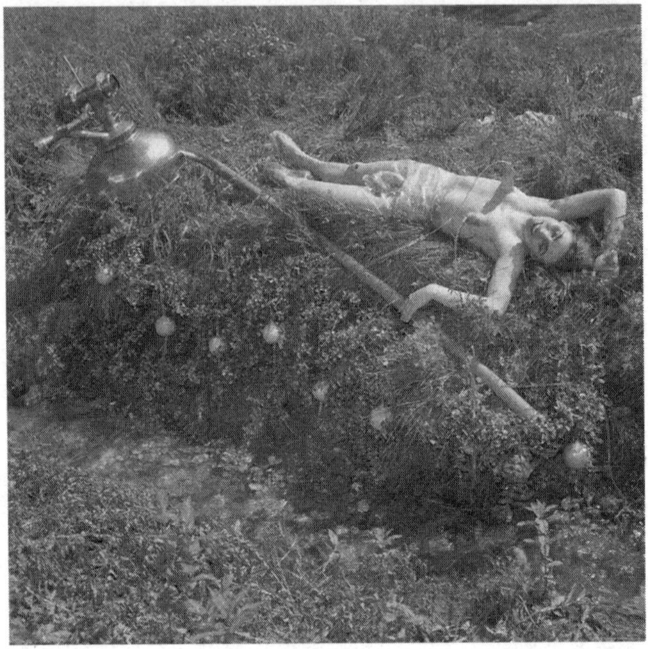

Image 9 Alicja Żebrowska, *Onone - Assimilatio*, 1995, series *Onone. The World after the World*, 1995–99, video installation, video still. Courtesy of the artist.

(which might be translated as *Heshe(s)*), combines Polish personal pronouns 'on', standing for 'he', 'ono' meaning 'it' and 'one', plural for 'them' (female). It suggests the inadequacy of language to describe gender identity, which cannot be defined with one word. Grammatical gender fits rigid categories that exist and are often enforced when using, for example, the pronoun 'he' in English to designate a person of unspecified sex. Sometimes even if a neutral pronoun is used, it still describes a gender, depending on antecedents and referents. Gender neutral language is developing and employs gender neutral pronouns that, however, are not widespread.

This chapter discusses the metaphor of the rose garden in *Alice in Wonderland*. When Alice entered the garden, she noticed three gardeners in the shape of playing cards ornamented with hearts, painting white roses red. Approached by Alice and asked why they were doing this, 'Two' replied that they had planted the white rose tree by mistake. If the Queen of Hearts discovered it, they would be executed and their heads would be cut off. This demonstrates the supremacy of binary logic, according to which things need to belong to either/or as the space in between is not acknowledged. The identification with what is red or white inscribes one into certain rigid structures that do not allow for negotiation of difference. Identification with the other, here represented by white roses, is believed to be erroneous. This victimises the body and can be fatal. Nonetheless, the rose garden can be a place of transformation which enables contesting bipolar structures to acknowledge both sides of the spectrum (male and female, active and passive, light and dark and so on). It is where everything is possible, where creatures such as Onone, proposed by Żebrowska, can exist and where seduction replaces desire, enabling the recognition of difference. I call this space in between – to which I refer when discussing the 'into' and 'out of' the mirror – genderland. The threshold and boundary it offers becomes blurred.

The *Onone* video is spellbinding. In a series of idyllic, hypnotic, almost naive scenes we see a naked human being, a Onone, only partially wrapped in a transparent foil, in a moment as though of creation. This new life form reminds us of a woman, but the artificial additions such as implants and transparent foil as a second skin bring to mind contemporary artificiality and modification of the body. Her/his breasts are replaced with penises with nipples and the genitals combine female and male features. There is a penis-like tube attached to the glans. This god/dess is lying in a meadow that is covered in juicy lush grass and wildflowers. It looks like Eden, a heavenly garden and paradise where a new order is being established and where libidinal energy circulates freely. A constituted paradise-like idyll symbolising an unattainable dream in which the world is in harmony has a long tradition in art. For example, Henri Matisse, in *The Joy of Life* (1906), portrayed an Arcadian landscape populated by figures that are nude, but their sexuality or eroticism is not emphasised. This world is imagined and artificially created. It is a place of the different aspects of the joy of life, which are symbolised by each group of figures. In Żebrowska's meadow there is a pulsating bubbling creek with perhaps the nectar of life and it is connected to the body of the female/male and a mechanical pump placed nearby, similar to those used to milk cows. A small incision in the banks of the meadow were yellowish balls (apples?) are scattered is reminiscent of a vagina. The apples, the pump and the body are connected through pipes with water of the creek.

This human being is on the threshold of biological and symbolic sexes. It lives in a tranquil and soothing world that is tantalising and seductive. Even the electronic music, suggesting something terrestrial and hyper-real, is not persuasive enough to suggest that this world is a fiction. The genderless space beyond repressive structures of gendered realm governed by patriarchy seems real. Here neither women nor men are oppressed. The androgynous being is part of an energy flow among nature, human and technology. The water from the creek circulates and pulsates through different organisms, fertilising the earth and the body. The human being reminds one of Gaia, one of the Greek primordial deities personifying the Earth, who, together with Eros, was born from Chaos. She was the Mother Goddess who parthenogenetically (with no male intervention) gave birth to the Universe. In Żebrowska's video a new structure is also emerging in a world that is governed by genderless beings. By embracing concepts of androgyny and hermaphroditism, the artist creates a genderless space where female and male energies flow together, not opposing each other.

In *Onone* Żebrowska defines a new transhuman being that reminds us of Bakhtin's hybrid grotesque body situated beyond the clear divisions between the sexes. In this world the sexual energy circulates among nature, the body and technology referring to desire, which Deleuze and Guattari define in *Anti-Oedipus: Capitalism and Schizophrenia* as a positive force that enables emancipation and the production of reality.[1] It is not based solely on lack and acquisition as in the theories of Plato, Freud and Lacan. This positive account of desire deconstructs the Oedipal structure that colonises members of society and represses their desires. Instead, society is offered complexes that govern and organise it. Such an opening of desire, which is illustrated in Żebrowska's *Onone*, allows for transcending the bipolar Oedipal inscription of the body in gender but also in physicality, which refers to Deleuze and Guattari's concept of 'the body without organs'.[2]

Later in the video, the androgynous being explores the landscape, rolls in the grass, sits melancholically on a cliff, chin in hands, and dances frivolously and awkwardly. By using the title *Assimilatio*, Żebrowska calls this creature 'assimilation', 'adaptation' and 're(as)sembling'. In this androgynous body what is dissimilar becomes similar. Differences start corresponding to each other and distance between male and female and self and the other slowly starts blurring into oneness. Żebrowska has said she is fascinated by how identity is being constructed and how the self is being articulated and revealed through the outside. Through the artificial world created in *Assimilatio* in which holistic beings are multidimensional, self-sufficient and self-focused, Żebrowska questions human desire for rebirth, catharsis and rebuilding the self through exploring one's own intimacy.

The video installation was followed by a series of photographs depicting young angel-like human beings in interiors. They are no longer placed in nature but inhabit artificially created spaces. *Autoholos* (1996) portrays an androgynous human standing on a podium wrapped in silver foil. The being is wearing a transparent foil shaped as a cape or an outside skin that is detached from the body, magnifying it and further blurring anything that might suggest a specific sex. The body underneath is barely recognisable and its contours are blurred by the light reflections of the foil. Behind we can see a brick wall also covered in silver foil. The title, *Autoholos*, means 'he, who is complete unto himself'.[3] The creature's arms are spread, like wings. Its bust is pushed forward emphasising the phallic nipples and the male genitals originating in the female lap curve back to the vagina. It resembles an ancient sculpture or a cult idol that depicts not a particular individual but a type or an ideal to follow. It is as though a sacral object of worship is pure and self-sufficient. Its organs self-fertilise, allowing the sexual energy to autocirculate. Żebrowska plays with religious imagery that is cultivated and worshipped, in particular in Poland. She stretches it up to a point of ridicule, bringing together the sublime and the grotesque, which allows transgressing sacrality and turning towards other stories of creation that are not based on bipolar structures.

Another three photographs in the series are entitled *Affirmatio* (1995). Here, another Onone is situated on a podium wrapped in silver foil. The creature is naked with a ridiculously large penis coming out of its vagina. This time the torso is more male-like. On the first photograph Onone, wearing red lipstick and chin-length brown hair neatly combed behind the ears, is sitting with its profile sideways to the camera, arms wrapped around its drawn-up knees. The penis is lying on the podium as though supporting the posture. The second photograph illustrates the creature with unruly hair kneeling frontally, gazing into the camera, as though into a mirror. He or she is laughing, covering his or her lips with the right hand. The third and final photograph portrays Onone lying on one side, reminiscent of Venus's pose from *The Rokeby Venus* or *The Toilet of Venus* by Diego Velázquez (1647–51). Here he or she is not looking at his or her reflection. The mirror is placed at the back of his or her body and the creature is admiring its male and female genitals; a penis next to a vagina. *Affirmatio* refers to self-affirmation and exploration of one's own sexuality. Onone searches for the self in the mirror reflection, playing with Lacan's triad as though with a jigsaw puzzle. There is no fragmentation of identity as androgyny allows building the whole and affirming and celebrating the self. In *Autoconsummtio* (1995), the same Onone is lying on one side but this time the viewer sees the back of the creature and watches its ecstasy when its body is being stimulated by its fingers.

In the first photograph of *Continuo* (1996), we see two androgynous individuals wearing transparent foil capes and lying on their sides. They are placed in an interior, wrapped in silver foil. One of the figures has shorter hair and its oversized penis is almost piercing through the foil. The other has long blonde/ blond wavy hair and both figures are looking ahead into a void. In the second photograph the couple stands side by side, their hands placed on top of one another and their eyes closed. The penis of the longhaired creature with cone-shaped nipples reaches backwards to its vagina. In the third photograph, they are standing next to each other with their arms widespread. Their hair is slickly backcombed and their eyes are wide open, staring directly into the camera. The title of the photographs refers to the Latin word 'continuare', which means to bridge, to gap, to do without pause or to extend and renew.[4] The concept of androgyny is concerned with this continuation over and through borders, and the location of the body beyond binaries towards what is polymorphous, ambiguous and fluid. The double Onone portrayed in *Continuo* emphasises the double gaze and a double reading of a subject. It allows the viewer to decode gendered structures and recognise the dissolved borders of the body. The foil capes, functioning as skin, delineate the threshold between physicality and the outside world. At the same time, they enable transition between the inside and the outside through skin and its pores absorbing, expelling and excreting inner and outer fluids. The surface of the body is porous and mediating, extending borders. Even if it is wrapped in artificial foil or garments, the skin functions as a medium between two realms.

In *Synchron* (1996) and *Sexfantilis* (1996), the androgynous beings are no longer motionless. Böhme suggests that Żebrowska portrays them in the aesthetic of the *tableau vivant*, living pictures. It is worth remembering that nude *tableaux vivants* were particularly popular in the nineteenth century, when they provided erotic entertainment. In *Synchron* the creatures lie exhausted; perhaps they fell asleep, side-by-side with their eyes closed. In *Sexfantilis*, the shorthaired Onone is sitting cross-legged and holding an inflated sex doll that wears garish red dress, looking child- or teenage-like. The doll's mouth is wide open, ready to offer sexual pleasure to its user. Her presence suggests a fetishisation of sexuality, where objects serve as intermediaries and substitutes allowing disengagement from socio-cultural relationships in order to create an artificial world of one's desires. The title emphasises this lack of human connection, the corresponding sexual infantilism and the saturation of visual culture with images of women-children that blur boundaries between perversion and sexual fantasies. By referring to the *tableau vivant* Żebrowska points to our desires and dreams, in this case our longing for transgressing gender binaries. She also refers to the fetishisation of the phallus, which is oversized and exaggerated in her series of Onone installations. The fetish is this *tableau vivant*, the living dead, the Other that can only come to life if it is animated in the fantasies of the fetishist.

In *Hypnosis* (1997) we see the artist herself lying on her back, as though peacefully asleep, on an ornamented chaise longue placed in a dark room. Her face is lit by a floor lamp standing next to the furniture. The area of her vagina growing into a thick penis is wrapped in transparent foil and her breasts have some attachments shaping them into phallic cones. She is holding her belly, which seems swollen; perhaps she is pregnant? We can also see some elongated elliptical objects suspended from the ceiling. At the foot of the chaise longue, in a dim light, a man is sitting on a chair observing the naked body, or rather looking at it piercingly. He might be the hypnotist. The scene is reminiscent of paintings of naked women subjected to the gaze of the artist and the audience or a theatrical stage. The couch and armchair also evoke nineteenth-century therapeutic hypnotic sessions undergone by women suffering from hysteria and orchestrated by men. This dark room suggests magic, spiritualism and charlatanism rather than science. The naked body is as though in a trance, transforming itself into an androgynous being. In the second photograph in the series, the creature is no longer passive and asleep. She is positioned on the chaise longue looking down at her deflated belly. The man is still sitting on the chair but we only see the back of his head. The room is now well lit and the exhausted androgynous body is clearly visible.

Other photographs in the series are entitled *Autonekrophagos* (1998), portraying a doll-like body with the mouth wide open, as the sex doll from *Sexfantilis*, wearing a dark foam suit, floating in space or water; *Nekroinfanaticus* (1998), presenting a boy's body lying on the upper level of a bunk bed in a purple-lit room; and *Rebis-Versum* (1998), depicting a white interior looking like an operating theatre or a doctor's office, in which we can notice an androgynous figure sitting on a chair in one photograph and lying in a lace and frills covered canopy bed in the second.

In the project *Onone. The World after the World* fantasy, dreams and hypnotic visions of a different realm, perhaps subconscious, interlace. Żebrowska builds a utopian space where the body functions beyond sexual identity. It is the other side of the looking-glass, down the rabbit hole, where one is allowed to enter and explore one's own body and psyche. The artist invites the viewer on a journey towards oneness represented by the androgynous creature of Onone where the Other and the Self meet in the search of lost identity. It is a reincarnation of the Androgyne, the One, the embodiment of Jungian animus and anima, primary anthropomorphic archetypes of the unconscious mind, the masculine and the feminine archetype. This non-gendered utopian being created by Żebrowska's genderland embodies healing from pain originating in binary structures forced upon humans. As discussed earlier, the primary being was an entity, the One and was split into two halves initiating bipolar thinking about the body, sex and gender. Żebrowska's Onone is liberated from the suppressing structures. It offers a social construct worshipping completeness and embracing differences within one body. The androgynous being is presented in the video imagining the Garden of Eden and in a series of photographs which portray the journey from passive existence, through self-affirmation, bridging of differences, undergoing therapy or hypnosis sessions and becoming more active, towards the final release into a cosmic realm where Onone is no longer covered in foil as a second skin but embraces the Self with no artificial additions.

The creature inhabits genderland, a world responding to the deepest fears, anxieties, longings and desires regarding humans' sexual disorientation and frustration. It is another dimension similar to the one imagined by Alice in Wonderland where a new species, neither male not female but entire is born. Genderland forms part of Ettinger's matrixial realm with its transformational potentiality for the subject. It is a hospitable and generous space inviting nonsymmetrical relations and identities. It is a new paradise in which maleness and femaleness are suspended and freed from original sin and expulsion; a realm that enables exploration of other life forms and one's own identity beyond bipolar thinking, responding to the Platonic concept of 'oneness' and love. Żebrowska's Onone is a transgressive body that weakens what Butler describes as power structures based on binary politics.[5] Genderland is governed by fulfilment, freedom and safety. It is a space where the construction of one's own body and gender is a choice reflecting thinking about identity, which is fluid and does not necessarily need to conform to any restraining definitions. In genderland roles are reversed and identity and the body become a hybrid. It is possible to play with one's own gender and meanings imposed by social constructions of femininity and masculinity, dress it up in masks and construct identity against stereotypical gender codes. This reinforces the need to abort binary thinking about the body and gender and move towards designing identity. Other Polish artists who create apparent conflicting dispersed or scattered identities include Marta Deskur, Monika Zielińska, Barbara Konopka and Katarzyna Górna. They ironically mix sacrum and profanum, similarly to Żebrowska's *Original Sin*. These threads are also undertaken in the artistic practice of Katarzyna Kozyra, who questions dichotomous divisions in the series discussed previously, *In Art Dreams Come True*.

Jean Baudrillard suggests that '[t]he orgy is over'.[6] Sexuality has entered a new era when the search for liberation and sex has been replaced by explorations in the field of gender. As Michel Foucault states, sexuality is processed *inter alia* as the production of desire.[7] This new direction focuses on sexual identity and undefinedness or the mixing of genders, what Baudrillard calls 'gender benders' – neither masculine nor feminine, but not homosexual either'.[8] He calls the current situation of art, culture, politics and social body 'after the orgy'[9] – the orgy of modernity that liberated reality, sexuality and critique. After Baudrillard we might want to ask: 'What do we do after the orgy?' He suggests we have entered the state of simulation and we can only revisit everything, as has already happened. 'The aestheticisation of the world is complete.'[10] My suggestion is to go on a journey *through* to the other side of the mirror and experience the crossing of boundaries. The space of this threshold is where everything is possible – the past, present and future, beauty merged with ugliness, Venus with Medusa, femininity with masculinity, and illusion with the real. This realm might be called genderland, in which bodies are mapped in an ungendered way and in which lack is not depreciating.

The concept of seduction is, according to Baudrillard, important for feminism as it engages in discussion on 'woman' as an object exchanged by man in which 'she' becomes a commodity to sacrifice and subordinate to the patriarchal order. Seduction allows subverting and contesting gender binaries. It does not refer to bisexuality in biological or Freudian terms; it rather intertwines and polarises, combining the feminine and the masculine. It is a threshold reversing and diverting gender codes. The term derives from *seducere*,[11] meaning leading away towards, as Cixous suggests, a new kind of Eros, 'other love'.[12] Cixous focuses on desire, but not as a drive towards the lack or absent, as in the Lacanian 'Symbolic',[13] but as a drive towards everything, which I will elaborate on below. This understanding implies the idea of wholeness, beings not differentiated by gender or absence, not complimentary but whole. She sees the penis no longer as a signifier of lack or its fulfilment. This view resonates with Silverman's suggestion about deconstructing 'the binary opposition of ideality and abjection' through the notion of the 'good enough' entangled with the concept of love or rather 'the conditions under which we might ethically love ourselves'.[14] She questions whether self-idealisation can only be challenged by self-revulsion and demonstrates ways of deconstructing it. She proposes: 'The "good enough" is a paradigm through which ideals can be simultaneously lived and deconstructed.'[15] According to Baudrillard, seduction offers the destruction of sexuality and the phallogocentric order. Its power is situated in the playing with appearances. It liberates eroticisation and moves towards gender binaries but also beyond androgyny. It draws upon Cixous's desire for everything, not Lacan's desire for the absent or lack. It also employs the metaphor of the mirror that allows Eros – the intertwinement of completeness and fragmentariness and the polarisation of the feminine and the masculine.

'Perpetual striptease, fantasies of exposed organs, sexual blackmail'[16] might well describe how the female body is being represented in contemporary visual culture and how Venus has appeared in many artworks, most often produced by male artists, as discussed in Chapter 3. Cixious's concept of the 'Medusa laugh',[17] which will be discussed below, together with the Baudrillardian idea of 'swallowing the mirror' offer a new way of looking at notions of desire, beauty and sexuality as transparent, referring to Venus and Medusa. Baudrillard's idea of the object operating in the world and refracting the subject – '*I will be your mirror!*'[18] is reflected in fragmentation and discontinuity, and a reversal of gender codes. Baudrillard argues: 'Nothing is less certain today than sex, behind the liberation of its discourse. And nothing today is less certain than desire, behind the proliferation of its images.'[19]

Seduction and desire

Judith Butler interrogates sex, gender and desire with relation to power structures. Gender is inscribed, according to Butler, in production, whereby the sexes are being established. Butler remarks:

> As a result, gender is not to culture as sex is to nature; gender is also the discursive/cultural means by which 'sexed nature' or 'a natural sex' is produced and established as 'prediscursive', prior to culture, a politically neutral surface *on which* culture acts.[20]

According to Michel Foucault,[21] sexuality derives from the process of production – of desire or discourse – rather deadly for seduction. Production and nature were the driving forces in the bourgeois era.[22] In Baudrillard's account it appeared with the liberation of sexuality and the blurring of the distinctions between genders.[23] Prior to the eighteenth century, all the distinctions between the male and the female were based on gender, not sex, resulting in political and legal ramifications. It seemed that the Renaissance belief in the existence of one sex was still strong and the absence of the word 'vagina' until the beginning of the eighteenth century articulates the patriarchalisation of desire and love. In the nineteenth century the female body was seen as both a vessel of morality and as a dirty disease. As it could not function as both, women were either good, pure, morally strong or bad, eroticised and perverted.[24] Desire was overshadowed and female sexuality became forbidden by cultural constraints that imposed morality on women. Patriarchal society increasingly confined the female to the domestic sphere and inscribed her as a mother. Especially during the nineteenth century, when the middle class grew significantly in Western Europe, the role of woman and her attachment to home was magnified.[25] Baudrillard's account of simulation refers to the existence of replicas of replicas, traces of the past where the original does not exist anymore. Desire and seduction, as concepts referring to sexuality, need to be contextualised in the current socio-political space.

According to Baudrillard, seduction requires artifice and ritual. It is a force often equated with femininity, which is perceived as changeable. It seems it allows for a deconstruction of rigid gender binaries and enables margins that are ambiguous, fluid and function as thresholds governed by the logic of 'trans'. Baudrillard addresses seduction as a liberated desire differentiated from the eighteenth-century aristocratic association of the concept with honour and valour. This Enlightenment interpretation is no longer viable and functions as a myth that cannot currently exist. The bourgeois era, following the French Revolution, focused on nature and production that eclipsed seduction. However, as according to Baudrillard, seduction intertwines with artifice rather than nature and with signs and rituals rather than energy, it still belongs to the system of production in which we live.[26]

Seduction awaits reversibility, chaos, the collapse of desire and production, destruction of sexuality or masculine predominance. It corresponds with femininity or even androgyny and eroticisation of the cultural, the social and the political, being embedded within gender and the body, between the feminine and the masculine, in the idea of wholeness built from separate, independent and total fragments. It builds upon Cixous's desire for everything. It encapsulates beings defined not by difference or gender but by completeness. They will no longer be complementary, but each of them will constitute an individual, independent, whole being. In a way this is the initiation of a new kind of Eros, 'other love'[27] that welcomes the other. Silverman suggests that even though love is often associated with the function of idealisation, subjects are mobile and cannot be compartmentalised. They should be interpreted in multiple ways considering versatile forms of difference including age, sex, gender and class. Idealisation should be used in new ways,[28] suggested for example by Luce Irigaray in her previously mentioned concept of mimesis. Existing systems of ideals need to be challenged, as Joanna Rajkowska does in *Satisfaction Guaranteed*, in order to demystify stereotypes and suggest new ways of thinking also about the past and commonly recognised tropes of femininity such as Venus and Medusa. In Cixous's account:

> To love, to watch-think-seek the other in the other, to despecularise, to unhoard. Does this seem difficult? It's not impossible and this is what nourishes life – a love that has no commerce with the apprehensive desire that provides against the lack and stultifies the strange; the love that rejoices in the exchange that multiplies … In one another we will never be lacking.[29]

'Merger type sexuality'

In her essay *The Laugh of Medusa*, Hélène Cixous explores female representations in history through their bodies as a medium of communication. Using the metaphor of a dark, unexplored room, she talks about female fears – of language and sexuality – resulting from the male dominance and the myths and images they imposed, for instance, of Medusa and the abyss. She discusses bisexuality in culture, subjecting it to a phallogocentric order, which establishes constraining structures that do not allow women to reclaim their voice. Cixous's discourse is abstracted from the Freudian Oedipal trajectory that is divided into two sexual halves – hetero and homo –both of which are placed under the control of castration fear.

The separation between male and female and the subordination and repression of the feminine by the masculine leads towards a 'new sexuality', which Cixous calls the 'other bisexuality', annulling the division between sexes and their implied differences. Deconstructing the 'slash' between the sexes dissolves the split. Cixous uses 'bisexual' (and hence neuter) to refer to the concept of bisexuality based on the castration fear and the idea of the total being composed of two halves. Here, neutrality dissolves all the power associated with the individual's sex. This conception of the 'merger type sexuality' is opposed to the 'other bisexuality',[30] which is liberated from phallocentric representationalism but emphasises differences rather then annulling them. In the 'merger type sexuality' the dichotomy of the self and the other does not exist and all oppositions forming the binary are erased and fused. There is no uniform and homogenous, classified sexuality – male or female, presence or absence, language or silence, light or dark, active or passive, good or evil. This other bisexuality does not meld the masculine and the feminine together, but rather dissolves the distinctions and draws sexuality from any body and any time. Cixous states:

> Bisexuality: that is, each one's location in self of the presence … of both sexes, non-exclusion either of the difference or of one sex, and, from this "self-permission", multiplication of the effects of the inscription of desire, over all parts of my body and the other body.[31]

This concept of the 'other bisexuality'– an ungendered space yet allowing for individuality, dissolving dichotomies, contextualised in Derrida's and Lacan's poststructuralist ideas – corresponds to Wendy Steiner's, Leslie Heywood's or Judith Butler's and Luce Irigaray's[32] idea of androgyny. The term 'androgyny' comes from ancient Greek and, in a broad sense, defines the one, which is composed from two parts – *andro*, signifying the male and *gyn* defining the female.[33] It describes a condition where the confines between sexes are re-appropriated and transgressed. The dynamism between the feminine and the masculine refers not only to their interaction and their embracing of one another but also to their oppositions within differences. This co-existence of antagonisms and lack of distinguishing boundaries is best embodied in the god Eros – 'the sexual passion'[34] – who 'was double-sexed and golden-winged and, having four heads, sometimes roared like a bull or a lion, sometimes hissed like a serpent or bleated like a ram'.[35] As the incarnation of Love, Eros disregards all social constraints and gender-based conventions. He is a harmonious union of the feminine and the masculine polarities within the psyche, setting the universe in motion.

The notion of androgyny is approached by Aleksandra Polisiewicz, known as Aleka Polis (from Poland) in a video *Bestiarium podświadomości*

(*The Bestiary of Subconscious*, 2003–04). The title of the work refers to medieval illustrated bestiaries that presented images of ordinary and fantastical animals that epitomised Christian morals. The film is composed of three parts in which the viewer is confronted first with a trunk of a body. The headless fragmented figure, dressed in a shirt, is submerged in water. In between the legs, that replace the arms, we can see a fish swimming towards the orifice of the neck. The fish is hunting red worms coming out of the hole. In the second part of the video the headless body is presented in another view, in which blood spurts from the orifice. This vision is accompanied with images of dogs licking, lacerating and/or feeding off the wounds/flesh. In the final part of the video the viewer is confronted with the same body spurting blood, which pours towards a glass with white liquid (milk?). Images delivered by Polis are disturbing and provoke anxiety. The placement of the body and its rotation (up and down) turns into a graphic sign resembling X and Y chromosomes. The artist portrays processes of separation, joining and transforming. She references the fears linked with carnality, drawing on Kristeva's concept of the abject. Body parts are replaced (arms with legs) and it is not clear that the hole left by the head is not a vagina. Polis questions gender marked by symbolic and carnal signs, which here are subverted.

The archetype of androgyny has demonstrated its presence throughout history and is one of the oldest, only second to the one of the Absolute.[36] The idea of duality shaped the Platonic Western tradition, but is also a basis of Buddhism (dual state of consciousness), Taoism (yin and yang) or Hinduism (mind and matter). Even in the Book of Genesis, God created the female and the male in His own image, that of the androgyne – 'so God created man in his own image, in the image of God he created him; male and female he created them'.[37] This image of God threatened the patriarchal principle and was consequently eliminated from the Judeo-Christian tradition. Yet, it often appears in artworks referring to this pre-sexuality, the non-differentiated structure of gender's complementarities.

In Plato's *Symposium* (dated *c*.385–370 BC) the figure of the androgyne is mentioned during a discussion on the nature of Love and its modes of expression. Aristophanes tells a story of circular beings that existed before the split into masculine and feminine halves.

> For the original human nature was not like the present, but different. In the first place, the sexes were originally three in number, not two as they are now; there was man, woman and the union of the two, having a name corresponding to this double nature; this once had a real existence, but is now lost, and the name only is preserved as a term of reproach.[38]

The three original wholes that existed – the male/the sun, the female/the earth and the male and female in one being/the moon[39] – were searching for their other parts, which could be of the same or different sex. They desired to become 'One' again and loosen all the boundaries. The 'primordial oneness', joining the two beings, created the harmonious life, beyond pure sexuality.[40]

According to Carolyn Heilbrun, even the myth of Oedipus has androgynous implications. The murdering of the father and the marrying of the mother might lead to the exposure of the feminine element.[41] June Singer questions the concept of androgyny as an archetype inscribed in the human psyche witnessing the primal unity.[42] She refers to Jung's concept of an archetype based on Plato's 'eidos', which indicates the existence of a primordial, universal type. Singer sees androgyny as precisely that kind of archetype, constantly represented in myths and various sociocultural signs, 'primordial cosmic unity, having existed in oneness and wholeness, before any separation was made'. The 'One' embraces all oppositions that arc not yet recognised. At a certain point in time, wholeness is broken open and there exist the 'two' distinct entities that polarise. All the differentiations – as the mind and the body or light and dark – derive from these opposites that join in pairs. The binary of the male and the female represent the energetic power of creation. The two beings were separated before rejoining and formed one body, 'unity-totality' – 'the Primordial Androgyne'.[43] It consisted of all the opposites and potentialities of duality.

Androgyny is often confused with bisexuality and hermaphroditism. The latter – deriving from the myth of Hermaphroditus, a double-sexed being, the son of Aphrodite and Hermes[44] – implies the shifting of sex qualities, including internal and external characteristics, towards the opposite sex. It refers to the appearance of the sexually distinct features that are blurred, the physical sex that is undifferentiated. It embodies ideas of ambiguity and confusion. Bisexuality, on the contrary, describes the confusion regarding gender identification – masculinity or femininity. Androgyny has often also been mistaken for the Romantic image of a young boy with girlish features or a woman with a boyish figure.[45] Sontag defines it as one of camp's main sensibilities – 'sexless bodies' and 'androgynous vacancy behind the perfect beauty'.[46] According to Singer, androgyne is not extreme, either in terms of emphasising one's sex or of differentiating sexes interpersonally. She remarks: '[The concerns] of the androgyne are mainly *intrapsychic*. The androgyne consciously accepts the interplay of the masculine and the feminine aspects of the individual psyche. One is the complement of the other.'[47] Its images are often imperfect and incomplete, re-instating the vision of the double-sexed god Dionysus, whose borderline nature between the masculine and the feminine is represented as mad, sexual, but still uniting the opposites.

Fashioning the body

Sexuality is strongly reliant on the phallus and castration. As Baudrillard remarks:

> Within our body we experience not one sex, not two, but a multitude of sexes. We do not see a man, or a woman, but a human being, anthropomorphic ... Our bodies are tired of all the stereotyped cultural barriers, all the psychological segregation.[48]

According to Baudrillard, feminism opposes the phallocratic structure in terms of the body, language, autonomy, speech, writing and pleasure but not seduction. Its connotation with the external, the outside form, is considered to be shameful. Seduction's power lies in governing the universe of signs, not only the real. Baudrillard considers seduction as a weapon that plays with appearances, reverses them constantly, making reality vulnerable and fragile. It is far from the sexualisation of the body and the phallic incarnations.

Variations on bodily exposure are best exemplified in fashion by the changing silhouette and proportions of fashion mannequins. From the 1920s they were natural; accentuating the bust, waistline and the hips, and then the buttocks and the stomach were gradually flattened, but still defined the body. From the 1950s and predominantly in the 1960s, the new vision of the body – elongated, angular, static and androgynous – was established. It opened the arena for various physical types, broadening the criteria of what might be considered beautiful.[49] Dorothy Schefer asks if androgyny became the new beauty ideal.[50] 'Trans' (-gender, -sexuality, -body) awareness has increased in the mass media, embodying the experience of existing between male and female genders. In 2010s, female models such as Casey Legler or Elliott Sailors, among others, have been working as male models. Erika Linder has appeared in both female and male campaigns and Andreja (formerly Andrej) Pejić started as a male model in womenswear runway shows. At the beginning of 2014 Pejić underwent sex reassignment surgery. On 1 June 2015 Caitlyn Jenner (formerly known as Bruce Jenner, an American athlete known for winning the men's decathlon at the 1976 Summer Olympics) announced on her webpage, Facebook and Twitter and in other social media her transformation from man to woman, 'I'm so happy after such a long struggle to be living my true self. Welcome to the world Caitlyn. Can't wait for you to get to know her/me.'[51] Since then she has posted news about the transgender community and her experience, including stories about her journey and lack of acceptance but also about getting to grips with the new body (a picture and a video of her applying nail varnish from a 9 July 2015 post is captioned: 'Still getting the hang of this. What do you think of the colour?'). This playing with gender and not conforming with gender binaries but also acknowledging one's gender identity to fight gender dysphoria is becoming more visible within the fashion world. Harold Koda remarks:

> With the cultural relaxation of rules of appropriate body exposure, a universal standard of beauty became increasingly problematic, no matter how inclusive it was in relation to the past. The refuge of wearing foundation garments to re-form the body was obsolete, and the greater tyranny emerged of an ideal of beauty with the impossibility of recourse to artifice. In no other century has the ideal form of the body been in such a flux.[52]

Together with the production of the new silhouette and the corresponding designs, art too has assimilated concepts deriving from fashion, such as gender, the body and production. Also, the notion of beauty has been addressed in terms of its components, relevance and the application of the universal canon.[53] Art quickly absorbed the idea of the costume as a mechanism to transform the body and explore it as an entity built from separate, yet whole, parts. The body became mutilated and dressed in tropes and canons. It could even be said that it became 'fashionised', as the reorganisation of the figure and its proportions is the principal element constituting fashion as dress. The mechanism also works analogously, as fashion has incorporated critical theories. The variations of the notion of beauty and the subversion of the dichotomy between the beautiful and the ugly, the feminine and the masculine were also inscribed in the body. It became an androgynous site of producing narratives, engaging with gender issues, ambiguous sexuality and the critique of the cultural and the political.

Joanna Rajkowska's earlier practices are preoccupied predominantly with the body, which is transformed, fashioned and readjusted in the search of its own identity. She is interested in the threshold between physicality and self-knowledge and deliberately uses her own physicality to problematise the body. In *Rzeczy Które Robię Wieczorem w Alejach Jerozolimskich* (Things I do in the Evenings in Aleje Jerozolimskie) (1999) Rajkowska played with her identity and tested her body in different identifications and roles. She made a series of photographs that have been manipulated so that she appears in different sexual scenarios (pornographic images, oil paintings, clubs etc.) in which she functions as male and female. She becomes an Onone, everyone, a universal symbol for female empowerment, blurring the border between celebration and objectification. Rajkowska has also created a series of hybrid figures, including life-size mannequins and miniature clay figurines, as in *Bibliotekarze z Ziemi Ognistej* (Librarians in the Land of Fire) (1997), situated in different group scenarios, that are neither male nor female. The figures, scaled to human proportions, are based on the artist's body and some of the 'Librarians' 'wear' her face. They are 'masked' to obscure their identity and toy with multiplicity of options for the self. Rajkowska's actual identity is removed from the work and replaced with performative alter egos. She is curious about how she would feel in their role questioning her 'self'. She is cruel to them. They have their heads chopped off, and their limbs are mutilated or deformed. This physical disintegration portrays a disturbed mental state that often arises from sexual anxieties and forced identification with the 'appropriate' sex. The figures portray androgynous beings that refuse to identify with either/or sexuality. Their identity is undefined, fluid and dispersed and requires new incarnations that would acknowledge otherness and difference.

Binary oppositions

Self-identification is based on gender and sexuality, still imprisoned in a rigid system of biology and morphology. Yet self-recognition goes beyond sexes and often cannot be classified according to the dominating distinction between female, male or neutral. It is a fluid process that requires the liberating of gender and a recognition of different transmutations. At the same time, this encourages going beyond heavily loaded connotations such as 'she-male' or 'transsexual'. Some proposed pronouns, such as 'ze', 'zer' or 'mer', 'ey', 'em', 'eir'[54] or 'hir penis', 'hes vagina'[55] have slowly appeared as substitutes for the traditional linguistic constructs.

The erasure of distinctions between the male and the female destroys other differences associated with binary oppositions. Gender studies refer to the binary or multiplication systems, distinguishing two or more genders. Butler remarks:

> Gender is not exactly what one 'is' nor is it precisely what one 'has'. Gender is the apparatus by which the production and the normalization of the masculine and feminine take place along with the interstitial forms of hormonal, chromosomal, psychic, and performative that gender assumes.[56]

Gender goes beyond the traditional binary of the masculine and the feminine, which does not allow any trans- or cross-gender permutations. According to Butler, gender is a mechanism, transmuting, naturalising and producing the female and the male. She explores gender and sexuality together with sexual difference. This issue, also raised by Irigaray and called the 'sexuate difference',[57] inaugurates a certain problematic within contemporary sociopolitical culture, interrogating the status and roles of the female and the male. The notion does not need to be re-established biologically. It poses questions concerning the psychic, the discursive and the social – where they begin and end. Butler recognises sexual difference as 'the site where a question concerning the relation of the biological to the cultural is posed and re-posed, where it must and can be asked, but where it cannot, strictly speaking, be answered'. She revisits the concept as a locum, where 'psychic, somatic and social dimensions'[58] intertwine, but do not collapse into one another. Irigaray, however, sees sex as a category between the biological or the social, and thus distinct from gender, located in the linguistic.

Cixous describes female sexuality as not being centralised, in the way that its male equivalent is, and not subordinated to a larger whole. 'Female' is a totality composed of whole parts, completely independent subdivisions, not organised around some central fragment. Cixous argues: 'I do desire the other for the other, whole and entire, male or female ... Castration? Let others toy with it. What's a desire originating from lack? A pretty meagre desire.'[59]

Gender has become fragmented. Finally, the norms describing its boundaries have the potential to loosen and open, inviting us to revisit the idea of wholeness and completeness. As Baudrillard proposes:

> Either the structure remains the same, with the female being entirely absorbed by the male, or else it collapses, and there is no longer either female or male – the degree zero of the structure. This is very much what is happening today: erotic polyvalence, the infinite potentiality of desire, different connections, diffractions, libidinal intensities – all multiple variants of a liberatory alternative coming from the frontiers of a psychoanalysis free of Freud, or from the frontiers of desire free of psychoanalysis. Behind the effervescence of the paradigm of sex, everything is converging towards the non-differentiation of the structure and its potential neutralisation.[60]

Cixous's 'merger type sexuality' affords a view of the body as a compilation of the feminine and the masculine, beautiful and ugly, psychical and physical. It inscribes the body in an ungendered space.

New sexual politics

Sex has lost its singularity; as Baudrillard remarks: 'This is the era of the Transsexual, where the conflicts linked to difference – and even the biological and anatomical signs of difference – survive long after the real otherness of the sexes has disappeared.'[61] The new sexual politics, encompassing gender and sexual identities, brings together notions of difference and otherness and the socially-structured body in which femaleness should no longer be opposed to maleness. It is indicative of an important issue confronted at the end of twentieth and and beginning of the twenty-first centuries by women artists, whose practices are indebted to Adrian Piper, Abramović, Valie Export and Schneemann, among others (such as in Żebrowska's project). These artists use their identity to celebrate the slippery status of gender, acknowledging the twenty-first century cultural milieu that makes this possible. The male and female roles as performed dissociate culture from biological imperatives. Similarly to Shakespeare's plays, where men took on female roles, gender becomes fluid and identity is constructed by oscillating between female and male genders. The body is used to transform and move between genders. It allows for the inside and the outside persona to be reassessed and appropriately expressed beyond the traditional notions of sexuality and gender. It is a fluid and malleable medium, in a constant flux that can be forged in order to depict the inner self. Its mutations, hybrids or metamorphoses externalise the identity residing inside. The body can be transformed, remade, reshaped and re-adopted to express the inner self. Gender identity is a shifting presence, oscillating between femininity and masculinity.

At the *Troubling Desire(s) in Art* symposium in November 2009,[62] which was hosted in conjunction with the *SHOUT* festival in Birmingham – a series of events dedicated to the bisexual, transgender and homosexual community and focused on queer theory and practice – speakers investigated the phenomenon of the 'queer' as a new kind of inclusive politics, which was taken as bringing together gender and sexual identities. Gavin Butt, the chair of the symposium, used the term 'theatricalised politics' to encapsulate the prevailing situation within the domain of sexual politics, where attention increasingly focused on the extent to which the socially-structured body and identity incorporate notions of physical difference.

The concept of seduction has been extended to incorporate interchanging identities functioning in a composite matrix of the social, the political and the cultural. The corporeal, located in this context, becomes loaded with notions of intimacy, pleasure and desire. Jonathan Katz, in his symposium paper 'Art, Eros and the sixties', explored desire as a utopian dream, a political platform, but most importantly as a loosening identity and a bridging of differences. This contemporary liberation, under the sign of Eros, was once defined by Herbert Marcuse as 'the political potential of Eros [that] turned on its ability to free the mind through a return to the body and its disruptive pleasures'.[63] Katz suggested that the Freudian concept of 'boundarylessness' inscribed in Eros, refers to the intertwinement of the physical and the psychical.

The body, associated with the flesh and functionalism, is, in fact, a polymorphous organism, seductive and pleasure-seeking/dispensing. Eros, with its liberating potential, explores the erotic of the social body – as it is latent in such contemporary classifications as gay, hetero, trans, inter and others. Katz argued that the groundbreaking exhibition *This is Tomorrow* at the Whitechapel Gallery in London in 1956, and specifically the collage by Richard Hamilton *Just What is it that Makes Today's Homes So Different, So Appealing?* (1956), contributed enormously to sexual fluidity and the disappearing distinction of the social codes. It created a dream of individual identities liberated from the destructive forces of capitalism. The new image of the body does not deny Eros and bodily pleasures. The flesh and form – perfect, classical, seducing, fragmented, sexual – becomes a material, a jubilation of the erotic, where the female and the male resonate in one physical body. This intersubjectivity equalises sexes on the sociopolitical level. The differentiations transform into togetherness and interconnectedness, which characterise the constitution of a universalised Eros.

The artist Volcano Del LaGrace (born in California), who also participated in the symposium in Birmingham, in the final presentation entitled 'Hermaphroditic Desires and the Impossible Dream', explored the notion of 'intersex bodies', which are neither exclusively male nor female, constituted of both sexes, nonetheless exhibiting substantial differences from trans-bodies. Del LaGrace challenged the 'known', asking whether she/he is doing gender or gender is doing her/him? Born as Debra Dianne Wood, Del LaGrace functioned as a multiple self, blurring the boundaries between genders. The body is used as a primal material, defined and domesticised by clothes and make-up. 'What you see' becomes deconstructed by 'what you get'. In a statement Volcano says:

> *I name myself. A gender* abolitionist. A part time gender terrorist. An intentional mutation and intersex by design, (as opposed to diagnosis), in order to distinguish my journey from the thousands of intersex individuals who have had their 'ambiguous' bodies mutilated and disfigured in a misguided attempt at 'normalization'. I believe in crossing the line as many times as it takes to build a bridge we can all walk across.[64]

Volcano described herself/himself as not gender and not age appropriate. She/he becomes some gender, a hybrid, a question. On her/his wall on Facebook, she/he wrote: 'I refuse the concept of the body beautiful, that there is only one acceptable body type. Mutations come in many forms ....'[65]

In transvestism, biology is separated from signs and so there is no more sex. The signs are seduced and reduplicated. The binary of the inside and the outside contest the relation of the seen and the known. Butler remarks:

> The heterosexualisation of desire requires and institutes the production of discrete and asymmetrical oppositions between 'feminine' and 'masculine', where these are understood as expressive attributes of 'male' and 'female'. The cultural matrix through which gender identity has become intelligible requires that certain kinds of 'identities' cannot 'exist' – that is, those in which gender does not follow from sex and those in which the practices of desire do not 'follow' from either sex or gender.[66]

The essential foundations of the body are questioned and recomposed in the context of identity. The ethics and aesthetics of the self also demand a new body – trans-body, as I would like to propose – which encapsulates social contradictions. The corporeal does not oppose the mind but becomes an active medium. Baudrillard sees the liberated body as 'omnipresent', evoking obsessions and cults of the physical, even substituting the search for the soul in terms of ideology and function. 'The body is a *cultural* fact.'[67] The liberation of the body, tackled in 1970s radical feminist art by, for example, Schneemann, Valie Export, Maria Pinińska-Bereś, Natalia LL, Ewa Partum and Krystyna Piotrowska, has been revisited by women artists such as Chişa, Tkáčová, Grupa Sędzia Główny, Kozyra, Rajkowska, Rossa and Żebrowska, among others. They continue the legacy of challenging taboos through the body and through playing with the notion of gender as a fixed perspective.

According to Baudrillard, the subject – in the present structures of production – is split into the corporeal representation as the capital and as fetish, the consumer object. He also suggests that beauty and eroticism constitute a new attitude towards corporeality. It is suspended between two contrary poles – the feminine and the masculine – that could be named 'phryneism' and 'athleticism' – but also becomes an imperative, applied not only to describe woman or man, but the body or the object. Beauty's ethics, parallel to the ethics of fashion, decreases the specific bodily values, for instance sexual, to a single 'exchange-value', embodying the concept of desire and pleasure. In Baudrillard's account: 'For beauty is nothing more than sign material being exchanged. It *functions* as sign value.'[68] Additionally, the new sexuality and, consequently, the notion of trans-beauty it has generated, rediscover the body, which becomes theatricalised.

Returning to Venus/Aphrodite, the 'Goddess of Desire',[69] she represents love, sexuality and beauty. She is the reflection of Eros. According to both Cixous and Anne Koedt, woman is defined sexually by what pleases men, what originated in the myth of a liberated woman and vaginal orgasm.[70] Venus functions as the archetypal *femme fatale*, the ideal woman engendered by means of a masculine projection of femininity, periodically resimulated as Medusa, Lolita, Alice in Wonderland or the Playboy Bunny, what Baudrillard calls 'a hysterical and supernatural metaphor', 'realized utopia',[71] deriving from the 'Romantic Eros'. Woman has vanished, not physically, but instead she mirrors the masculine idea of the feminine reflecting the 'male gaze', and answers to the archetype of sexual attraction. In Baudrillard's account:

> The *femme fatale* is never *fatale* as a natural element, but as artifice, as seductress or as the projective artefact of male hysteria. The absent woman, ideal or diabolic, but always fetishised, that constructed woman, that machinic Eve, that mental object, scoffs at the difference of the sexes. She scoffs at desire and the subject of desire. More feminine than the feminine: the woman object.[72]

Nonetheless, the female body can seduce with tropes and tempt with the imagined, projected representations that at the same time challenge and subvert the male gaze and go beyond gendered constructions. Baudrillard asks: 'Is the female gender capable today of producing – since it no longer wishes to personify it – this same seductive otherness? Is the female gender still hysterical enough to invent the other?'[73] Different strategies exist for the female body to challenge the patriarchal structures. Some, such as Żebrowska in *Original Sin*, employ, for example, Julia Kristeva's 'abject' which 'disturbs identity, system, order, what does not respect borders positions, rules'.[74] The baseness of the body, with all its fluids and ambiguity, questions traditional aesthetic categories and often includes references to various medical conditions associated with woman, such as hysteria, or to the limiting of the female on various levels, as for instance female circumcision or wearing corsets.

Dissolution of myths

The myth of Medusa, discussed in Chapter 3, refers to female sexuality and represents the duality of the inside and the outside as well as the binary between beauty and ugliness. Cixous contends that all myths associated with female sexuality – including that of woman as a black abyss or the Medusa myth – inevitably dissolve. Freud, in his 1922 essay 'Medusa's head', interpreted the snakes writhing in Medusa's hair as penises that, because of their absence, evoked horror.[75] The head enveloped in snakes represented the female genitals crowned by hair. The terror she induced was a consequence of thc fact that she had too many, rather than too few of them, thus feeding man's castration fear.[76] Her terror represented the terror of castration associated with seeing something. According to Freud, the sight of Medusa's head made the spectator stiff and thus erect that implied the existence of the penis. Therefore, Athena's application of the symbol to her clothing – as a substitute for the female genitals – made the goddess frightening, unapproachable and unsubjected to sexual desires.[77]

Cixous discusses those myths in the context of phallogocentrism and men's fear of losing one's penis in confrontation with women, who have either none or too many of them. Only by women showing their 'sexts' is it possible to explain female sexuality as not orientated on penises, either none or too many. Therefore Cixous suggests that: 'You only have to look at the Medusa straight on to see her. And she's not deadly. She's beautiful and she's laughing.'[78]

Baudrillard suggests:

> If desire exists – as modernity hypothesizes – then nothing must interfere with its natural harmony, and cosmetics are hypocritical. But if desire is a myth – as seduction hypothesizes – then nothing can prevent it from being put to use by signs, unrestrained by natural limits.[79]

Cixous account of desire leading *towards* the lack implies the possibility of difference in sexuality and sexual identity.[80] Perniola suggests there exist two sexualities: a vitalistic one – differentiating sexes, erotic and hedonic; and an inorganic one – beyond the distinction between the female and the male, i.e. neutral. This latter type does not synthesise or reunite, but enables variations.[81] Both sexualities offer a new identity and the body, which can be continuously readjusted.

Zbigniew Libera illustrates the rigid construction of gender through culturally specific social training. His 1987 video *Jak tresuje się dziewczynki* (How to Train Little Girls) portrays an adult woman teaching a 5-year-old girl how to use a lipstick, a mirror, jewellery, etc. The training familiarises the girl with techniques she should be adapting in her life to embody the desirable behaviours and looks of a woman (represented by the figure of Venus). She is being taught to learn to control her body and adjust it to conform to cultural standards. Her looks will secure her position as a woman and her physical attractiveness will determine her success in life. Libera portrays the different ways in which gender is constructed in culture. Women should strive to be beautiful through embellishing and controlling their bodies and removing any signs of masculinity (such as pubic and armpit hair, which is demonstrated in his 1995 work representing ten dolls in cardboard boxes *Możesz ogolić dzidziusia*, You Can Shave the Baby). Similarly, men should aspire to build muscular and strong bodies, as portrayed in *Body Master dla dzieci od lat pięciu* (Body Master for Children Up to the Age of 9), from 1995. The work presents a multi-gym with bodybuilding equipment, which is accompanied by a chart demonstrating the ideal the user should aim to achieve. The toy trains the body and the mind to conform to societal standards of masculinity and fit existing paradigms of appearance. Apart from being physically disciplined, the body should also be trained for social roles. The *Universal Penis Expander* (1995) is a penis-expanding device, which enables the penis to expand to 100cm in length. The toy refines male sexual effectiveness. Another work, *Łóżeczko porodowe* (*Birth Bed*), from 1996, looks like a doll's stroller and is aimed at preparing girls for their role as mothers. Libera emphasises that both the female and male bodies are culturally constructed and disciplined to fit social standards and stereotypes concerning femininity and masculinity. These stereotypes can and should be challenged.

The body that once defined and imprisoned woman becomes a medium that affords the transcending of corporeal boundaries.[82] The myths, predominantly of Medusa and the abyss, need little probing to expose the patriarchal manipulation around which they are structured. The abyss represents the space that is 'too dark to be explorable'[83] and Medusa illustrates the external, preventing one from exploring the darkness and the monster that is, in fact, beautiful. After all, as Sontag remarks, 'beauty is theatrical, it is for being looked at and admired'.[84] Looking directly at Medusa is not deadly. The monstrous image – related to ugliness, sublimity, fetishisation and perversion – is a costume, a façade, a lavish display of theatricality. When Medusa was killed, beauty was reborn with Pegasus. This beauty came from the inside, disregarding the ugliness and terror of appearance. Medusa seduces as though saying 'I'll be your temptation'.

The look is mobile. The privileged looks attached to idealised bodies and negating the socially devalued bodies can be tested and challenged through Silverman's 'good enough' paradigm. The dichotomous structure of ideality and abjection needs deconstruction in order for the body to live and contest ideals at the same time. Silverman proposes that it is necessary to look at things again, re-view them, which is 'a necessary step in the coming of the subject to an ethical or nonviolent relation to the other'.[85] Irigaray's concept of mimesis also emphasises the need to lift the spell bound to cultural representations and roles attached to women. The different sorts of misrecognition require re-viewing and demystifying.

Waking up

When Alice wakes up from her dream of the other side of the 'looking-glass', she says:

> Let's consider who it was that dreamed it all … it must have been either me or the Red King. He was part of my dream, of course – but then I was part of his dream, too! … Which do you think it was?[86]

Venus, or her contemporary embodiments such as Barbie, Lolita, Alice and so on, portray patterns of femininity pertaining to ideals of beauty and illustrating the perfect 'woman' generated by Western standards and consumer culture. She also represents a paradox. Tropes of femininity standardise ideal female beauty on one hand, and the impossibility of fulfilling it, or perhaps even inability to do so, on the other. 'Her' body evaluates and corrects accepted and entrenched ideas about gender issues in history, in both the context of art and scholarly discourse. Nonetheless, it also presents itself in a new historical and topographical context of post-modern culture and beyond, and also encompasses femininity envisioned in the male gaze and revisioned in the conscious external form. The female body functions as a prerequisite for future interpretations of gender issues in art and their social function but also for the cultural gaze imposing bipolar heteronormative images on the female body.

The ideal image of the female is grounded in classical canons of the sculptured body, and expands beyond that towards its further idealisations centred on phallogocentric stances and challenged in feminist arguments. The 'trans' incorporative logic re-visioning the mirror stage enables seeing the body as a congregate of identities. One of the most immediately recognised symbols of feminine beauty – Venus – can be used to contest female representations, but to do so it needs to be seen through the cultural mirror, which provides a valuable perspective on an otherwise unchangeable imprisoned image. Going and looking through the mirror liberates the body, which can finally experience various optical illusions and inversions.

The transformation of the ideal Venus into an excessive contemporary Medusa is a step towards self-definition against culturally constructed images of the female body that are instrumentalised in a variety of illustrations, both theoretical and practical, of gender construction. I hope that this transformation might be seen as an invitation towards alternative and subversive gazes, counter regimes of femaleness and maleness demasking patriarchal ideas and allowing 'trans' logic. Hybridity, which emerges, recreates and re-appropriates the image of woman and other gender orientations on the crossroads of tradition, doctrines and individualism. This is a first step towards looking through the 'looking-glass' – its mirror, surface and screen – and entering multiplicity of genderland. Hopefully, genderland offers a space that destabilises labels attached to the image of 'woman' and corporeality that have been glued to either Venus or Medusa. Venus has never really been looked at *through* Medusa, which seems to generate new meanings and a new opticality, a Baudrillardian 'inversion of vision'.[87] I have demonstrated some analogies between those two mythological figures. They are interesting in their own right, and working through mimesis, as Irigaray proposes, enables re-viewing not only the female body attached to both representations but also the myths that have been constructed as a result.

The Venus/Medusa rationale emphasises the still powerful burden of the male gaze. The proposed dialectic is disturbing, merging myths and disciplines beyond art history, but it encourages a fresh new hybrid perspective. It is fascinating and at the same time terrifying how the female appearance is created outside of 'her' and how powerful it can be. It is important to note that my arguments on beauty cannot be categorised as either positive or negative. The category is visually challenging precisely in its incompleteness, monstrosity and excess. I hope to open up a possibility of re-viewing some of the marginalised and conventional modes of looking that could be utilised to liberate the female body from the imprisonment in Venus's image. Breaking, swallowing or revising the mirror offers an opportunity for transformation which 'un-' and 'de-'feminises and masculinises the body itself, negotiating its identity towards cross and trans logic.

Baudrillard's account of seduction and his political economy of the sign and symbolic exchange prove the absurdity of the concept of the calculability of sex. Furthermore, sexual difference constructed on binary dichotomies within modern Western cultural tradition is also inscribed in the idea of the number of sexes and hence mythic final identities. As Baudrillard remarks: 'Of all the prostheses that punctuate the history of the body, the double is doubtless the most ancient. The double, however, is not properly speaking a prosthesis at all. Rather, it is an imaginary figure.'[88]

The phallic as the absolute signifier needs to be annulled eventually. By utilising Baudrillard's proposed explosion of the exchange between the real and the imaginary into the symbolic, identity becomes multiple, borderless, fluid and hybrid. Signs, also of sex, are traded and all signifiers are able to cross any difference and align their own identity as desired. They are located in the order of challenges, not representation, and are subjected to constant transformation. In symbolic exchange fetishes are destabilised and so 'woman' becomes defetishised. The shift in logic concerns neutrality and the annulment of all archetypal separations. After Baudrillard, I would suggest that the implosion of everything transforms the subject, functioning currently both within and without. There are no homogenous groups, such as 'women' or 'men'. All distinctions disperse into many pieces. The 'fractal logic'[89] and fragmentariness beyond wholeness governs genderland. As transcendence and immanence belong to the order of femininity, this new subject identifies itself with the maternal and the mother's phallus.

What is on the other side of the mirror?

The other side of the mirror inscribes into Baudrillard's transparency and the merging and blurring of the boundaries in between objects and identities. The subject, as the self-same, is invited to the other side of the mirror with its depth and transcendence. The concept of seduction enables identity to become uncodified.

The external appearance, either perfect or monstrous, is like a costume that seduces with its surface. Form becomes a fetish and a primordial union that incarcerates the subject, the Lacanian *object petit a* – an object of origin of desire, not satisfaction – which needs to be lost in order to liberate the subject. The external form functions as a substitute and a displacement. It is inscribed into a politics of desire, where sexuality unites and binds in Eros. Beauty is like a mirror image, a Freudian game of disappearance and return,[90] where the object reappears constantly, providing pleasure and satisfaction.

It might be argued that the current cultural moment is what Baudrillard calls 'the paroxystic phase',[91] which marks a moment just before the end. The mirror has been broken and swallowed, as suggested by Baudrillard. He goes even further in implying that '[p]erhaps this represents an opportunity, for, in the fragments of this broken mirror, all the singularities re-emerge. The ones we thought threatened survive; the ones we thought had disappeared revive.'[92]

Further, Baudrillard declares that '[r]eality is a bitch'[93] while talking about reality's apparent perfection, as though masking hidden incompleteness. What I have been trying to demonstrate in my discussion is exactly this re-emergence of fragments in the new incomplete completeness. The 'One' (such as Żebrowska's imagined Onone), offering the possibility of otherness and individuality, replaces binary systems. It functions in Cixous's 'merger type sexuality' and Ettinger's 'matrixial realm', in the trans logic governing the body, which is liberated from the subjection to the male gaze. Irigaray suggests that multiplicity enables movement towards an otherness of new singularities.[94] The current hybridisation of the body, beauty, religions, races, politics and economy moves us in the direction of a 'trans' stage – a phase of indistinction, ambiguity, sexual indifference. It falls under the regime of the lost and reclaimed image. It returns from the other side of the mirror, blurring the threshold between realities, making everything transparent.

Baudrillard once asked 'what do we do after the orgy?'[95] He suggests: 'After the orgy, then, a masked ball. … Diffusion of … transsexual kitsch in all its glory … where sexuality is lost in the theatrical excess of its ambiguity.'[96] It seems as if the only possibility is an endless reproduction of the self-same in the screen as subjectivity becomes fractal. However, then Baudrillard adds:

> I forgot to say that this expression – 'after the orgy' – comes from a story full of hope: it is the story of a man who whispers in the ear of a woman during an orgy, 'What are you doing after the orgy?'[97]

This post-orgy reality becomes possible through postmodern subjectivity destroying heteronormative ideologies. The body has become porous, interacting not only with other bodies but with otherness. This new body, inhabiting genderland and subjected to the trans logic, desires to go beyond the post-modern subject that, even though fluid in its subjectivity, is still entrapped in a physical body. It destabilises the border, inviting Eros – desire with its ability to construct true relationships beyond physicality. As such, the body transgresses being just an erotic spectacle to be looked at. Finally, as Luce Irigaray says, we need to respect the difference to reach individuation.[98] According to Irigaray, our sexual identity is inscribed in our nature, which is autonomous, neither opposing nor complementing femaleness with maleness. Therefore, sex resides in duality not dualism, implying androgyny. This contradicts our humanity. Hence, here I am proposing, instead of bisexuality, Cixous's 'merger type sexuality' and Irigaray's 'sex's individuation'.

Desire can be supported by the beautiful body but beyond imposed stereotypes and canons. It invites difference in monstrosity, the carnivalesque or fragmentation. As such, desire is shared, according to Irigaray, in difference, reviving energy and starting a new epoch in culture, sharing with 'the other' globally. In order to cultivate Eros, we need new relations.[99] Here, I proposed the 'trans' enabling specificity or, rather, singularity. So, after all, perhaps reality needs Eros, as after Baudrillard: 'This is perhaps a way of exacting vengeance on its partisans: by throwing them back on their own desire. In the end, it is perhaps more a sphinx than a bitch.'[100]

Dispersal of identities into trans

Baudrillard remarks that the body has travelled from being a metaphor for the soul then sex to the current stage, when it can be anything or, as I would like to suggest any-body – the trans-body associated with Eros and metamorphosed beyond femininity and masculinity. Everything becomes 'trans'. In Baudrillard's account:

> The possibility of metaphor is disappearing in every sphere. This is an aspect of a general tendency towards transsexuality which extends way beyond sex, affecting all disciplines as they loose their specificity and partake of a process of confusion.[101]

And further, 'this state of affairs is epitomised by a single feature: the transpolitical, the transsexual, the transaesthetic.'[102] We are now experiencing a peripateia of sex and identity. The logic of explosion, characterised by the outward movement, is replaced by the implosion, merging and collapsing of opposing poles, such as reality and appearance into simulation of female and male into the 'One'. The 'trans' destabilises gender binary and deconstructs the paradigm of sex/gender difference. Our specific social, historical and political conditions – described as 'posttransexual' by Susan Stryker and Sandy Stone,[103] or as 'performance in trans' by Kate

Bornstein[104] – makes the body a site of identification rather than otherness. The game with the commutability of appearance and sex invites a trans-body with its disrupting boundaries, situated in a Baudrillardian phase of fluidity and resignification of genders, beyond the phallic law of identity/difference. It enters the maternal logic of implosion and the fusion of identities into any-body. It needs to be clear, however, that this is not a playground for baroqueness and a lack of specificity, where erotic becomes carnivorous. The trans logic is an attempt, at the same time, to restore 'otherness' lost by creation of 'the hell of the Same'. According to Baudrillard:

> Alienation is no more: the Other as gaze, the Other as mirror, the Other as opacity – all are gone. Henceforward it is the transparency of others that represents absolute danger. Without the Other as mirror, as reflecting surface, consciousness of the self is threatened with irradiation in the void.[105]

'Off with their heads'

I end by discussing three performance pieces, two by Jess Dobkin and one by Katarzyna Kozyra, emphasising the body as a construct reflecting self-identity – whether sexual, gendered, national or any other. For the first time I bring into my analysis an artist not attached to the Central and Eastern European territory (Dobkin is from Canada) as an afterthought to open up discussion on the exploration of alternate geographies and realities.

When I watched Dobkin's and Lex Vaughn's *It's Not Easy Being Green* performance (2009), re-interpreting Kermit the Frog's song of the same title, I thought of the carnivalesque, monstrosity and puppets. The piece starts with a naked Dobkin sitting motionless, as though she were a marionette, on a bar stool, fashioning herself as Kermit the Frog, painted green except from her red lips, white eyes and a small triangle around her genitals. Cabaret-like music plays loudly, creating a cheerful atmosphere. Next comes Vaughn, dressed as a man, who rubs lube over her hand, which disappears into Dobkin's perineum. At that moment Dobkin lip-synchs Kermit's signature song of learning self-acceptance:

It's not easy bein' green
It seems you blend in with so many other
ordinary things
And people tend to pass you over 'cause you're
not standing out like flashy sparkles in the water –
or stars in the sky.[106]

Here, Dobkin performs genital tricks singing about green identity. The puppeteer directs the marionette but is also playing a straight man. Who is running the show? Is the lip-synching woman mastered by the trans-vested man? Is she defined and directed by the male gaze? Or is it femininity playing masculinity? Is the male gaze annulled by the act of trans-vesting? Does it become unimportant due to 'greenness'? Everything seems twisted and merged into a body, which is both performed and performs. In the end, the final words of Kermit's song are:

When green is all there is to be
It could make you wonder why, but why wonder why? Wonder,
I am green and it'll do fine,
it's beautiful!
And I think it's what I want to be.[107]

Another of Dobkin's performances, *Composite Body* (2003), portrayed a woman's head and hands located in cut out holes in a white board. The artist created a self-constructed body by drawing its contours. Firstly, she drew small breasts, a waist, a belly button and genitals. But then she erased the waist and made it thinner. Next, she enlarged her breasts and added abdominal muscles to make her stomach look more toned up. Afterwards, Dobkin adjusted the muscles, thinned the waist even more and made the breasts even bigger. She constantly edited, redrew and erased the contours of the body, closely considering its lines and imagined physique. She dressed the body in a patriarchal costume. The investigation of the stereotypical female form, its realities and its subjection to the ubiquitous canons becomes obsessive. The continuous re-adjustment and re-forming questions the body and its construction according to common standards.

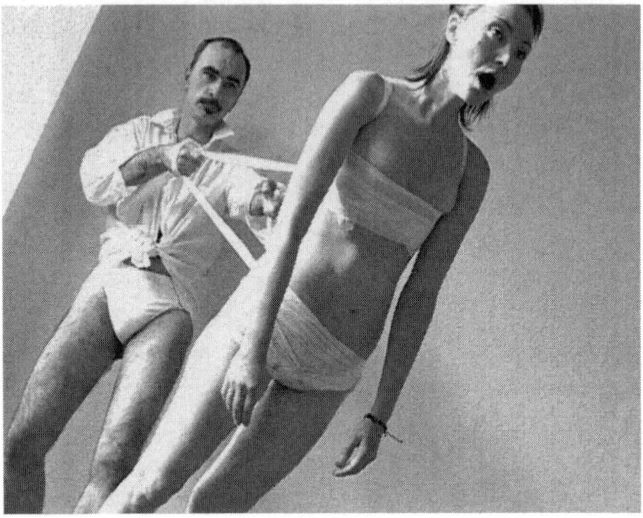

Image 10 Katarzyna Kozyra, *Non so piu, W sztuce marzenia stają się rzeczywistością* (series In Art Dreams Come True), 2004, ten-channel video installation (colour), loop, 4:3 PAL, sound, video still. Courtesy of the Katarzyna Kozyra Foundation.

In another action entitled *Non so piu cosa son, cosa faccio...* (*I No Longer Know What I Am or What I Do*) (2004), part of the series In Art Dreams Come True, Katarzyna Kozyra continues experiencing different identities and situations of the Berlin drag queen scene and the world of opera. The multichannel video portrays her infiltrating two seemingly opposing realities. She learns tricks and rituals of femininity, female behaviour and actions from Gloria Viagra, who in her view symbolises the perfect female body, and Maestro teaches her opera singing, preparing her for performance of an aria from Mozart's *Marriage of Figaro* (1786). The title of the work refers to the first line of Cherubino's aria from the opera.[108] These seemingly contrary circles of drag and opera merge into an artificial spectacle composed from a movie trailer and nine videos, *Makijaż* (Make up), *Sven*, *Backstage*, *Zakupy* (Shopping), *Kluby* (Clubs), *Callas*, *The Maestro*, *Diabeł* (The Devil) and *Kitkat*, that can be viewed in no particular order and which were initially presented in a maze-like space. Kozyra created a fairy tale, describing unfulfilled dreams concerning one's identity. She questions who is who and attempts to blur and undo gender boundaries. Kozyra presents us with gender identities, which she argues do not need to exclude each other.

The three performances summarise my argument and demonstrate the power embedded in the look, the gaze and the screen, all of which are performative and belong to the order of the spectacle. They can be opened and can allow for imagining the female body differently, not as lack and not as a male fantasy but as plentitude that is not reflected in the gaze of the other but spreads to engage with multidimensional opticality. The realm in which this female body functions is inviting and hospitable, and understands the flaws of binary logic. It is also permeable in the sense it moves towards difference that encompasses belonging. It is a passage to the other side that disrupts borders and boundaries. This threshold and this site of 'into' and 'out of' enables us to explore the 'what if …'.

Postscript

This book focuses on the female body and, through the metaphor of the looking-glass and the proposed concept of genderland, discusses the importance of gender and place in shaping female identity. Although it prioritises the role of theory within interpretation, it applies and tests a range of theories to analyse contemporary art concerned with processes and strategies of embodiment and representation. The book explores the relationship between theory and art practice; in its methodology it refutes this binary split and engages with practice-led research, not from the point of view of a practitioner but a theorist.

Citing art practices by contemporary women artists from Central and Eastern Europe, my discussion raises questions around the politics of place, the construction of the body, the implications of gender discourses, and the performativity of female identity. The artworks that are analysed confront the sexual politics around women's freedoms and experiences and the visual tropes and narratives from the Alice books facilitate the articulation of my concept of 'genderland'. I propose genderland as a space where dualism or oppositional concepts can achieve a balance of differences within the formulation of particular activist and aesthetic commitments.

The body discussed in relation to gender (and genderland), problematises issues around identity and the emergence of the 'self'. The need to have a voice and be a 'some body' is articulated in the practices of the Central and Eastern European women artists I have introduced. They explore how incapacitation imposed largely by culture can be reclaimed. They address and often simulate mechanisms of consumerism and popular culture to demonstrate how the female body is tamed, trained and disciplined to conform to ideals and gender roles defined as universal. Such norms exclude difference, otherness and alternative forms of identity that do not fit agreed standards. Thus the body and the self, the most personal 'possessions' we own, are subjected to manipulation and control. Women artists intervene, often violently, in such articulations of the body and enable us to see it differently.

For women artists beyond Western Europe, the new post-1989 European political reality promoted sociocultural and economic changes and these were reflected in artistic practices. Capitalist development and consumer culture were introduced, to a greater or lesser extent, in Central and Eastern Europe. New freedoms were welcomed by fragile and underdeveloped democracies but this change also presented new threats. Freedoms of expression and creativity, and freedom in relation to the influence of the Catholic Church, were once again raised and tested in artistic practice. Democracy enabled artists to confront and dispute issues of difference, concerning gender, sexuality, religion, politics, and so on.

Women artists in Central and Eastern Europe had not passively digested the totalitarian structures in state socialism but had critiqued the power of the Stalinist model, the overarching power from 'above', and from the 'centre', imposed by the State or the Communist parties. Post-1989 they continued observing, challenging and subverting gender relations in their homes and communities, and representing them in visual arts. Their actions exemplify the complex relationships that exist between cultural values, the role of the female body, place and time.

My narrative tells a story of the female body seen through the looking-glass, which enables searching for the 'self' and establishing one's identity. It presents the art practices of women artists who negotiate the complex terrain of genderland. Going through the space in between the looking-glass and the other side, genderland is inviting, generous, hospitable and multiple. It is under the rule of 'trans', where identity is flexible and the look is mobile. The mirror, as looking-glass, allows us to question the relationship and dynamics between the gaze and the look, and between viewing and being viewed. It can uncover difference, which does not need to be marginalised but can be recognised and cherished. Identity, formed in this space in between, escapes from restraining Oedipalisation, becoming flexible. Embodiment, exercised by women artists, enhances body subjectivity, enabling women to claim their rights to their bodies and to their selves. Perhaps this is utopian thinking but, as Baudrillard suggests: 'There is always the hope of a new seduction.'[1] Perhaps dreams can come true, not only in art.

Notes

Introduction

1 Lewis Carroll, *Alice's Adventures in Wonderland; and, Through the Looking-Glass, and What Alice Found There*, ed. and intro. Hugh Haughton (London: Penguin, 1998).

2 Femen website. Available at http://femen.org (accessed 31 July 2014).

3 Ibid.

4 Slavoj Žižek, 'The true blasphemy', 2012. Available at http://chtodelat.wordpress.com/2012/08/07/the-true-blasphemy-slavoj-zizek-on-pussy-riot/ (accessed 19 May 2014).

5 This is demonstrated by exhibitions such as *Gender Check* in the Museum of Modern Art (MUMOK) in Vienna in 2009 and publications including Amelia Jones (ed.), *The Feminism and Visual Culture Reader* (New York and London: Routledge, 2003); Gayatri Chakravorty Spivak, 'Three women's texts and a critique of imperialism' [1985], in Bill Ashcroft, Gareth Griffiths and Helen Tiffin (eds), *Post-colonial Studies Reader* (New York and London: Routledge, 1995), pp. 43–61; Gayatri Chakravorty Spivak, 'Can the subaltern speak?' [1988], in Ashcroft, Griffiths and Tiffin, *Post-colonial Studies Reader*, pp. 28–37; Trinh T. Minh-ha, *Woman, Native, Other: Writing Postcoloniality and Feminism* (Bloomington, IN: Indiana University Press, 1989); Sara Suleri, 'Women skin deep: Feminism and the post-colonial condition' [1992], in Ashcroft, Griffiths and Tiffin, *Post-colonial Studies Reader*, pp. 246–49; Kadiatu Kanneh 'Feminism and the colonial body', ibid., pp. 250–5, among others.

6 Susan Gal and Gail Kligman, (eds), *The Politics of Gender after Socialism: A Comparative-Historical Essay* (Princeton, NJ: Princeton University Press, 2000) and Janet Elise Johnson and Jean C. Robinson (eds), *Living Gender After Communism* (Bloomington, IN: Indiana University Press, 2006).
7 The following scholars elaborate on this issue: ibid.; Ella Shohat, *Talking Visions: Multicultural Feminism in a Transnational Age* (Cambridge, MA: MIT Press, 1998); Edit András, 'Gender minefield: The heritage of the past', *n.paradoxa* 11 (1999), pp. 4–9.
8 Ibid. and Ekaterina Dyogot, 'How to qualify for post-colonial discourse', *ARTMargins*, 1 November 2001. Available at http://www.artmargins.com/index.php/archive/325-how-to-qualify-for-postcolonial-discourse (accessed 23 November 2015).
9 Naomi Wolf, *The Beauty Myth: How Images of Beauty are Used Against Women* (London: Vintage, 1991).
10 Ulf Brunnbauer, 'From equality without democracy to democracy without equality. Women and transition in South-East Europe', *South-East Europe Review* 3/3 (2000), pp. 151–8.
11 Luce Irigaray, *This Sex Which is Not One* (Ithaca, NY: Cornell University Press, 1975).
12 Available for download at http://www.un.org/en/universal-declaration-human-rights/.
13 Jacques Lacan, *Écrits: A Selection* (New York: Norton, 1977); *The Seminar of Jacques Lacan. Book I: Freud's Papers on Technique 1953–1954*, ed. Jacques-Alain Miller, trans. John Forrester (New York and London: Norton, 1988)
14 Kaja Silverman, *The Acoustic Mirror: The Female Voice in Psychoanalysis and Cinema* (Bloomington, IN: Indiana University Press, 1988); and *The Threshold of the Visible World* (New York and London: Routledge, 1996).
15 Jacques Rancière, *The Emancipated Spectator* (London: Verso Books, 2009).
16 John Berger, *Ways of Seeing* [1972] (London: Penguin, 2008).
17 Laura Mulvey, 'Visual pleasure and narrative cinema' [1973], in Leo Braudy and Marshall Cohen (eds), *Film Theory and Criticism: Introductory Readings* (New York: Oxford University Press, 1999), pp. 833–44.
18 Bracha Ettinger, *The Matrixial Borderspace* (Minneapolis, MN: University of Minnesota Press, 2006).
19 Lennard J. Davis, (ed.), *The Disability Studies Reader* (London, New York: Routledge, 1997); and 'Visualizing the disabled body: The classical nude and the fragmented torso', in Mariam Fraser and Monica Greco (eds), *The Body: A Reader* (London and New York: Routledge, 2005), pp. 165–181.
20 Leslie Heywood, *Dedication to Hunger: The Anorexic Aesthetic in Modern Culture* (London: University of California Press, 1996).

21 Wendy Steiner, 'The sublime shudder', in Bill Beckley (ed.), *Sticky Sublime* (New York: Allworth Press, 2001), pp. 194–200; and *The Trouble with Beauty* (London: William Heinemann, 2001).
22 Hélène Cixous, 'The laugh of the Medusa', in Elaine Marks and Isabelle de Courtivron (eds), *New French Feminisms: An Anthology* (Brighton: The Harvester Press, 1981), pp. 245–64.
23 Luce Irigaray, *This Sex Which is Not One* (Ithaca, NY: Cornell University Press, 1975); and *Luce Irigaray: Key Writings* (London: Continuum, 2004).
24 Chapter 5, 'Wool and Water', in Carroll, *Through the Looking-Glass*.

Chapter 1

1 Lewis Carroll, 'Through the looking-glass, and what Alice found there', in Lewis Carroll, *Alice's Adventures in Wonderland* and *Through the Looking-Glass, and What Alice Found There* (London: Penguin Books, 1998), pp. 125–7.
2 Ibid., p. 127.
3 Gilles Deleuze, *The Logic of Sense* [1990] (London: Continuum, 2011), pp. 51, 52.
4 Ibid., p. 272.
5 Kaja Silverman, *The Threshold of the Visible World* (New York and London: Routledge, 1996), pp. 3, 4.
6 Ibid., p. 9.
7 Jacques Lacan, *Four Fundamental Concepts of Psycho-analysis*, trans. Alan Sheridan (New York: Norton, 1978), p. 106.
8 Sigmund Freud, *The Interpretation of Dreams*, trans. A. A. Brill (New York: Macmillan, 1913); and *Totem and Taboo* [1913] trans. J. Strachey (London: Routledge and Kegan Paul, 1950).
9 Silverman, *The Threshold*, pp. 132–5.
10 Ibid., pp. 26, 27.
11 Luce Irigaray, *Speculum of the Other Woman* (Ithaca, NY: Cornell University Press, 1974), pp. 25–7.
12 Sigmund Freud, 'Beyond the pleasure principle', in *The Standard Edition of the Complete Psychological Works of Sigmund Freud*, ed. and trans. James Strachey vol. 18 (London: Hogarth Press, 1955), pp. 15, 16.
13 Jacques Derrida, *The Post Card: From Socrates to Freud and Beyond* (Chicago, IL: University of Chicago Press, 1987), p. 311.
14 Jacques Derrida, *The Ear of the Other: Otobiography, Transference, Translation* (Lincoln, NE: University of Nebraska Press, 1988), p. 69.
15 Luce Irigaray, *This Sex Which is Not One* (Ithaca, NY: Cornell University Press, 1975) and *Speculum of the Other.*
16 John Berger, *Ways of Seeing* [1972] (London: Penguin, 2008), p. 47.

17 Łukasz Guzek, 'Alicja Żebrowska', in Grzegorz Borkowski, Adam Mazur and Monika Branicka (eds), *New Phenomena in Polish Art after 2000* (Centre for Contemporary Art Ujazdowski Castle: Warsaw, 2007), p. 326.
18 Michel Foucault, *Discipline and Punish: The Birth of the Prison*, trans. Alan Sheridan (London: Allen Lane, 1977).
19 Sigmund Freud, 'Some psychical consequences of the anatomical distinction between the sexes' [1925], in *The Standard Edition of the Complete Psychological Works of Sigmund Freud*, ed. and trans. James Strachey, vol. 19 (London: Hogarth Press, 1961), p. 252.
20 Jean-Joseph Goux, 'The phallus: Masculine identity and the "exchange of women"', *differences* 4/1 (1992), pp. 40–75, p. 49.
21 Silverman, *The Threshold*, p. 30.
22 Boryana Rossa, 'SZ-ZS performance', 2005. Available at http://boryanarossa.com/sz-zs-performance/ (accessed 14 September 2013).
23 See: Irigaray, *Speculum of the Other* and *This Sex Which is Not One*; Julia Kristeva, *Tales of Love* (New York: Columbia University Press, 1987); Elizabeth Grosz, *Jacques Lacan: A Feminist Introduction* (New York and London: Routledge, 1990); Christine Battersby, 'Just jamming: Irigaray, painting and psychoanalysis', in Katy Deepwell (ed.), *New Feminist Art Criticism: Critical Strategies* (Manchester: Manchester University Press, 1995), pp. 128–137; Hilary Robinson, 'Border crossings: Womanliness, body, representation', ibid., pp. 138–46; Silverman, *The Acoustic Mirror: The Female Voice in Psychoanalysis and Cinema* (Bloomington, IN: Indiana University Press, 1988); Anneke Smelik, *And the Mirror Cracked: Feminist Cinema and Film Theory* (Basingstoke: Palgrave Macmillan, 2001).
24 Jacques Lacan, *Écrits: A Selection* (New York: Norton, 1977).
25 Foucault, *Discipline and Punish*.
26 Bracha Ettinger, *The Matrixial Borderspace* (Minneapolis, MN: University of Minnesota Press, 2006); Atara Stein, 'Xena: Warrior Princess, the lesbian gaze, and the construction of a feminist heroine', 1998. Available at http://whoosh.org/issue24/stein1.html (accessed 15 August 2010); bell hooks, 'Oppositional gaze. black female spectators', in bell hooks, *Black Looks: Race and Representation* (New York: South End Press, 1992); Silverman, *The Acoustic Mirror*; Smelik, *And the Mirror Cracked*.
27 Michel Foucault, 'Of other spaces', *Diacritics* 16/1 (1987), pp. 22–7, p. 24.
28 ——, *The Order of Things: An Archaeology of the Human Sciences* (London and New York: Routledge, 2002).
29 Ibid., p. 22.
30 Foucault, 'Of other spaces', p. 26.
31 Ibid., p. 24.
32 Jorge Luis Borges, 'Fauna of mirrors', in Jorge Luis Borges, *The Book of Imaginary Beings* (London: Vintage, 2002), pp. 67–8.

33 Sigmund Freud, 'On narcissism: An introduction', in *The Standard Edition of the Complete Psychological Works of Sigmund Freud*, ed. and trans. James Strachey, vol. 14 (London: Hogarth Press, 1957), pp. 73–102.
34 Hélène Cixous, 'The laugh of the Medusa', in Elaine Marks and Isabelle de Courtivron (eds), *New French Feminisms: An Anthology* (Brighton: The Harvester Press, 1981), pp. 245–64, p. 254.
35 Mieke Bal, *Travelling Concepts in the Humanities: A Rough Guide* (Toronto and London: University of Toronto Press, 2002), p. 90.
36 Ibid., p. 251.
37 Ibid., p. 208.
38 Rosalind Krauss, *The Optical Unconscious* (London: MIT Press, 1993), p. 23.
39 Freud, 'On narcissism: An introduction', pp. 73–102.
40 Ibid., p. 75.
41 Ibid., p. 88–91.
42 Ibid., p. 94.
43 Lacan's theory of the mirror phase constantly evolved and thus resulted in several versions. For a precise description of the variations between the consequent stages of this development, see Jacques Lacan, *The Seminar of Jacques Lacan. Book I: Freud's Papers on Technique 1953–1954*, ed. Jacques-Alain Miller, trans. John Forrester (New York and London: Norton, 1988).
44 Darian Leader and Judy Groves, *Introducing Lacan* (Cambridge: Icon Books, 2000), pp. 88–96.
45 Pierce aligns the imaginary with the 'icon', an image apprehended with little mediation (Charles Sanders Pierce, 'Logic as semiotic: The theory of signs', in *Philosophical Writings of Pierce*, ed. Justus Buchler (New York: Dover Publications, Inc., 1955). Saussure attributes the imaginary to the 'signified' symbolised by a sign (Ferdinand de Saussure, 'Linguistic value', in Ferdinand de Saussure, *Course in General Linguistics* (New York: McGraw Hill, 1966).
46 Leader and Groves, *Introducing Lacan*, pp. 18–61.
47 See Althusserian ideological state apparatuses in Louis Althusser, 'Ideology and ideological state apparatuses', in Louis Althusser, *Lenin and Philosophy and Other Essays* (New York: Monthly Review Press, 1968).
48 Marsha Meskimmon, *Contemporary Art and the Cosmopolitan Imagination* (London and New York: Routledge, 2011), p. 35.
49 Ibid., p. 35.
50 Rossa, 'SZ-ZS performance'.
51 Silverman, *The Threshold*, pp. 2–3.
52 Ibid., p. 11.
53 Ibid.
54 Ibid., p. 3.

55 Ibid.
56 Ibid., p. 2.
57 Ibid.
58 Ibid., p. 10.
59 Ibid., p. 15.
60 Ibid., pp. 16, 17.
61 Anetta Mona Chişa & Lucia Tkáčová, 'Vessel', 2012. Available at http://www.chitka.info/vessel.html (accessed 14 September 2013).
62 Bojana Pejić, 'i aM a venus, A conch, a kiT, a Cat, a Lot', 2012. Available at http://rotwandgallery.com/exhibitions/anetta-mona-Chişa-lucia-tkáčová-2012 (accessed 17 April 2014).
63 Jacques Derrida, *The Politics of friendship*, trans. George Collins (London, New York: Verso, 2005), p. 279.
64 The politics of friendship, hospitality and migration in relation to transnationalisms and belonging is the main focus of my current research project.
65 Pejić, 'i aM a venus'.
66 Laura Mulvey, 'Visual pleasure and narrative cinema' [1973], in Leo Braudy and Marshall Cohen (eds), *Film Theory and Criticism: Introductory Readings* (New York: Oxford University Press, 1999), pp. 833–44, p. 843.
67 Maurice Merleau-Ponty, *The Visible and the Invisible* (Evanston, IL: Northwestern University Press, 1968), pp. 141–3.
68 Meskimmon, *Contemporary Art*, p. 38.
69 Silverman, *The Threshold*, p. 13.
70 Marjorie Garber, *Vested Interests: Cross-Dressing and Cultural Anxiety* (London: Routledge 1997), p. 11.
71 Ibid., p. 12.
72 Mikhail Bakhtin, *The Dialogic Imagination* (Austin, TX: University of Texas Press, 1981).
73 Jean Baudrillard, 'Aesthetic illusion and disillusion', in Jean Baudrillard, *The Conspiracy of Art: Manifestos, Interviews, Essays*, ed. Sylvère Lotringer, trans. Ames Hodges (New York: Semiotext(e), 2005), p. 120.
74 Both names are used in mythology. For more information, refer to Robert Graves, *The Greek Myths* (Manchester: Carcanet, 2001).
75 Jean Baudrillard, *Seduction* (New York: St Martin's Press, 1990), p. 69.
76 ——, 'Aesthetic illusion', p. 122 (emphasis original).
77 ——, *Seduction*, p. 69 (emphasis original).
78 Luce Irigaray and Margaret Whitford, *The Irigaray Reader* (Oxford: Blackwell, 1991), pp. 6, 7.
79 For more information refer to: Hilary Robinson, 'Whose beauty? Women, art, and intersubjectivity in Lucy Irigaray's writings', in Peg Brand Zeglin, *Beauty Matters* (Bloomington and Indianapolis, IN: Indiana University Press, 2000), pp. 224–51.

80 Luce Irigaray, *Luce Irigaray: Key Writings* (London: Continuum, 2004), p. 121.
81 Cixous, 'The laugh of the Medusa', p. 248.
82 Ibid., pp. 255, 256, 259.
83 Ibid., p. 259.
84 Ibid., p. 261.
85 Jean Baudrillard, *The Mirror of Production* (St Louis: Telos Press, 1975).
86 —–, *The Perfect Crime* (London, New York: Verso, 2008), p. 87.
87 Ibid., p. 150.
88 Harald Fricke, 'Gender trouble and fairytales: On Katarzyna Kozyra's *In Art Dreams Come True*', in Hanna Wróblewska, *In Art Dreams Come True. Katarzyna Kozyra*. (Wrocław: BWA Wrocław, 2007), pp. 35–41, p. 37.

Chapter 2

1 John Berger, *Ways of Seeing* [1972] (London: Penguin, 2008).
2 Guy Debord, *The Society of the Spectacle* (New York: Zone Books, 1994).
3 Ibid., p. 1.
4 Jean Baudrillard, *The Transparency of Evil* [1990], trans. James Benedict (London and New York: Verso, 2002).
5 Ibid., p. 159.
6 Izabela Kowalczyk, 'The ambivalent beauty', in Edit Andras, Keti Chukrov and Branko Dimitrijevia, *Gender Check. Femininity and Masculinity in the Art of Eastern Europe*, exhibition catalogue (Cologne: Buchhandlung Walther König GmbH & Co. KG. Abt. Verlag, 2009), pp. 38–45.
7 Ibid., p. 45.
8 Ibid., p. 33.
9 Ibid., pp. 42, 43.
10 Such as, for instance, in the works of Orlan who, through undergoing a series of plastic surgeries, aims to reconstruct ideals of feminine beauty promoted and imposed on women by men.
11 Naomi Wolf, *The Beauty Myth: How Images of Beauty are Used Against Women* (London: Vintage, 1991).
12 For a contrasting account of how the male body is explored in relation to the notion of beauty, see Susan Bordo, 'Beauty (re)discovers the male body', in Peg Brand Zeglin (ed.), *Beauty Matters* (Bloomington and Indianapolis, IN: Indiana University Press, 2000), pp. 112–68.
13 Saul Ostrow, 'The eternal problem of beauty's return', *Art Journal* 62/3 (2003), pp. 113–115, p. 113.
14 Rasheed Araeen, 'Cultural imperialism: observations on cultural situation in the Third World', in Dave Beech (ed.), *Beauty* (London: MIT Press, 2009), pp. 175–179, p. 175.

15 Eleanor Heartney, 'Foreword: Cutting two ways with beauty', in Brand Zeglin, *Beauty Matters*, pp. xiii–xv, p. xiii.

16 Dana Benson, 'Beauty optional', 2003. Available at http://issuu.com/riceuniversity/docs/rice_summer_2003/49 (accessed 1 November July 2015).

17 Wolfgang Welsch, 'The return of beauty', *Filozofski Vestnik* 28/2 (2007), pp. 15–26, p. 7.

18 Neal David Benezra, Olga M. Viso, and Arthur C. Danto, *Regarding Beauty: A View of the Late Twentieth Century*, exhibition catalogue (Washington DC: Hirshhorn Museum and Sculpture Garden, Smithsonian Institution, 1999), p. 106.

19 Heartney, 'Foreword', p. xv.

20 Jean-François Lyotard, *Lessons on the Analytic of the Sublime (Kant's 'Critique of Judgment' Sections 23–29)*, trans. Elizabeth Rottenberg (Stanford, CA: Stanford University Press, 1994).

21 Benezra et al., *Regarding Beauty*, p. 101.

22 Suzanne Perling Hudson, 'Beauty and the status of contemporary criticism', in Beech, *Beauty*, pp. 50–58, p. 57.

23 Dave Hickey, *The Invisible Dragon: Four Essays on Beauty* (Los Angeles, CA: Art Issues Press, 1993), p. 11.

24 Ibid., pp. 11, 12.

25 Paul Goldberger, 'Klaus Kertess and the Making of the Whitney Biennial', *The New York Times Magazine*, February 26 (1995), p. 61

26 Peg Brand Zeglin, Introduction', in Brand Zeglin, *Beauty Matters*, p. 6.

27 Ibid.

28 Arthur C. Danto, *The Abuse of Beauty: Aesthetics and the Concept of Art* (Chicago, IL: Open Court, 2003).

29 Ibid., p. xxv.

30 Ibid., p. 7.

31 James Kirwan, *Beauty* (Manchester: Manchester University Press, 1999), pp. 5–6.

32 Luce Irigaray, *This Sex Which is Not One* (Ithaca, NY: Cornell University Press, 1975) and *Speculum of the Other Woman* (Ithaca, NY: Cornell University Press, 1974).

33 Paul Schilder, *The Image and Appearance of the Human Body* (New York: International Universities Press, 1935).

34 Silverman, *The Threshold*, p. 13.

35 Meskimmon, *Contemporary Art*, p. 38.

36 Moira Gatens and Genevieve Lloyd, *Collective Imaginings: Spinoza Past and Present* (London and New York: Routledge, 1999), pp. 77, 123.

37 Meskimmon, *Contemporary Art*, pp. 39, 40.

38 Boryana Rossa, 'Ultrafuturo manifesto', 2004. Available at http://boryanarossa.com/ultrafuturo-manifesto-2/ (accessed 14 September 2013).

39 Mark Cousins, 'The ugly', *AA Files* 29 (1995), pp. 3–6, p. 3.
40 Ibid., pp. 3, 4.
41 Ibid., p. 5.
42 Ibid.
43 Ibid., p. 6.
44 Mieke Bal, *Quoting Caravaggio. Contemporary Art, Preposterous History* (Chicago, IL and London: University of Chicago Press, 1999).
45 Mark Cousins, 'The ugly', *AA Files* 30 (1995), pp. 65–8, pp. 67, 68.
46 Suzanne Ramljak, *A Disarming Beauty: 'The Venus the Milo in 20th-Century Art*, exhibition catalogue (St Petersburg: Salvador Dali Museum, 2001), pp. 11–43, p. 40.
47 William Jeffett, 'An obscure object of desire: The 'Venus the Milo', Surrealism and beyond', in Ramljak, *A Disarming Beauty*, pp. 51–79, p. 74.
48 Wendy Steiner, *The Trouble with Beauty* (London: William Heinemann, 2001).
49 Ibid., p. xxiv.
50 Wendy Steiner, *Venus in Exile: The Rejection of Beauty in Twentieth-Century Art* (New York: Free Press, 2001), p. xxv.
51 Ibid., p. 87.
52 Ibid., p. 52.
53 Ibid., p. 141.
54 Postmodernism was called 'Ornamentalism' by Jensen and Patricia Convay, see ibid., p. 119. For further reading on postmodernism, see Thomas Docherty, *Postmodernism. A Reader* (New York: Columbia University Press, 1993); Charles Jencks, *The Post-Modern Reader* (London and New York: Academy Editions, St Martin's Press, 1992); Keith Jenkins, *The Postmodern History Reader* (London: Routledge, 1997); Steven Connor, *Postmodernist Culture: An Introduction to Theories of the Contemporary* (Oxford: Blackwell, 1997); Hal Foster (ed.), *Postmodern Culture* (London: Pluto, 1985); Jean-François Lyotard, *The Postmodern Condition: A Report on Knowledge* (Minneapolis, MN: University of Minnesota Press, 1994); Stuart Sim, *Irony and Crisis: A Critical History of Postmodern Culture* (Cambridge: Icon, 2002).
55 Steiner, *Venus in Exile*, p. 140.
56 Michael Grant, *Myths of the Greeks and Romans* (London: Weidenfeld and Nicolson, 1962), pp. 110, 111.
57 Pierre Grimal, *A Concise Dictionary of Classical Mythology* (Oxford: Blackwell, 1990), pp. 143, 144.
58 Sigmund Freud, 'Beyond the pleasure principle', in *The Standard Edition of the Complete Psychological Works of Sigmund Freud*, ed. and trans. James Strachey, vol. 18 (London: Hogarth Press, 1955), p. 46.
59 Hal Foster, *Compulsive Beauty* (Cambridge, MA and London: MIT Press, 1995), p. 44.

60 Silverman, *The Threshold.*

61 Berger, *Ways of Seeing*, p. 48.

62 Jacques Rancière, *The Emancipated Spectator* (London: Verso Books, 2009), p. 6.

63 Susan Sontag, 'Notes on "Camp"', 1964. Available at http://interglacial.com/~sburke/pub/prose/Susan_Sontag_-_Notes_on_Camp.html (accessed 29 January 2010). More on 'camp' can be found in Umberto Eco, *On Ugliness* (London: Harvill Secker, 2007).

64 Anthony Haden-Guest, 'On the track of the "S" word: a reporter's notes', in Bill Beckley (ed.), *Sticky Sublime* (New York: Allworth Press, 2001), pp. 49–56, p. 53.

65 Sontag, 'Notes on "Camp"'.

66 Ibid.

67 Ibid.

68 Jean Baudrillard, *The Perfect Crime* (London, New York: Verso, 2008), p. xi.

69 Immanuel Kant, *The Critique of Judgement* [1790] (Oxford: The Clarendon Press, 1982), pp. 68, 69.

70 Derrida, *The Truth in Painting* (Chicago, IL: Chicago University Press, 1987), pp. 59–60.

71 Ibid., pp. 127, 131–2.

72 Bal, *Quoting Caravaggio*, p. 7.

73 Baudrillard, *Seduction* (New York: St Martin's Press, 1990), p. 69.

74 Artur Żmijewski, and Joanna Rajkowska, 'Art of public possibility. Joanna Rajkowska in conversation with Artur Żmijewski', 2010. Available at http://www.rajkowska.com/en/teksty/43 (accessed 15 February 2014).

75 Joanna Rajkowska, 'Satisfaction guaranteed', 2000. Available at http://www.rajkowska.com/en/inne/159 (accessed 8 March 2014).

76 ——, 'Satisfaction guaranteed: products, text', 2000. Available at http://www.rajkowska.com/en/inne/149 (accessed 9 March 2014).

77 Stach Stabłowski, 'The story of a chocolate bar – the light art of Joanna Rajkowska', in *Satisfaction Guaranteed*, exhibition catalogue (Warsaw: Centrum Sztuki Współczesnej Zamek Ujazdowski, 2000), pp. 2–5, p. 3.

78 Ibid.

79 Margaret Atwood, *The Edible Woman* (London: Virago Press, 1997).

80 Ibid., pp. 270, 271.

81 Stach Szabłowski, 'Discreet return', 2000. Available at http://www.rajkowska.com/en/inne/151 (accessed 9 March 2014).

82 ——, 'The story of a chocolate bar', p. 3.

83 Ewa Gorządek, Stach Stabłowski, and Joanna Rajkowska, 'They are cutting my fing'rs', in *Satisfaction Guaranteed*, exhibition catalogue, pp. 8–11, pp. 9, 11.

84 Dorota Jarecka and Joanna Rajkowska, 'Joanna Rajkowska. Palma mnie przerosła', 2007. Available at http://www.wysokieobcasy.pl/wysokie-obcasy/1,53581,4495611.html?as=3 (accessed 17 March 2014).

85 Szabłowski, 'The story of a chocolate bar', p. 3.
86 Gorządek et al., 'They are cutting my fing'rs', p. 9.
87 Jarecka and Rajkowska, 'Palma mnie przerosła'.
88 Gorządek et al., 'They are cutting my fing'rs', p. 9.
89 Szabłowski, 'The story of a chocolate bar', p. 5.
90 Irigaray, *This Sex Which is Not One*.
91 ——, *Speculum of the Other Woman*.
92 Roland Barthes, *Camera Lucida* (New York: Hill and Wang, 1981), p. 41.
93 Griselda Pollock, 'Modernity and the spaces of femininity', in Nicholas Mirzoeff (ed.), *The Visual Culture Reader* (London and New York: Routledge, 1988), pp. 74–84, p. 77.
94 Baudrillard, 'Disneyworld company', p. 200.
95 Rancière, *The Emancipated Spectator*, p. 107.

Chapter 3

1 Jean Baudrillard *The Transparency of Evil* [1990], trans. James Benedict (London and New York: Verso, 2002), p. 111.
2 Jean Baudrillard, *The Perfect Crime* (London, New York: Verso, 2008), p. 89.
3 Silverman discusses 'excorporative' and 'heteropathic' identification in the context of identifying the self with another. Referring to Lacan's mirror stage, she explores the relationship between the subject and the ego-ideal, which results in the idealisation of the bodily image (in Kaja Silverman, *The Threshold of the Visible World* (New York and London: Routledge, 1996)).
4 Jean Baudrillard, 'The finest consumer object. The body', in Mariam Fraser and Monica Greco (eds), *The Body. A Reader* (London and New York: Routledge, 2005), pp. 277–82, p. 280.
5 Baudrillard, 'The finest consumer object', p. 281.
6 Silverman, *The Threshold*, p. 27.
7 Ibid., p. 18.
8 Ibid., p. 19.
9 Ibid.
10 Ibid., p. 23.
11 Jacques Lacan, 'The mirror stage as formative of the function of the I as revealed in psychoanalytic experience', in *Écrits: A Selection* (New York: Norton, 1977), pp. 1–7, p. 4.
12 Silverman, *The Threshold*, p. 21.
13 Ibid., p. 25.
14 Ibid., pp. 24, 25.
15 Bill Readings, *Introducing Lyotard: Art and Politics* (London: Routledge, 1991), pp. 25–8.

16 Ibid., p. 27.

17 Jean-François Lyotard, *The Postmodern Condition: A Report on Knowledge* (Minneapolis, MN: University of Minnesota Press, 1994), p. 82.

18 Mieke Bal, *Quoting Caravaggio: Contemporary Art, Preposterous History* (Chicago, IL and London: University of Chicago Press, 1999), p. 198.

19 Ibid., p. 135.

20 Craig Owens, 'The discourse of others: feminists and postmodernism', in Hal Foster (ed.), *Postmodern Culture* (London: Pluto, 1985), pp. 57–82.

21 'Leaning forward, Narcissus extends his body into our space', Bal remarks while discussing a painting of Caravaggio on the subject. The painted Narcissus reflects the narrative, reversing the mirror phase, extending the imaginary body instead of the real one. The illusion is the only possibility after the disappearance of everything comes to the outer space, annihilating the real. It offers 'the fragmentation of the body … the prosthetic illusion of wholeness that props the self up into existence, as a fiction, framed as a representation' (Bal, *Quoting Caravaggio*, pp. 245, 246).

22 Ibid., p. 261.

23 Laura Mulvey, 'Visual pleasure and narrative cinema' [1973], in Leo Braudy and Marshall Cohen (eds), *Film Theory and Criticism: Introductory Readings* (New York: Oxford University Press, 1999), pp. 833–44.

24 Ibid., p. 835.

25 Paul Nalini, 'Other ways of looking: The female gaze in Jean Rhys' *Wide Sargasso Sea*', *eSharp*, 2004. Available at http://www.gla.ac.uk/research/az/esharp/issues/2/paul/ (accessed 9 November 2015); Eva-Maria Jacobsson, 'A female gaze?', 1999. Available at http://cid.nada.kth.se/pdf/cid_51.pdf (accessed 11 August 2010); Jean-Claude Lebensztejn and Kate Cooper, 'Photorealism, kitsch and Venturi', *SubStance* 10/31 (1981), pp. 75–104; Atara Stein, 'Xena: Warrior Princess, the lesbian gaze, and the construction of a feminist heroine', 1998. Available at http://whoosh.org/issue24/stein1.html (accessed 15 August 2010); Mary Louise Pratt, *Imperial Eyes: Travel Writing and Transculturation* (London, New York: Routledge, 1992); bell hooks, 'Oppositional gaze. Black female spectators', in *Black Looks: Race and Representation* (New York: South End Press, 1992), pp. 115–31. For more information on other gazes, e.g. 'medical gaze', refer to Michel Foucault, *The Birth of the Clinic: An Archaeology of Medical Perception* (New York: Random House, 1963); for 'queer gaze', Tim Wray, 'The queer gaze', 2003. Available at http://e-pub.uni-weimar.de/volltexte/2008/1335/pdf/wray.pdf (accessed 11 August 2010); for 'lesbian gaze', Reina Lewis, 'Looking good: the lesbian gaze and fashion imagery', *Feminist Review* 55 (1997), pp. 92–109.

26 Bracha Ettinger (ed.), *The Matrixial Borderspace* (Minneapolis, MN: University of Minnesota Press, 2006).

27 For a discussion on the 'matrixial gaze', refer to Noreen Giffney, Anne Mulhall and Michael O'Rourke, 'Seduction into reading: Bracha L. Ettinger's *The Matrixial Borderspace*', *Studies in the Maternal* 2 (2009), pp 1–15.

28 Griselda Pollock, 'Introduction. Femininity: aporia or sexual difference?', in Ettinger, *The Matrixial Borderspace*, pp. 1–38, p. 11.

29 John Berger, *Ways of Seeing* [1972] (London: Penguin, 2008).

30 For more information on scopophilia, see Sigmund Freud, *Three Essays on the Theory of Sexuality* [1905] (London: Hogarth, 1962).

31 In case of Mulvey's article, it is the illusion of the cinema.

32 Mulvey, 'Visual pleasure', p. 843.

33 Ibid.

34 Roland Barthes, 'The world as object', in his *Critical Essays*, trans. Richard Howard (Evanston, IL: Northwestern University Press, 1972), p. 12.

35 Foucault, "Of other spaces', *Diacritics* 16/1 (1987), pp. 22–7, p. 26.

36 Mulvey, 'Visual pleasure', p. 837.

37 Lennard J. Davis, 'Visualizing the disabled body: The classical nude and the fragmented torso', in Fraser and Greco, *The Body*, pp. 165–181, p. 168.

38 Marquard Smith, 'The uncertainty of placing: prosthetic bodies, sculptural design, and unhomely dwelling in Marc Quinn, James Gillingham, and Sigmund Freud', 2009. Available at http://www.artbrain.org/the-uncertainty-of-placing-prosthetic-bodies-sculptural-design-and-unhomely-dwelling-in-marc-quinn-james-gillingham-and-sigmund-freud/ (accessed 17 March 2010). For extensive research on the social history of the body and disability studies, refer to David T. Mitchell and Sharon L. Snyder (eds), *The Body and Physical Difference. Discourses of Disability* (Ann Arbor, MI: The University of Michigan Press, 1997); Lennard J. Davis (ed.), *The Disability Studies Reader* (London, New York: Routledge, 1997); Another more recently published book offers a comprehensive survey of the cultural and social history of the body: William Bynum and Linda Kalof (eds), *A Cultural History of the Human Body*, vols 1–6 (Oxford: Berg/Palgrave, 2010).

39 Smith, 'The uncertainty'.

40 For the articulation of identities that are located in difference, monstrosity and the grotesque, see Marsha Meskimmon, 'The monstrous and the grotesque. On the politics of excess in women's self portraiture', *Make: The Magazine of Women's Art* (1996), pp. 6–10.

41 bell hooks, *Feminist Theory From Margin to Center* (Boston, MA: South End Press, 1984) and *The Will to Change: Men, Masculinity, and Love* (New York: Atria Books, 2004).

42 Martha L. Edwards, 'Construction of physical disability in the Ancient Greek world: the community concept', in Mitchell and Snyder, *The Body*, pp. 35–50, p. 35.

43 Anita Silvers, 'From the crooked timber of humanity, beautiful things can be made', in Peg Brand Zeglin, *Beauty Matters* (Bloomington and Indianapolis, IN: Indiana University Press, 2000), pp. 197–221.
44 Mikhail Bakhtin, *Rabelais and his World* (Bloomington, IN: Indiana University Press, 1984).
45 For instance, pens produced by *Venus Pencils* in 1940s and 1950s. Suzanne Ramljak, 'Survival of the fittest: the reproductive triumph of the "Venus the Milo"', in *A Disarming Beauty: The Venus the Milo in 20th-Century Art*, exhibition catalogue (St Petersburg: Salvador Dali Museum, 2001), pp. 11, 20.
46 For an overview of the history of the figure, see Gregory Curtis, *Disarmed. The Story of the 'Venus the Milo'* (Phoenix Mill: Sutton Publishing, 2003); for various representations of Venus, see Francis Haskell and Nicholas Penny, *Taste and the Antique: The Lure of Classical Sculpture 1500–1900* (New Haven, CT and London: Yale University Press, 1982), pp. 316–33.
47 The Greek goddess Venus functioned in Roman myths as Aphrodite.
48 Curtis, *Disarmed*, p. 170.
49 For an overview of various types of representation, see for instance Pierre Grimal, *A Concise Dictionary of Classical Mythology* (Oxford: Blackwell, 1990), pp. 181–2.
50 Quoted in William Jeffett, 'An obscure object of desire: The "Venus the Milo," Surrealism and beyond', in Suzanne Ramljak, *A Disarming Beauty: 'The Venus the Milo in 20th-Century Art*, exhibition catalogue (St Petersburg: Salvador Dali Museum, 2001), pp. 51–79, p. 63.
51 For more on the act of restoration and how it led to the focus on the antique fragment, see James Hall, 'The classical ideal and sculpture's lack of modernity', in his *The World as Sculpture: The Changing Status of Sculpture from the Renaissance to the Present Day* (London: Chatto and Windus, 1999), pp. 147–71.
52 Hall offers a closer look at the notion of touch: Hall, 'Sight versus touch', ibid., pp. 80–103.
53 Edmund Burke, *Philosophical Enquiry into the Origin of Our Ideas of the Sublime and Beautiful* [1759] (Oxford: Oxford University Press, 2008), part II, sections 14 and 20, pp. 73, 77.
54 Ramljak, 'Survival of the fittest', pp. 13–5.
55 Quoted ibid., p. 16.
56 Wilhelm Jensen, *Gradiva* (Berlin: S. Fischer Verlage, 1903).
57 Jeffett, 'An obscure object', pp. 67, 68.
58 Ibid., p. 68.
59 The moon was the primal double-sexed being. See Plato, *Symposium and Phaedrus* [*c.*360BC], trans. Benjamin Jowett (1871) (New York: Dover Publications, 1993), p. 17.
60 Grimal, *A Concise Dictionary*, p. 164

61 For more on carnality and prosthesis see: Marquard Smith and Joanne Morra (eds), *The Prosthetic Impulse From a Posthuman Present to a Biocultural Future* (Cambridge, MA: MIT Press, 2006).
62 Caroline Alexander, 'Faces of war', 2007. Available at http://www.smithsonianmag.com/history-archaeology/mask.html (accessed 13 July 2009).
63 Davis, 'Visualizing the disabled body', p. 174.
64 Darian Leader and Judy Groves, *Introducing Lacan* (Cambridge: Icon Books, 2000), p. 22.
65 Susan Sontag, 'Notes on "Camp"', 1964. Available at http://interglacial.com/~sburke/pub/prose/Susan_Sontag_-_Notes_on_Camp.html (accessed 29 January 2010).
66 Philip Shaw, *The Sublime* (London and New York: Routledge, 2008), pp. 148, 149.
67 Ibid., pp. 48–71.
68 Immanuel Kant, 'Analytic of the sublime' in *The Critique of Judgement* [1790] (Oxford: The Clarendon Press, 1982), pp. 90, 91.
69 Kant distinguished two modes of representing the object as sublime, the 'mathematical sublime' and the 'dynamical sublime'. In both cases, the sublime led the mind to realise the totality of freedom, the *a priori* ground for cognition. Kant's 'mathematical sublime', where the imagination referred to the 'faculty of cognition', was exemplified by a starry sky giving a sensation of magnitude and infinity; something that went beyond sensibility and, therefore, was grasped by imagination and intuition. It was the mind's ability to yield to formlessness. In the 'dynamical sublime' imagination referred to desire, as for instance during a storm, when the soul and the will were overpowered and the sensible in human became humbled. This disturbance was compensated for by moral greatness, independent from nature's powers. It was the ability to value one's own weaknesses and distance oneself from them, while facing nature. (Ibid., pp. 94–117).
70 Thomas McEvilley, 'Turned upside down and torn apart', in Bill Beckley (ed.), *Sticky Sublime* (New York: Allworth Press, 2001), pp. 57–83, p. 74; For an extensive reading on the history of the sublime, see: Shaw, *The Sublime*, Beckley, *Sticky Sublime* and also Umberto Eco, 'Romanticism and the redemption of ugliness', in his *On Ugliness* (London: Harvill Secker, 2007), ch. x.
71 Shaw, *The Sublime*, pp. 3, 116.
72 Theodor W. Adorno, *Aesthetic Theory* (London: Routledge and Kegan Paul, 1986), quoted in McEvilley, 'Turned upside down', p. 76.
73 Jean-François Lyotard, *Lessons on the Analytic of the Sublime (Kant's 'Critique of Judgment' Sections 23–29)*, trans. Elizabeth Rottenberg (Stanford, CA: Stanford University Press, 1994).
74 Lyotard, *The Postmodern Condition*, p. 81.
75 For example by Luce Irigaray in 'Paradox a priori', in *Speculum of the Other Woman* (Ithaca, NY: Cornell University Press, 1974), pp. 203–13, Christine Battersby in *The Phenomenal Woman: Feminist Metaphysics and the Pattern*

of Identity (London: Polity Press, 1990), Jane Kneller in *Autonomy and Community* (Albany, NY: State University of New York, 1993), Joanna Zylinska in *Spider, Cyborgs and Being Scared: The Feminine and the Sublime* (Manchester: Manchester University Press, 2001), Carolyn Korsmeyer in *Gender and Aesthetics* (New York: Routledge, 2004) or Bonnie Mann in *Women's Liberation and the Sublime* (Oxford: Oxford University Press, 2006), among others.

76 McEvilley, 'Turned upside down', p. 77.

77 Jeremy Gilbert-Rolfe, 'I'm not sure it is sticky', in Beckley, *Sticky Sublime*, pp. 83–93, p. 88.

78 Wendy Steiner, 'The sublime shudder', ibid., pp. 194–200, p. 199.

79 Shaw, *The Sublime*, pp. 48–71.

80 Ibid., p. 25

81 Eco, *On Ugliness*, p. 16; For more on the history of ugliness and beauty, see also Umberto Eco (ed.), *History of Beauty*, trans. Alastair McEwen (New York: Rizzoli, 2005).

82 Victor Hugo, *The Hunchback of Notre Dame* (1831); Mary Shelley, *Frankenstein; or, The Modern Prometheus* (1818); Oscar Wilde, *The Picture of Dorian Gray* (1890).

83 Quoted in Eco, *On Ugliness*, p. 352.

84 Mark Cousins, 'The ugly', *AA Files* 28 (1995), pp. 61–4; Cousins, 'The ugly', *AA Files* 29 (1995), pp. 3–6 and 30 (1995), pp. 65–8.

85 Cousins, 'The ugly', *AA Files* 28, p. 61.

86 Ibid., p. 63.

87 Mario Vargas Llosa, 'Botero: A sumptuous abundance', in Mario Vargas Llosa, *Making Waves* (New York: Farrar, Straus & Giroux, 1996), pp. 254–67, p. 264.

88 Cousins, 'The ugly', *AA Files* 28, p. 64.

89 Ibid.

Chapter 4

1 Charles Darwin, *On the Origin of Species* (1859).

2 Anetta Mona Chişa & Lucia Tkáčová, 'The descent of man, and selection in relation to sex', 2012. Available at http://www.chitka.info/descent.html (accessed 23 September 2013).

3 Mieke Bal, *Narratology. Introduction to the Theory of Narrative* (Toronto: University of Toronto Press, 1985).

4 This new perspective embodies Judith Butler's ideas of performativity and gender. It also resonates with the concept of volatile bodies. For more information, see Judith Butler, *Undoing Gender* (New York: Routledge, 2004) and *Gender Trouble* (New York: Routledge, 1990); Elizabeth Grosz, *Volatile Bodies. Toward a Corporeal Feminism* (Bloomington, IN: Indiana University Press, 1994).

5 Lewis Carroll, *Alice's Adventures in Wonderland; and, Through the Looking-Glass, and What Alice Found There*, ed. and intro. Hugh Haughton (London: Penguin, 1998), p. 56.
6 Victoria Grace, *Baudrillard's Challenge. A Feminist Reading* (London: Routledge, 2000), pp. 37, 38.
7 Butler, *Gender Trouble.*
8 Volcano Del LaGrace, 'Dynamics of desire (an excerpt)', 1992. Available at http://www.dellagracevolcano.com/text1.html (accessed 22 March 2010).
9 The concept of 'anorexic logic' lays foundations for the term 'anorexic aesthetics'. Heywood's discourse is closely linked to androgyny, the myth of an abyss and black hole, which will be discussed in relation to ideas of Cixous, Steiner, Butler and Irigaray.
10 Wendy Steiner, *The Trouble with Beauty* (London: William Heinemann, 2001).
11 Leslie Heywood, *Dedication to Hunger. The Anorexic Aesthetic in Modern Culture* (London: University of California Press, 1996), p. 14.
12 Ibid., pp. xi, xii.
13 Plato, *Symposium*, trans. Benjamin Jowett (New York: Dover, 1993). Plato's notion of 'Forms' was based on the idea of fixed, permanent essence that was repeated by materiality as a copy.
14 Heywood, *Dedication to Hunger*, pp. 16–21.
15 René Descartes, *Meditations on First Philosophy*, trans. Laurence J. Lafleur (New York: Macmillan, 1985), p. 22.
16 Georg W. F. Hegel, *The Phenomenology of Spirit*, trans. A. V. Miller (Oxford: Oxford University Press, 1977), p. 270.
17 Heywood, *Dedication to Hunger*, pp. 19, 21–5.
18 Sigmund Freud, *Sexuality and the Psychology of Love*, ed. Phillip Rieff (New York: Collier, 1963), p. 198.
19 Ibid., p. 39.
20 Ibid., p. 9.
21 Ibid., p. 39
22 Boryana Rossa, 'The last valve', 2004. Available at http://boryanarossa.com/the-last-valve/ (accessed 15 September 2013).
23 Boryana Rossa, 'Ultrafuturo manifesto', 2004. Available at http://boryanarossa.com/category/manifestos/ (accessed 15 September 2013).
24 There are different types of female genital mutilation including removal (partial or total) of clitoris or prepuce, labia minora, labia majora, sealing the vaginal opening by repositioning the labia and stitching, or other harmful practices such as incising or piercing. It is estimated that currently female genital mutilation concerns approximately 125 million girls (most of them between infancy and the age of 15) and women in 29 countries in Africa and some countries in Asia and the Middle East. More information can be found on the World Health Organization and United Nations websites

(http://www.who.int/en/ and http://www.un.org/en/index.html) and in the revised report 'Female genital mutilation: proposals for change' written by Efua Dorkenoo and Scilla Elworthy (Minority Rights Group International, Report 92/3 (1992)).

25 World Health Organization, 'Female genital mutilation', 2014. Available at http://www.who.int/mediacentre/factsheets/fs241/en/ (accessed 28 July 2014).

26 Vladimir Ilyich Lenin, 'The last valve', 1912. Available at http://www.marxists.org/archive/lenin/works/1912/aug/05.htm (accessed 17 April 2014).

27 Rossa, 'The last valve'.

28 Ibid.

29 Carroll, *Alice's Adventures in Wonderland*, p. 13.

30 Kaja Silverman, *The Threshold of the Visible World* (New York and London: Routledge, 1996), p. 28.

31 Ibid., p. 31.

32 Sigmund Freud, 'Femininity [1933]', in *The Standard Edition of the Complete Psychological Works of Sigmund Freud*, ed. and trans. James Strachey, vol. 22 (London: Hogarth Press, 1964), pp. 112–35 and 'Female sexuality [1931]', in *The Standard Edition of the Complete Psychological Works of Sigmund Freud*, ed. and trans. James Strachey, vol. 21 (London: Hogarth Press, 1964), pp. 223–34.

33 Silverman, *The Threshold*, p. 32.

34 Ibid., pp. 32, 33. Silveman elaborates this further in *The Acoustic Mirror: The Female Voice in Psychoanalysis and Cinema* (Bloomington, IN: Indiana University Press, 1988).

35 Silverman, *The Threshold*, p. 34.

36 Sigmund Freud, 'On narcissism: an introduction', in *The Standard Edition of the Complete Psychological Works of Sigmund Freud*, ed. and trans. James Strachey, vol. 14 (London: Hogarth Press, 1957), pp. 88, 89.

37 Silverman, *The Threshold*, p. 35.

38 Laura Mulvey, 'Visual pleasure and narrative cinema' [1973], in Leo Braudy and Marshall Cohen (eds), *Film Theory and Criticism: Introductory Readings* (New York: Oxford University Press, 1999), pp. 833–44; Theresa de Lauretis, *Alice Doesn't: Feminism, Semiotics, Cinema* (Bloomington, IN: Indiana University Press, 1984).

39 Karol Sienkiewicz, 'Interview with Aleksandra Kubiak and Karolina Wiktor', in *Grupa Sędzia Główny*, exhibition catalogue (Zielona Góra: Galeria BWA, 2008), pp. 56–67, p. 57.

40 Ibid., p. 65.

41 Karol Sienkiewicz, 'Young, pretty and eager to strip!', in *Grupa Sędzia Główny*, p. 19.

42 *Grupa Sędzia Główny*, p. 142.

43 Silverman, *The Threshold*, pp. 163, 164.

44 Luce Irigaray, 'Women's exile: Interview with Luce Irigaray', trans. Couze Venn, *Ideology and Consciousness* 1 (1977), pp. 62–76, p. 64.

45 Luce Irigaray, *This Sex Which is Not One* (Ithaca, NY: Cornell University Press, 1975) and *Speculum of the Other Woman* (Ithaca, NY: Cornell University Press, 1974).
46 Jacques Derrida, 'La question du style', *Nietzsche aujourd'hui*, 2 vols, vol. 1 (Paris: Union générale d'éditions, 1973), pp. 235–87.
47 Carolyn Burke, 'Irigaray through the looking glass', *Feminist Studies* 7/2 (1981), pp. 293–4.
48 Gayatri Chakravorty Spivak, 'Translator's preface', in Jacques Derrida, *Of Grammatology* (Baltimore, MD and London: Johns Hopkins University Press, 1976), pp. viii–lxxiv.
49 Jacques Derrida, *Dissemination*, trans. Barbara Johnson (Chicago, IL: University of Chicago Press, 1981).
50 Spivak, 'Translator's preface', p. lxvi.
51 Luce Irigaray, 'The Looking Glass, from the Other Side', in *This Sex*, pp. 9–22.
52 ——, *This Sex*, p. 9.
53 Ibid., p. 30.
54 The *Langenort* was a mobile clinic, sailed by the Dutch organisation Women on Waves, to offer safe abortions to women in countries where abortion was illegal. On board the ship all the activities are legal and subject to Dutch law. National penal legislation applies only to territorial waters within the 12-mile radius or two hours sailing. More information can be found at Women on Waves, 2015. Available at http://www.womenonwaves.org/en/page/2582/ship-campaigns (accessed 13 December 2015).
55 Sienkiewicz, 'Interview', p. 63.
56 Dorota Jarecka, 'Performerska Grupa Sędzia Główny', 2006. Available at http://www.wysokieobcasy.pl/wysokie-obcasy/1,53581,3396504.html (accessed 22 April 2014).
57 Sienkiewicz, 'Interview', p. 61.
58 *Grupa Sędzia Główny*, p. 106.
59 Piotr Rypson, 'Intimare' in *Grupa Sędzia Główny*, p. 79.
60 Małgorzata Ludwisiak, 'The grammar of embarrassment', in *Grupa Sędzia Główny*, p. 110.
61 *Grupa Sędzia Główny*, p. 138.
62 Maurice Merleau-Ponty, *The Visible and the Invisible* (Evanston, IL: Northwestern University Press, 1968).
63 Silverman, *The Threshold*, p. 37.

Chapter 5

1 Gilles Deleuze and Félix Guattari, *Anti-Oedipus: Capitalism and Schizophrenia* [1972] (Minneapolis, MN: University of Minnesota Press, 1983).

2 The 'body without organs' and the 'organs-partial objects' are mobilised by Deleuze and Guattari, ibid.
3 Hartmut Böhme, 'A journey into the body and beyond: The art of Alicja Zebrowska', *Magazyn Szutki* 16/3–4, pp. 89–102. Available at http://www.culture.hu-berlin.de/hb/static/archiv/volltexte/texte/Alicja_english.html (accessed 24 April 2014).
4 *Oxford Latin Dictionary* (Oxford: Oxford University Press, 1982).
5 Judith Butler, *Gender Trouble* (New York: Routledge, 1990), pp. 18–34.
6 Jean Baudrillard, *America* (London: Verso, 1989), p. 46.
7 For reading on Foucault's discourse on sexuality, refer to Michel Foucault, *The History of Sexuality*, vol. 3: *The Care of the Self* (London: Penguin, 1990), *The History of Sexuality*, vol. 2: *The Use of Pleasure* (London: Penguin, 1992), and vol. 1: *The Will to Knowledge* (London: Penguin, 1998).
8 Jean Baudrillard, *America*, p. 47.
9 ——, 'Towards the vanishing point of art', in *The Conspiracy of Art* (New York: Semiotext(e), 2005), p. 104.
10 Ibid., pp. 104, 105.
11 'Seducere' – to lead away, to lead astray, according to the *Online Etymology Dictionary* (2001). Available at http://www.etymonline.com/index.php?search=seducere&searchmode=none (accessed 2 October 2009).
12 Hélène Cixous, 'The laugh of the Medusa', in Elaine Marks and Isabelle de Courtivron (eds), *New French Feminisms: An Anthology* (Brighton: The Harvester Press, 1981), pp. 245–64, p. 263.
13 Mary Klages, 'Hélène Cixous: "The laugh of the Medusa"', 1997. Available at http://www.webpages.uidaho.edu/~sflores/KlagesCixous.html (accessed 24 September 2009).
14 Kaja Silverman, *The Threshold of the Visible World* (New York and London: Routledge, 1996), p. 4.
15 Ibid.
16 Jean Baudrillard, 'The conspiracy of art', p. 26.
17 Cixous, 'The laugh of the Medusa', pp. 245–64.
18 Jean Baudrillard, 'Aesthetic illusion and disillusion', in *The Conspiracy of Art: Manifestos, Interviews, Essays*, ed. Sylvère Lotringer, trans. Ames Hodges (New York: Semiotext(e), 2005), pp. 111–32, p. 122 (emphasis original).
19 Jean Baudrillard, *Seduction* (New York: St Martin's Press, 1990), p. 5.
20 Butler, *Gender Trouble*, p. 7.
21 Foucault, *The History of Sexuality*, vols 1, 2 and 3.
22 Here I refer to the bourgeoisie of the late eighteenth century in the Marxist context. The 'bourgeois' describes a social class whose power derives from capital and means of production.
23 Jean Baudrillard, *Seduction*.

24 Cindy LaCom, '"It is more than lame": female disability, sexuality, and the maternal in the nineteenth-century novel', in David T. Mitchell, and Sharon L. Snyder (eds), *The Body and Physical Difference: Discourses of Disability* (Ann Arbor, MI: The University of Michigan Press, 1997), pp. 191–3.
25 Elizabeth Wilson, *The Sphinx in the City: Urban Life, the Control of Disorder, and Woman* (London: Virago, 1991).
26 Baudrillard, *Seduction*, pp. 1, 2.
27 Cixous, 'The laugh of the Medusa', p. 263.
28 Silverman, *The Threshold*, pp. 1, 2.
29 Cixous, 'The laugh of the Medusa', p. 264.
30 Ibid., p. 254.
31 Ibid.
32 Wendy Steiner, *Venus in Exile: The Rejection of Beauty in Twentieth-Century Art* (New York: Free Press, 2001); Leslie Heywood, *Dedication to Hunger. The Anorexic Aesthetic in Modern Culture* (London: University of California Press, 1996); Luce Irigaray, *Luce Irigaray: Key Writings* (London: Continuum, 2004); Judith Butler, *Undoing Gender* (New York: Routledge, 2004); Butler, *Gender Trouble*; Luce Irigaray and Margaret Whitford, *The Irigaray Reader* (Oxford: Blackwell, 1991).
33 Carolyn G. Heilbrun, *Toward a Recognition of Androgyny* (New York and London: W.W. Norton, 1993), p. x. This is a very useful source overviewing different theories of androgyny.
34 Robert Graves, *The Greek Myths* (Manchester: Carcanet, 2001), p. 58.
35 Ibid., p. 30.
36 June Singer, *Androgyny: Towards a New Theory of Sexuality* (New York: Anchor Press, 1976), p. 20.
37 Genesis 1:27 in Robert Carroll and Stephen Prickett (eds), [1611] *The Bible: Authorized King James Version* (Oxford: Oxford University Press, 2008), p. 2.
38 Plato, 'Symposium', in Plato *Symposium and Phaedrus* [*c*.360BC], trans. Benjamin Jowett [1871] (New York: Dover Publications, 1993), p. 15.
39 'That double nature, which was once called Androgynous', ibid., p. 17.
40 Singer, *Androgyny*, p. 120.
41 Heilbrun, *Toward a Recognition*, p. 12.
42 Singer, *Androgyny*, p. 20.
43 Ibid., pp. 20, 21.
44 Graves, *The Greek Myths*, p. 68.
45 Singer, *Androgyny*, pp. 30, 32. For an overview of Freud and Jung's theory of bisexuality and androgyny, see ibid., pp. 38–45; for mythic connotations, ibid., pp. 55–66.
46 Susan Sontag, 'Notes on "Camp"', 1964. Available at http://interglacial.com/~sburke/pub/prose/Susan_Sontag_-_Notes_on_Camp.html (accessed 29 January 2010).

47 Singer, *Androgyny*, p. 34 (emphasis original).
48 Judith Belladonna, Barbara Penton, *Libé*, July 1978, quoted in Baudrillard, *Seduction*, p. 24.
49 Harold Koda, *Extreme Beauty: The Body Transformed* (New York: Metropolitan Museum of Art, 2003), p. 9.
50 Dorothy Schefer, *What is Beauty?: New Definitions from the Fashion Vanguard* (London: Thames and Hudson, 1997), p. 9.
51 Caitlyn Jenner, 'The journey begins', updated 29 July 2015. Available at http://caitlynjenner.com/category/my-story/ (accessed 15 July 2015).
52 Koda, *Extreme beauty*, pp. 9, 10.
53 Ibid., p. 10.
54 Those are just two examples of sexless pronouns. For an overview of various gender-neutral pronouns, see Richard Creel, 'Ze, Zer, Mer', 1977. Available at http://web.archive.org/web/20080418000432/http://www.apa.udel.edu/apa/archive/newsletters/v97n1/teaching/ze.asp (accessed 30 May 2010; no longer available).
55 Marc Quinn and Joachim Pissarro, 'The journey not the destination', in *Marc Quinn. Allanah, Buck, Catman, Chelsea, Michael, Pamela and Thomas*, exhibition catalogue (London: White Cube, 2010), p. 106.
56 Butler, *Undoing Gender*, p. 42.
57 Irigaray, *Luce Irigaray*, pp. ix, x, xii.
58 Butler, *Undoing Gender*, p. 186.
59 Cixous, 'The laugh of the Medusa', p. 262.
60 Baudrillard, *Seduction*, p. 6.
61 Jean Baudrillard, *The Perfect Crime* (London, New York: Verso, 2008), p. 117.
62 '"Troubling Desire(s) in Art": Queer Symposium', Birmingham City University Department of Art, 14 November 2009 (http://www.aah.org.uk/post/109).
63 Herbert Marcuse, *Eros and Civilization* (Boston, MA: Beacon Press, 1955), quoted in Jonathan D. Katz, 'Art, Eros and the sixties', 2009. Available at http://www.aah.org.uk/post/109 (accessed 10 March 2010).
64 Volcano Del LaGrace, 'Statement', 2005 (emphasis original). Available at http://www.dellagracevolcano.com/statement.html (accessed 22 March 2010).
65 Volcano Del LaGrace, 20 November 2009. Available at http://www.facebook.com/pages/Del-LaGrace-Volcano/18754989764?ref=ts&v=wall (accessed 22 March 2010).
66 Butler, *Gender Trouble*, p. 17.
67 Jean Baudrillard, 'The finest consumer object. The body', in Mariam Fraser and Monica Greco (eds), *The Body. A Reader* (London and New York: Routledge, 2005), pp. 277–82, p. 277 (emphasis original).
68 Ibid., p. 280 (emphasis original).
69 Graves, *The Greek Myths*, p. 49.

70 Anne Koedt, 'The myth of the vaginal orgasm', 1970. Available at http://www.uic.edu/orgs/cwluherstory/CWLUArchive/vaginalmyth.html (accessed 17 March 2010).
71 Baudrillard, *The Perfect Crime*, p. 116.
72 Ibid., p. 119.
73 Ibid., p. 120.
74 Quoted in Andrew Causey, *Sculpture since 1945* (Oxford: Oxford University Press, 1998), p. 259.
75 Sigmund Freud, 'Medusa's head' [1922], in *The Standard Edition of the Complete Psychological Works of Sigmund Freud*, ed. and trans. James Strachey, vol. 18 (London: Hogarth Press, 1955), p. 273.
76 Klages, 'Hélène Cixous'.
77 Freud, 'Medusa's head', pp. 273, 274.
78 Cixous, 'The laugh of the Medusa', p. 255.
79 Baudrillard, *Seduction*, pp. 93-94.
80 See also Roland Barthes's concept of difference radicalised in the 'critique of desire' and 'the text as a thing' in *Roland Barthes* (Basingstoke: Palgrave Macmillan, 1988) and *The Pleasure of the Text* (New York: Farrar, Straus & Giroux, 1975).
81 Mario Perniola, 'Feeling the difference', in James E. Swearingen and Joanne Cutting-Gray (eds), *Extreme Beauty: Aesthetics, Politics, Death* (New York, London: Continuum, 2002), pp. 7–9.
82 For an overview of narratives concerning the sexed body image, refer to Elizabeth Grosz, *Volatile Bodies. Toward a Corporeal Feminism* (Bloomington, IN: Indiana University Press, 1994) and Gail Weiss, *Embodiments as Intercorporeality* (London and New York: Routledge, 1998).
83 Cixous, 'The laugh of the Medusa', p. 255.
84 Susan Sontag, 'An argument about beauty', *Daedalus* (2002), pp. 21–6, p. 24.
85 Silverman, *The Threshold*, p. 3.
86 Lewis Carroll, *Alice's Adventures in Wonderland; and, Through the Looking-Glass, and What Alice Found There*, ed. and intro. Hugh Haughton (London: Penguin, 1998), pp. 239, 240.
87 Jean Baudrillard, *The Transparency of Evil* [1990], trans. James Benedict (London and New York: Verso, 2002), p. 56.
88 Ibid., p. 113.
89 Baudrillard, *The Perfect Crime*, p. 5.
90 Sigmund Freud, 'Beyond the pleasure principle', in *The Standard Edition of the Complete Psychological Works of Sigmund Freud*, ed. and trans. James Strachey, vol. 18 (London: Hogarth Press, 1955), p. 15.
91 Jean Baudrillard, *Paroxysm: Interviews with Philippe Petit* (London: Verso, 1998), p. 35.

92 Ibid., p. 13
93 Baudrillard, *The Perfect Crime*, p. 3
94 Luce Irigaray, *This Sex Which is Not One* (Ithaca, NY: Cornell University Press, 1975) and *Speculum of the Other Woman* (Ithaca, NY: Cornell University Press, 1974).
95 Baudrillard, 'Towards the vanishing point', p. 110.
96 ——, *The Transparency*, p. 23.
97 ——, 'Towards the vanishing point', p. 110.
98 At the Human Condition Series third international interdisciplinary conference *Eros* in Bracebridge, Canada (20–22 May 2010), Luce Irigaray presented a paper, 'Perhaps cultivating Eros could provide for our safety', which has not yet been published and will contribute to a new publication by the author. Here I refer to Irigaray's paper.
99 Ibid.
100 Baudrillard, *The Perfect Crime*, p. 101
101 ——, *The Transparency*, p. 7.
102 Ibid., p. 10.
103 Susan Stryker, 'Transgender studies: Queer Theory's evil twin', *GLQ: A Journal of Lesbian and Gay Studies* 10/2 (2004), pp. 212–5; Sandy Stone, 'The 'empire' strikes back: a posttransexual manifesto', [1984] 1987. Available at http://sterneck.net/gender/stone-posttranssexuel/index.php (accessed 15 August 2010).
104 Kate Bornstein, *Gender Outlaw: On Men, Women, and the Rest of Us* (London: Routledge, 1994).
105 Baudrillard, *The Transparency*, p. 122.
106 Joe Raposo, 'It's not easy being green', 1970. Available at http://lyricsplayground.com/alpha/songs/i/itsnoteasybeinggreen.shtml (accessed 9 July 2010).
107 Ibid.
108 Hanna Wróblewska, *In Art Dreams Come True. Katarzyna Kozyra.* (Wrocław: BWA Wrocław, 2007), p. 32.

Postscript

1 Jean Baudrillard, 'Towards the vanishing', in *The Transparency of Evil* [1990], trans. James Benedict (London and New York: Verso, 2002), p. 110.

Bibliography

Adorno, Theodor W., *Aesthetic Theory* (London: Routledge and Kegan Paul, 1986).

Alexander, Caroline, 'Faces of war', 2007. Available at http://www.smithsonianmag.com/history-archaeology/mask.html (accessed 13 July 2009).

Althusser, Louis, *Lenin and Philosophy and Other Essays* (New York: Monthly Review Press, 1968).

András, Edit, 'Gender minefield: the heritage of the past', *n.paradoxa* 11 (1999), pp. 4–9.

Araeen, Rasheed, 'Cultural imperialism: Observations on cultural situation in the Third World', in Dave Beech (ed.), *Beauty* (London: MIT Press, 2009), pp. 175–9.

Atwood, Margaret, *The Edible Woman* (London: Virago Press, 1997).

Bakhtin, Mikhail, *The Dialogic Imagination* (Austin, TX: University of Texas Press, 1981).

______ *Rabelais and his World* (Bloomington, IN: Indiana University Press, 1984).

Bal, Mieke, *Narratology. Introduction to the Theory of Narrative* (Toronto: University of Toronto Press, 1985).

______ *Quoting Caravaggio. Contemporary Art, Preposterous History* (Chicago, IL and London: University of Chicago Press, 1999).

______ *Travelling Concepts in the Humanities: A Rough Guide* (Toronto and London: University of Toronto Press, 2002).

Barthes, Roland, *Critical Essays*, trans. Richard Howard (Evanston, IL: Northwestern University Press, 1972).

______ *The Pleasure of the Text* (New York: Farrar, Straus & Giroux, 1975).

______ *Camera Lucida* (New York: Hill and Wang, 1981).

______ *Roland Barthes* (Basingstoke: Palgrave Macmillan, 1988).

Battersby, Christine, *The Phenomenal Woman: Feminist Metaphysics and the Pattern of Identity* (London: Polity Press, 1990).

______ 'Just jamming: Irigaray, painting and psychoanalysis', in Katy Deepwell (ed.), *New Feminist Art Criticism: Critical Strategies* (Manchester: Manchester University Press, 1995), pp. 128–137.

Baudrillard, Jean, *The Mirror of Production* (St Louis: Telos Press, 1975).

______ *America* (London: Verso, 1989)

______ *Seduction* (New York: St Martin's Press, 1990).

______ *Paroxysm: Interviews with Philippe Petit* (London: Verso, 1998).

______ *The Transparency of Evil* [1990], trans. James Benedict (London and New York: Verso, 2002).

______ *The Conspiracy of Art: Manifestos, Interviews, Essays, ed. Sylvère Lotringer, trans. Ames Hodges* (New York: Semiotext(e), 2005).

______ 'The finest consumer object. The body', in Mariam Fraser and Monica Greco (eds), *The Body. A Reader* (London and New York: Routledge, 2005), pp. 277–82.

______ *The Perfect Crime* (London, New York: Verso, 2008).

Benezra, Neal David, Olga M. Viso, and Arthur C. Danto, *Regarding Beauty: A View of the Late Twentieth Century*, exhibition catalogue (Washington DC: Hirshhorn Museum and Sculpture Garden, Smithsonian Institution, 1999).

Benson, Dana 'Beauty optional', 2003. Available at http://issuu.com/riceuniversity/docs/rice_summer_2003/49 (accessed 1 November July 2015).

Berger, John, *Ways of Seeing* [1972] (London: Penguin, 2008).

Böhme, Hartmut, 'A journey into the body and beyond: The art of Alicja Zebrowska', *Magazyn Szutki* 16/3–4, pp. 89–102. Available at http://www.culture.hu-berlin.de/hb/static/archiv/volltexte/texte/Alicja_english.html (accessed 24 April 2014).

Bordo, Susan, 'Beauty (re)discovers the male body', in Peg Brand Zeglin, *Beauty Matters* (Bloomington and Indianapolis, IN: Indiana University Press, 2000), pp. 112–68.

Borges, Jorge Luis, *The Book of Imaginary Beings* (London: Vintage, 2002).

Bornstein, Kate, *Gender Outlaw: On Men, Women, and the Rest of Us* (London: Routledge, 1994).

Brand Zeglin, Peg (ed.), *Beauty Matters* (Bloomington and Indianapolis, IN: Indiana University Press, 2000).

Brunnbauer, Ulf, 'From equality without democracy to democracy without equality: Women and transition in South-East Europe', *South-East Europe Review* 3/3 (2000), pp. 151–8.

Burke, Carolyn, 'Irigaray through the looking glass', *Feminist Studies* 7/2 (1981), pp. 293–4.

Burke, Edmund, *Philosophical Enquiry into the Origin of Our Ideas of the Sublime and Beautiful* [1759] (Oxford: Oxford University Press, 2008).

Butler, Judith, *Gender Trouble* (New York: Routledge, 1990).

______ *Undoing Gender* (New York: Routledge, 2004).

Bynum, William and Linda Kalof (eds), *A Cultural History of the Human Body*, vols 1–6 (Oxford: Berg/Palgrave, 2010).

Carroll, Lewis, *Alice's Adventures in Wonderland; and, Through the Looking-Glass, and What Alice Found There*, ed. and intro. Hugh Haughton (London: Penguin, 1998).

Carroll, Robert and Stephen Prickett (eds), *The Bible: Authorized King James Version* [1611] (Oxford: Oxford University Press, 2008).

Causey, Andrew, *Sculpture since 1945* (Oxford: Oxford University Press, 1998).

Chişa, Anetta Mona & Lucia Tkáčová, 'The descent of man, and selection in relation to sex', 2012. Available at http://www.chitka.info/descent.html (accessed 23 September 2013).

______ 'Vessel', 2012. Available at http://www.chitka.info/vessel.html (accessed 14 September 2013).

Cixous, Hélène, 'The laugh of the Medusa', in Elaine Marks and Isabelle de Courtivron (eds), *New French Feminisms: An Anthology* (Brighton: The Harvester Press, 1981), pp. 245–64.

Connor, Steven, *Postmodernist Culture: An Introduction to Theories of the Contemporary* (Oxford: Blackwell, 1997).
Cousins, Mark, 'The ugly', *AA Files* 28 (1995), pp. 61–4.
______ 'The ugly', *AA Files* 29 (1995), pp. 3–6.
______ 'The ugly', *AA Files* 30 (1995), pp. 65–8.
Creel, Richard, 'Ze, Zer, Mer', 1977. Available at http://web.archive.org/web/20080418000432/http://www.apa.udel.edu/apa/archive/newsletters/v97n1/teaching/ze.asp (accessed 30 May 2010; no longer available).
Curtis, Gregory, *Disarmed. The Story of the 'Venus the Milo'* (Phoenix Mill: Sutton Publishing, 2003).
Danto, Arthur C., *The Abuse of Beauty: Aesthetics and the Concept of Art* (Chicago, IL: Open Court, 2003).
Davis, Lennard J. (ed.), *The Disability Studies Reader* (London, New York: Routledge, 1997).
______ 'Visualizing the disabled body: The classical nude and the fragmented torso', in Mariam Fraser and Monica Greco (eds), *The Body. A Reader* (London and New York: Routledge, 2005), pp. 165–181.
Debord, Guy, *The Society of the Spectacle* (New York: Zone Books, 1994).
Deleuze, Gilles, *The Logic of Sense* [1990] (London: Continuum, 2011).
______ and Félix Guattari, *Anti-Oedipus: Capitalism and Schizophrenia* [1972] (Minneapolis, MN: University of Minnesota Press, 1983).
Derrida, Jacques, 'La question du style', in *Nietzsche aujourd'hui*, 2 vols, vol. 1 (Paris: Union générale d'éditions, 1973), pp. 235–87.
______ *Dissemination*, trans. Barbara Johnson (Chicago, IL: University of Chicago Press, 1981).
______ *The Post Card: From Socrates to Freud and Beyond* (Chicago, IL: University of Chicago Press, 1987).
______ *The Truth in Painting* (Chicago, IL: Chicago University Press, 1987).
______ *The Ear of the Other: Otobiography, Transference, Translation* (Lincoln, NE: University of Nebraska Press, 1988).
______ 'Politics of friendship', *American Imago* 50/3 (1993), pp. 353–91.
______ *The Politics of Friendship*, trans. George Collins (London, New York: Verso, 2005).
de Saussure, Ferdinand, *Course in General Linguistics* (New York: McGraw Hill, 1966).
Descartes, René, *Meditations on First Philosophy*, trans. Laurence J. Lafleur (New York: Macmillan, 1985).
Docherty, Thomas, *Postmodernism. A Reader* (New York: Columbia University Press, 1993).
Dorkenoo, Efua and Scilla Elworthy, 'Female genital mutilation: Proposals for change', Minority Rights Group International, Report 92/3 (1992).
Eco, Umberto (ed.), *History of Beauty*, trans. Alastair McEwen (New York: Rizzoli, 2005).
______ *On Ugliness* (London: Harvill Secker, 2007).
Edwards, Martha L., 'Construction of physical disability in the Ancient Greek world: The community concept', in David T. Mitchell, and Sharon L. Snyder (eds), *The Body and Physical Difference: Discourses of Disability* (Ann Arbor, MI: The University of Michigan Press, 1997), pp. 35–50.
Ettinger, Bracha, *The Matrixial Borderspace* (Minneapolis, MN: University of Minnesota Press, 2006).
Foster, Hal (ed.), *Postmodern Culture* (London: Pluto, 1985).
______ *Compulsive Beauty* (Cambridge, MA and London: MIT Press, 1995).
Foucault, Michel, *The Birth of the Clinic: An Archaeology of Medical Perception* (New York: Random House, 1963).

______ *Discipline and Punish: The Birth of the Prison*, trans. Alan Sheridan (London: Allen Lane, 1977).

______ 'Of other spaces', *Diacritics* 16/1 (1987), pp. 22–7.

______ *The History of Sexuality*, vol. 3: *The Care of the Self* (London: Penguin, 1990), *The History of Sexuality*, vol. 2: *The Use of Pleasure* (London: Penguin, 1992), and vol. 1: *The Will to Knowledge* (London: Penguin, 1998).

______ *The Order of Things: An Archaeology of the Human Sciences* (London and New York: Routledge, 2002).

Freud, Sigmund, *The Interpretation of Dreams*, trans. A.A. Brill (New York: Macmillan, 1913).

______ *Totem and Taboo* [1913] trans. J. Strachey (London: Routledge and Kegan Paul, 1950).

______ 'Beyond the pleasure principle', in *The Standard Edition of the Complete Psychological Works of Sigmund Freud*, ed. and trans. James Strachey, vol. 18 (London: Hogarth Press, 1955).

______ 'Medusa's Head' [1922], in *The Standard Edition of the Complete Psychological Works of Sigmund Freud*, ed. and trans. James Strachey, vol. 18 (London: Hogarth Press, 1955).

______ 'On narcissism: An introduction' [1914] in *The Standard Edition of the Complete Psychological Works of Sigmund Freud*, ed. and trans. James Strachey, vol. 14 (London: Hogarth Press, 1957).

______ 'Some psychical consequences of the anatomical distinction between the sexes' [1925], in *The Standard Edition of the Complete Psychological Works of Sigmund Freud*, ed. and trans. James Strachey, vol. 19 (London: Hogarth Press, 1961).

______ *Three Essays on the Theory of Sexuality* [1905] (London: Hogarth, 1962).

______ *Sexuality and the Psychology of Love*, ed. Phillip Rieff (New York: Collier, 1963).

______ 'Female sexuality [1931]', in *The Standard Edition of the Complete Psychological Works of Sigmund Freud*, ed. and trans. James Strachey, vol. 21 (London: Hogarth Press, 1964), pp. 223–34.

______ 'Femininity [1933]', in *The Standard Edition of the Complete Psychological Works of Sigmund Freud*, ed. and trans. James Strachey, vol. 22 (London: Hogarth Press, 1964), pp. 112–35.

Fricke, Harald, 'Gender trouble and fairytales: On Katarzyna Kozyra's *In Art Dreams Come True*', in Hanna Wróblewska, *In Art Dreams Come True. Katarzyna Kozyra*. (Wrocław: BWA Wrocław, 2007), pp. 35–41.

Gal, Susan and Gail Kligman, (eds), *The Politics of Gender after Socialism: A Comparative-Historical Essay* (Princeton, NJ: Princeton University Press, 2000).

Garber, Marjorie, *Vested Interests: Cross-Dressing and Cultural Anxiety* (London: Routledge 1997).

Gatens, Moira and Genevieve Lloyd, *Collective Imaginings: Spinoza Past and Present* (London and New York: Routledge, 1999), pp. 77, 123.

Giffney, Noreen, Anne Mulhall and Michael O'Rourke, 'Seduction into reading: Bracha L. Ettinger's *The Matrixial Borderspace*', *Studies in the Maternal* (2009), pp 1–15.

Gilbert-Rolfe, Jeremy, 'I'm not sure it is sticky', in Bill Beckley (ed.), *Sticky Sublime* (New York: Allworth Press, 2001), pp. 83–93.

Goldberger, Paul, 'Klaus Kertess and the Making of the Whitney Biennial', *The New York Times Magazine*, February 26 (1995), p. 61.

Gorządek, Ewa, Stach Stabłowski, and Joanna Rajkowska, 'They are cutting my fing'rs', in *Satisfaction Guaranteed*, exhibition catalogue (Warsaw: Centrum Sztuki Współczesnej Zamek Ujazdowski, 2000), pp. 9–11.

Goux, Jean-Joseph, 'The phallus: Masculine identity and the "exchange of women"', *differences* 4/1 (1992), pp. 40–75.

Grace, Victoria, *Baudrillard's Challenge. A Feminist Reading* (London: Routledge, 2000).

Grant, Michael, *Myths of the Greeks and Romans* (London: Weidenfeld and Nicolson, 1962).

Graves, Robert, *The Greek Myths* (Manchester: Carcanet, 2001).

Grimal, Pierre, *A Concise Dictionary of Classical Mythology* (Oxford: Blackwell, 1990).

Grosz, Elizabeth, *Jacques Lacan: A Feminist Introduction* (New York and London: Routledge, 1990).

______ *Volatile Bodies: Toward a Corporeal Feminism* (Bloomington, IN: Indiana University Press, 1994).

Grupa Sędzia Główny, exhibition catalogue (Zielona Góra: Galeria BWA, 2008).

Guzek, Łukasz, 'Alicja Żebrowska', in Grzegorz Borkowski, Adam Mazur and Monika Branicka (eds), *New Phenomena in Polish Art after 2000* (Centre for Contemporary Art Ujazdowski Castle: Warsaw, 2007), pp. 326–7.

Haden-Guest, Anthony, 'On the track of the "S" word: a reporter's notes', in Bill Beckley (ed.), *Sticky Sublime* (New York: Allworth Press, 2001), pp. 49–56.

Hall, James, *The World as Sculpture. The Changing Status of Sculpture from the Renaissance to the Present Day* (London: Chatto and Windus, 1999).

Haskell, Francis and Nicholas Penny, *Taste and the Antique. The Lure of Classical Sculpture 1500–1900* (New Haven, CT and London: Yale University Press, 1982).

Heartney, Eleanor, 'Foreword: cutting two ways with beauty', in Peg Brand Zeglin, *Beauty Matters* (Bloomington and Indianapolis, IN: Indiana University Press, 2000), pp. xiii–xv.

Hegel, Georg W.F., *The Phenomenology of Spirit*, trans. A. V. Miller (Oxford: Oxford University Press, 1977).

Heilbrun, Carolyn G., *Toward a Recognition of Androgyny* (New York and London: W.W. Norton, 1993).

Heywood, Leslie, *Dedication to Hunger. The Anorexic Aesthetic in Modern Culture* (London: University of California Press, 1996).

Hickey, Dave, *The Invisible Dragon: Four Essays on Beauty* (Los Angeles, CA: Art Issues Press, 1993).

hooks, bell, *Feminist Theory From Margin to Center* (Boston, MA: South End Press, 1984).

______ *Black Looks: Race and Representation* (New York: South End Press, 1992).

______ *The Will to Change: Men, Masculinity, and Love* (New York: Atria Books, 2004).

Hudson, Suzanne Perling, 'Beauty and the status of contemporary criticism', in Dave Beech (ed.), *Beauty* (London: MIT Press, 2009), pp. 50–58.

Irigaray, Luce, *Speculum of the Other Woman* (Ithaca, NY: Cornell University Press, 1974).

______ *This Sex Which is Not One* (Ithaca, NY: Cornell University Press, 1975).

______ 'Women's exile: interview with Luce Irigaray', trans. Couze Venn, *Ideology and Consciousness* 1 (1977), pp. 62–76.

______ *Luce Irigaray: Key Writings* (London: Continuum, 2004).

______ and Margaret Whitford, *The Irigaray Reader* (Oxford: Blackwell, 1991).

Jacobsson, Eva-Maria, 'A female gaze?', 1999. Available at http://cid.nada.kth.se/pdf/cid_51.pdf (accessed 11 August 2010).

Jarecka, Dorota, 'Performerska Grupa Sędzia Główny', 2006. Available at http://www.wysokieobcasy.pl/wysokie-obcasy/1,53581,3396504.html (accessed 22 April 2014).

______ and Joanna Rajkowska, 'Joanna Rajkowska. Palma mnie przerosła', 2007. Available at http://www.wysokieobcasy.pl/wysokie-obcasy/1,53581,4495611.html?as=3 (accessed 17 March 2014).

Jeffett, William, 'An obscure object of desire: The 'Venus the Milo', Surrealism and beyond', in Suzanne Ramljak, *A Disarming Beauty: 'The Venus the Milo in 20th-Century Art*, exhibition catalogue (St Petersburg: Salvador Dali Museum, 2001), pp. 51–79.

Jencks, Charles, *The Post-Modern Reader* (London and New York: Academy Editions, St Martin's Press, 1992).

Jenkins, Keith. *The Postmodern History Reader* (London: Routledge, 1997).

Jenner, Caitlyn, 'The journey begins', updated 29 July 2015. Available at http://caitlyn-jenner.com/category/my-story/ (accessed 15 July 2015).

Jensen, Wilhelm, *Gradiva* (Berlin: S. Fischer Verlage, 1903).

Johnson, Janet Elise and Jean C. Robinson (eds), *Living Gender After Communism* (Bloomington, IN: Indiana University Press, 2006).

Jones, Amelia (ed.), *The Feminism and Visual Culture Reader* (New York and London: Routledge, 2003).

Kanneh, Kadiatu, 'Feminism and the colonial body', in Bill Ashcroft, Gareth Griffiths and Helen Tiffin (eds), *Post-colonial Studies Reader* (New York and London: Routledge, 1995), pp. 250–5.

Kant, Immanuel, *The Critique of Judgement* [1790] (Oxford: The Clarendon Press, 1982).

Katz, Jonathan D., 'Art, Eros and the sixties', 2009. Available at http://www.aah.org.uk/post/109 (accessed 10 March 2010).

Kirwan, James, *Beauty* (Manchester: Manchester University Press, 1999).

Klages, Mary, 'Hélène Cixous: "The laugh of the Medusa"', 1997. Available at http://www.webpages.uidaho.edu/~sflores/KlagesCixous.html (accessed 24 September 2009).

Kneller Jane, *Autonomy and Community* (Albany, NY: State University of New York, 1993).

Koda, Harold, *Extreme Beauty: The Body Transformed* (New York: Metropolitan Museum of Art, 2003).

Koedt, Anne, 'The myth of the vaginal orgasm', 1970. Available at http://www.uic.edu/orgs/cwluherstory/CWLUArchive/vaginalmyth.html (accessed 17 March 2010).

Korsmeyer, Carolyn, *Gender and Aesthetics* (New York: Routledge, 2004).

Kowalczyk, Izabela, 'The ambivalent beauty', in Edit Andras, Keti Chukrov and Branko Dimitrijevia, *Gender Check: Femininity and Masculinity in the Art of Eastern Europe*, exhibition catalogue Cologne: Buchhandlung Walther König GmbH & Co. KG. Abt. Verlag, 2009), pp. 38–45.

Krauss, Rosalind, *The Optical Unconscious* (London: MIT Press, 1993).

Kristeva, Julia, *Tales of Love* (New York: Columbia University Press, 1987).

Lacan, Jacques, 'Of structure as the inmixing of an otherness prerequisite to any subject whatever', in Richard Macksey and Eugenio Donato (eds), *The Languages of Criticism and the Sciences of Man: The Structuralist Controversy* (Baltimore, MD: Johns Hopkins Press 1970), pp. 186–200.

______ *Écrits: A Selection* (New York: Norton, 1977).

______ *Four Fundamental Concepts of Psycho-analysis*, trans. Alan Sheridan (New York: Norton, 1978).

______ *The Seminar of Jacques Lacan. Book I: Freud's Papers on Technique 1953–1954*, ed. Jacques-Alain Miller, trans. John Forrester (New York and London: Norton, 1988).

LaCom, Cindy, '"It is more than lame": female disability, sexuality, and the maternal in the nineteenth-century novel', in David T. Mitchell, and Sharon L. Snyder (eds), *The Body and Physical Difference. Discourses of Disability* (Ann Arbor, MI: The University of Michigan Press, 1997), pp. 191–3.

LaGrace, Volcano Del, 'Dynamics of desire (an excerpt)', 1992. Available at http://www.dellagracevolcano.com/text1.html (accessed 22 March 2010).

______ 'Statement', 2005. Available at http://www.dellagracevolcano.com/statement.html (accessed 22 March 2010).

______ 20 November 2009. Available at http://www.facebook.com/pages/Del-LaGrace-Volcano/18754989764?ref=ts&v=wall (accessed 22 March 2010).

Lauretis, Theresa de, *Alice Doesn't: Feminism, Semiotics, Cinema* (Bloomington, IN: Indiana University Press, 1984).

Leader, Darian and Judy Groves, *Introducing Lacan* (Cambridge: Icon Books, 2000).

Lebensztejn, Jean-Claude and Kate Cooper, 'Photorealism, kitsch and Venturi', *SubStance* 10/31 (1981), pp. 75–104.

Lenin, Vladimir Ilyich, 'The last valve', 1912. Available at http://www.marxists.org/archive/lenin/works/1912/aug/05.htm (accessed 17 April 2014).

Lewis, Reina, 'Looking good: The lesbian gaze and fashion imagery', *Feminist Review* 55 (1997), pp. 92–109.

Ludwisiak, Małgorzata, 'The grammar of embarrassment', in *Grupa Sędzia Główny*, exhibition catalogue (Zielona Góra: Galeria BWA, 2008), pp. 110–112.

Lyotard, Jean-François, *Lessons on the Analytic of the Sublime (Kant's 'Critique of Judgment' Sections 23–29)*, trans. Elizabeth Rottenberg (Stanford, CA: Stanford University Press, 1994).

______ *The Postmodern Condition: A Report on Knowledge* (Minneapolis, MN: University of Minnesota Press, 1994).

Mann, Bonnie, *Women's Liberation and the Sublime* (Oxford: Oxford University Press, 2006).

Marcuse, Herbert, *Eros and Civilization* (Boston, MA: Beacon Press, 1955).

McEvilley, Thomas, 'Turned upside down and torn apart', in Bill Beckley (ed.), *Sticky Sublime* (New York: Allworth Press, 2001), pp. 57–83.

Merleau-Ponty, Maurice, *The Visible and the Invisible* (Evanston, IL: Northwestern University Press, 1968).

Meskimmon, Marsha, 'The monstrous and the grotesque. On the politics of excess in women's self portraiture', *Make: The Magazine of Women's Art* (1996), pp. 6–1.

______ *Contemporary Art and the Cosmopolitan Imagination* (London and New York: Routledge, 2011).

Minh-ha, Trinh T., *Woman, Native, Other: Writing Postcoloniality and Feminism* (Bloomington, IN: Indiana University Press, 1989).

Mitchell, David T. and Sharon L. Snyder (eds), *The Body and Physical Difference. Discourses of Disability* (Ann Arbor, MI: The University of Michigan Press, 1997).

Mulvey, Laura, 'Visual pleasure and narrative cinema' [1973], in Leo Braudy and Marshall Cohen (eds), *Film Theory and Criticism: Introductory Readings* (New York: Oxford University Press, 1999), pp. 833–44.

Nalini, Paul, 'Other ways of looking: the female gaze in Jean Rhys' *Wide Sargasso Sea*', *eSharp*, 2004. Available at http://www.gla.ac.uk/research/az/esharp/issues/2/paul/ (accessed 9 November 2015).

Ostrow, Saul, 'The eternal problem of beauty's return', *Art Journal* 62/3 (2003), pp. 113–115.

Owens, Craig, 'The discourse of others: feminists and postmodernism', in Hal Foster (ed.), *Postmodern Culture* (London: Pluto, 1985), pp. 57–82.

Oxford Latin Dictionary (Oxford: Oxford University Press, 1982).

Pejić, Bojana, 'i aM a venus, A conch, a kiT, a Cat, a Lot', 2012. Available at http://rotwandgallery.com/exhibitions/anetta-mona-Chişa-lucia-tkacova-2012 (accessed 17 April 2014).

Perniola, Mario, 'Feeling the difference', in James E. Swearingen and Joanne Cutting-Gray (eds), *Extreme Beauty: Aesthetics, Politics, Death* (New York, London: Continuum, 2002), pp. 7–9.

Pierce, Charles Sanders, *Philosophical Writings of Pierce*, ed. Justus Buchler (New York: Dover Publications Inc., 1955).

Plato, *Symposium and Phaedrus* [*c*.360BC], trans. Benjamin Jowett [1871] (New York: Dover Publications, 1993).

Pollock, Griselda, 'Modernity and the spaces of femininity', in Nicholas Mirzoeff (ed.), *The Visual Culture Reader* (London and New York: Routledge, 1988), pp. 74–84.

______ 'Introduction. Femininity: aporia or sexual difference?', in Bracha Ettinger, *The Matrixial Borderspace* (Minneapolis, MN: University of Minnesota Press, 2006), pp. 1–38.

Pratt, Mary Louise, *Imperial Eyes: Travel Writing and Transculturation* (London, New York: Routledge, 1992).

Quinn, Marc and Joachim Pissarro, 'The journey not the destination', in *Marc Quinn. Allanah, Buck, Catman, Chelsea, Michael, Pamela and Thomas*, exhibition catalogue (London: White Cube, 2010), p. 106.

Rajkowska, Joanna, 'Satisfaction guaranteed', 2000. Available at http://www.rajkowska.com/en/inne/159 (accessed 8 March 2014).

______ 'Satisfaction guaranteed: Products, text', 2000. Available at http://www.rajkowska.com/en/inne/149 (accessed 9 March 2014).

Ramljak, Suzanne, *A Disarming Beauty: 'The Venus the Milo in 20th-Century Art*, exhibition catalogue (St Petersburg: Salvador Dali Museum, 2001).

Rancière, Jacques, *The Emancipated Spectator* (London: Verso Books, 2009).

Raposo, Joe, 'It's not easy being green', 1970. Available at http://lyricsplayground.com/alpha/songs/i/itsnoteasybeinggreen.shtml (accessed 9 July 2010).

Readings, Bill, *Introducing Lyotard: Art and Politics* (London: Routledge, 1991).

Robinson, Hilary, 'Border crossings: womanliness, body, representation', in Katy Deepwell (ed.), *New Feminist Art Criticism: Critical Strategies* (Manchester: Manchester University Press, 1995), pp. 138–46.

______ 'Whose beauty? Women, art, and intersubjectivity in Lucy Irigaray's writings', in Peg Brand Zeglin, *Beauty Matters* (Bloomington and Indianapolis, IN: Indiana University Press, 2000), pp. 224–51.

Rossa, Boryana, 'The last valve', 2004. Available at http://boryanarossa.com/the-last-valve/ (accessed 15 September 2013).

______ 'Ultrafuturo manifesto', 2004. Available at http://boryanarossa.com/category/manifestos/ (accessed 15 September 2013).

______ SZ-ZS performance', 2005. Available at http://boryanarossa.com/sz-zs-performance/ (accessed 14 September 2013).

Rypson, Piotr, 'Intimare' in *Grupa Sędzia Główny*, exhibition catalogue (Zielona Góra: Galeria BWA, 2008), pp. 76–79.

Schefer, Dorothy, *What is Beauty?: New Definitions from the Fashion Vanguard* (London: Thames and Hudson, 1997).

Schilder, Paul, *The Image and Appearance of the Human Body* (New York: International Universities Press, 1935).

Shaw, Philip, *The Sublime* (London and New York: Routledge, 2008).

Shohat, Ella, *Talking Visions: Multicultural Feminism in a Transnational Age* (Cambridge, MA: MIT Press, 1998).

Sienkiewicz, Karol, 'Interview with Aleksandra Kubiak and Karolina Wiktor', in *Grupa Sędzia Główny*, exhibition catalogue (Zielona Góra: Galeria BWA, 2008), pp. 56–67.

______ 'Young, pretty and eager to strip!', in *Grupa Sędzia Główny*, exhibition catalogue (Zielona Góra: Galeria BWA, 2008), pp. 19–21.

Silverman, Kaja, *The Acoustic Mirror: The Female Voice in Psychoanalysis and Cinema* (Bloomington, IN: Indiana University Press, 1988).

______ *The Threshold of the Visible World* (New York and London: Routledge, 1996).

Silvers, Anita, 'From the crooked timber of humanity, beautiful things can be made', in Peg Brand Zeglin, *Beauty Matters* (Bloomington and Indianapolis, IN: Indiana University Press, 2000), pp. 197–221.

Sim, Stuart, *Irony and Crisis: A Critical History of Postmodern Culture* (Cambridge: Icon, 2002).

Singer, June, *Androgyny: Towards a New Theory of Sexuality* (New York: Anchor Press, 1976).

Smelik, Anneke, *And the Mirror Cracked: Feminist Cinema and Film Theory* (Basingstoke: Palgrave Macmillan, 2001).

Smith, Marquard, 'The uncertainty of placing: Prosthetic bodies, sculptural design, and unhomely dwelling in Marc Quinn, James Gillingham, and Sigmund Freud', 2009. Available at http://www.artbrain.org/the-uncertainty-of-placing-prosthetic-bodies-sculptural-design-and-unhomely-dwelling-in-marc-quinn-james-gillingham-and-sigmund-freud/ (accessed 17 March 2010).

______ and Joanne Morra (eds), *The Prosthetic Impulse From a Posthuman Present to a Biocultural Future* (Cambridge, MA: MIT Press, 2006).

Sontag, Susan, 'Notes on "Camp"', 1964. Available at http://interglacial.com/~sburke/pub/prose/Susan_Sontag_-_Notes_on_Camp.html (accessed 29 January 2010).

______ 'An argument about beauty', *Daedalus* (2002), pp. 21–6.

Spivak, Gayatri Chakravorty, 'Translator's preface', in Jacques Derrida, *Of Grammatology* (Baltimore, MD and London: Johns Hopkins University Press, 1976), pp. viii–lxxiv.

______ 'Can the subaltern speak?' [1988], in Bill Ashcroft, Gareth Griffiths and Helen Tiffin (eds), *Post-colonial Studies Reader* (New York and London: Routledge, 1995), pp. 28–37.

______ 'Three women's texts and a critique of imperialism' [1985], in Bill Ashcroft, Gareth Griffiths and Helen Tiffin (eds), *Post-colonial Studies Reader* (New York and London: Routledge, 1995), pp. 43–61.

Stabłowski, Stach, 'Discreet return', 2000. Available at http://www.rajkowska.com/en/inne/151 (accessed 9 March 2014).

______ 'The story of a chocolate bar – the light art of Joanna Rajkowska', in *Satisfaction Guaranteed*, exhibition catalogue (Warsaw: Centrum Sztuki Współczesnej Zamek Ujazdowski, 2000), pp. 2–5.

Stein, Atara, 'Xena: Warrior Princess, the lesbian gaze, and the construction of a feminist heroine', 1998. Available at http://whoosh.org/issue24/stein1.html (accessed 15 August 2010).

Steiner, Wendy, 'The sublime shudder', in Bill Beckley (ed.), *Sticky Sublime* (New York: Allworth Press, 2001), pp. 194–200.

______ *The Trouble with Beauty* (London: William Heinemann, 2001).

______ *Venus in Exile: The Rejection of Beauty in Twentieth-Century Art* (New York: Free Press, 2001).

Stone, Sandy, 'The 'empire' strikes back: A posttransexual manifesto', [1984] 1987. Available at http://sterneck.net/gender/stone-posttranssexuel/index.php (accessed 15 August 2010).

Stryker, Susan, 'Transgender studies: Queer Theory's evil twin', *GLQ: A Journal of Lesbian and Gay Studies* 10/2 (2004), pp. 212–5.

Suleri, Sara, 'Women skin deep: Feminism and the post-colonial condition' [1992], in Bill Ashcroft, Gareth Griffiths and Helen Tiffin (eds), *Post-colonial Studies Reader* (New York and London: Routledge, 1995), pp. 246–49.

Vargas Llosa, Mario, *Making Waves* (New York: Farrar, Straus & Giroux, 1996).
Weiss, Gail, *Embodiments as Intercorporeality* (London and New York: Routledge, 1998).
Welsch, Wolfgang, 'The return of beauty', *Filozofski Vestnik* 28/2 (2007), pp. 15–26.
Wilson, Elizabeth, *The Sphinx in the City: Urban Life, the Control of Disorder, and Woman* (London: Virago Press, 1991).
Wolf, Naomi, *The Beauty Myth: How Images of Beauty are Used Against Women* (London: Vintage, 1991).
Women on Waves, 2015. Available at http://www.womenonwaves.org/en/page/2582/ship-campaigns (accessed 13 December 2015).
World Health Organization, 'Female genital mutilation', 2014. Available at http://www.who.int/mediacentre/factsheets/fs241/en/ (accessed 28 July 2014).
Wray, Tim, 'The queer gaze', 2003. Available at http://e-pub.uni-weimar.de/volltexte/2008/1335/pdf/wray.pdf (accessed 11 August 2010).
Wróblewska, Hanna, *In Art Dreams Come True. Katarzyna Kozyra.* (Wrocław: BWA Wrocław, 2007), pp. 28–34.
Żmijewski, Artur and Joanna Rajkowska, 'Art of public possibility: Joanna Rajkowska in conversation with Artur Żmijewski', 2010. Available at http://www.rajkowska.com/en/teksty/43 (accessed 15 February 2014).
Zylinska, Joanna, *Spider, Cyborgs and Being Scared: The Feminine and the Sublime* (Manchester: Manchester University Press, 2001).

Index